Lecture Notes in Artificial Intelligence   2530
Edited by J. G. Carbonell and J. Siekmann

Subseries of Lecture Notes in Computer Science

T0171841

Springer
Berlin
Heidelberg
New York
Hong Kong
London
Milan
Paris
Tokyo

Gianluca Moro
Manolis Koubarakis (Eds.)

Agents and Peer-to-Peer Computing

First International Workshop, AP2PC 2002
Bologna, Italy, July 15, 2002
Revised and Invited Papers

Springer

Series Editors

Jaime G. Carbonell, Carnegie Mellon University, Pittsburgh, PA, USA
Jörg Siekmann, University of Saarland, Saarbrücken, Germany

Volume Editors

Gianluca Moro
University of Bologna
Department of Electronics, Computer Science and Systems
Via Rasi e Spinelli, 176
47023 Cesena (FC), Italy
E-mail: gmoro@deis.unibo.it

Manolis Koubarakis
Technical University of Crete
Department of Electronic and Computer Engineering
Intelligent Systems Laboratory
University Campus - Kounoupidiana
73100 Chania, Crete, Greece
E-mail: manolis@intelligence.tuc.gr

Cataloging-in-Publication Data applied for

A catalog record for this book is available from the Library of Congress.

Bibliographic information published by Die Deutsche Bibliothek
Die Deutsche Bibliothek lists this publication in the Deutsche Nationalbibliografie;
detailed bibliographic data is available in the Internet at <http://dnb.ddb.de>.

CR Subject Classification (1998): I.2.11, H.4, H.3, C.2, K.4.4

ISSN 0302-9743
ISBN 3-540-40538-0 Springer-Verlag Berlin Heidelberg New York

Springer-Verlag Berlin Heidelberg New York
a member of BertelsmannSpringer Science+Business Media GmbH

http://www.springer.de

© Springer-Verlag Berlin Heidelberg 2003
Printed in Germany

Typesetting: Camera-ready by author, data conversion by PTP-Berlin GmbH
Printed on acid-free paper   SPIN: 10873170   06/3142   5 4 3 2 1 0

Preface

Peer-to-peer (P2P) computing is currently attracting enormous media attention, spurred by the popularity of file-sharing systems such as Napster, Gnutella, and Morpheus. In P2P systems a very large number of autonomous computing nodes (the peers) rely on each other for services. P2P networks are emerging as a new distributed computing paradigm because of their potential to harness the computing power of the hosts composing the network, and because they make their underutilized resources available to each other.

In P2P systems, peer and Web services in the role of resources become shared and combined to enable new capabilities greater than the sum of the parts. This means that services can be developed and treated as pools of methods that can be composed dynamically. The decentralized nature of P2P computing makes it also ideal for economic environments that foster knowledge sharing and collaboration as well as cooperative and non-cooperative behaviors in sharing resources. Business models are being developed that rely on incentive mechanisms to supply contributions to the system and methods for controlling free riding. Clearly, the growth and the management of P2P networks must be regulated to ensure adequate compensation of content and/or service providers. At the same time, there is also a need to ensure equitable distribution of content and services.

The wealth of business opportunities promised by P2P networks has generated much industrial interest recently, and has resulted in the creation of various projects, startup companies, special interest groups, and a working group for standardization activities. Compared to industry, the academic community has been somewhat slow in reacting to the P2P wave. Although researchers working in distributed computing, multiagent systems, databases, and networks have been using similar concepts for a long time, it is only recently that papers motivated by the current P2P paradigm have started appearing in high-quality conferences and workshops.

Research in agent systems in particular appears to be most relevant to P2P computing because, since their inception, multiagent systems have always been thought of as networks of equal peers. The multiagent paradigm can thus be superimposed on the P2P architecture, where agents embody the description of the task environments, the decision-support capabilities, the collective behavior, and the interaction protocols of each peer. The emphasis in this context on decentralization, user autonomy, ease and speed of growth that gives P2P its advantages also leads to significant potential problems. Most prominent among these problems are coordination, the ability of an agent to make decisions on its own actions in the context of the activities of other agents, and scalability, the value of the P2P systems lies in how well they scale along several dimensions, including complexity, heterogeneity of peers, robustness, traffic redistribution, etc. It is important to scale up coordination strategies along multiple dimensions to enhance their tractability and viability, and thereby to widen the application domains. These two problems are common to many large-scale applications. Without coordination, agents may be wasting their efforts, squandering resources and failing to achieve their objectives in situations requiring collective effort.

This volume brings together the papers presented at AP2PC 2002, the 1st International Workshop on Agents and P2P Computing[1] that took place in Bologna on July 15, 2002 in the context of the 1st International Joint Conference on Autonomous Agents and Multi-Agent Systems (AAMAS 2002). AP2PC 2002 was devoted to the discussion of methodologies, models, algorithms and technologies, strengthening the connection between agents and P2P computing. This was realized by bringing together researchers and contributions from these two disciplines but also from more traditional areas such as distributed systems, networks and databases. In particular, the workshop aimed to address the following issues:

- Intelligent agent techniques for P2P computing
- P2P computing techniques for multiagent systems
- The Semantic Web, semantic coordination mechanisms and P2P systems
- Scalability, coordination, robustness and adaptability in P2P systems
- Self-organization and emergent behavior in P2P systems
- E-commerce and P2P computing
- Participation and contract incentive mechanisms in P2P systems
- Computational models of trust and reputation
- Community of interest building and regulation, and behavioral norms
- Intellectual property rights in P2P systems
- P2P architectures
- Scalable data structures for P2P systems
- Services in P2P systems (service definition languages, service discovery, filtering and composition, etc.)
- Knowledge discovery and P2P data mining agents
- Information ecosystems and P2P systems.

In response to the call for papers for AP2PC 2002, we received 19 papers. All submissions were thoroughly reviewed for scope and quality by the program committee. As a result of the review process, 9 full papers and 5 posters as short papers were accepted for presentation at the workshop. The volume was organized according to the following main aspects of agent and P2P computing covered by the accepted papers:

- P2P services
- Discovery and delivery of trustworthy services
- Search and cooperation in P2P agent systems
- Metadata management and content distribution

Among specific aspects we mention load balancing in P2P environments, market models for P2P systems, metadata in P2P systems, mobile agents and P2P systems, and specialized hardware for P2P computing.

---

[1] http://p2p.ingce.unibo.it/

Full revised versions of the papers, taking into account the comments and lively discussion that took place during the workshop, are included in this volume. The volume also includes three contributions invited by the panel Chair which address some issues raised in the context of the panel debate: namely whether agents can be a good abstraction for P2P systems, and which are the agent-based P2P emerging research challenges that will address the needs of real systems, such as semantics-based interoperability, cooperation and search, scalability and control decentralization, and self-organizing applications.

Finally, we are glad to thank the authors, the program committee members, the invited panelists Karl Aberer (EPFL, Switzerland), Sonia Bergamaschi (University of Modena and Reggio-Emilia), Paolo Ciancarini (University of Bologna), and Munindar P. Singh (North Carolina State University), the steering committee, and the two sponsors mentioned below that contributed with their support to the success of the workshop. To end, we would sincerely like to thank the more than 40 participants in this first edition of the workshop for their active contribution to the interesting debate during the presentations and the panel.

Gianluca Moro
Manolis Koubarakis
Aris M. Ouksel

Organization

Executive Committee

Program Chairs and Organizers: Gianluca Moro (University of Bologna, Italy)
Manolis Koubarakis (Technical University of Crete, Greece)

Panel Chair: Aris M. Ouksel (University of Illinois at Chicago, USA)

Steering Committee: Paul Marrow (BTexact Technologies, UK)
Aris M. Ouksel (University of Illinois at Chicago, USA)
Claudio Sartori (University of Bologna, Italy)

Program Committee

Karl Aberer	EPFL, Lausanne, Switzerland
Sonia Bergamaschi	University of Modena and Reggio-Emilia, Italy
Vassilis Christophides	Institute of Computer Science, FORTH, Greece
Paolo Ciancarini	University of Bologna, Italy
Costas Courcoubetis	Athens University of Economics and Business, Greece
Tawfik Jelassi	ENPC, Paris, France
Matthias Klusch	DFKI, Saarbrucken, Germany
Yannis Labrou	PowerMarket Inc., USA
Rolf van Lengen	DFKI, Germany
Dejan Milojicic	Hewlett-Packard Labs, USA
Luc Moreau	University of Southampton, UK
Jean-Henry Morin	University of Geneva, Switzerland
John Mylopoulos	University of Toronto, Canada
Christos Nikolau	University of Crete, Greece
Andrea Omicini	University of Bologna, Italy
Mike Papazoglou	Tilburg University, The Netherlands
Jeremy Pitt	Imperial College, UK
Dimitris Plexousakis	Institute of Computer Science, FORTH, Greece
Omer Rana	Cardiff University, UK
Esmail-Salehi Sangari	Lulea University, Sweden
Dan Suciu	University of Washington, USA
Katia Sycara	Robotics Institute, Carnegie Mellon University, USA
Thomas Tesch	GMD, Darmstadt, Germany
Peter Triantafillou	Technical University of Crete, Greece
Francisco Valverde-Albacete	Universidad Carlos III de Madrid, Spain

Sponsors

- EU Framework V project DIET (Decentralised Information Ecosystem Technologies – `http://www.dfki.de/diet`)
- D2I project of Italian MIUR and the Department of Electronic Computer Science and Systems of the University of Bologna – (`http://www.dis.uniroma1.it/~lembo/D2I`).

Table of Contents

Posters

Metadata Management and Content Distribution

Agents and Peer-to-Peer Computing: A Promising Combination of Paradigms

Gianluca Moro[2,3], Aris M. Ouksel[1], and Claudio Sartori[2,4]

[1] Department of Information and Decision Sciences, University of Illinois at Chicago
2402 University Hall, 601 South Morgan Street
M/C 294 Chicago, IL 60607-7124, USA
aris@uic.edu
[2] Department of Electronics, Computer Science and Systems, University of Bologna
[3] Via Rasi e Spinelli, 176, I-47023 Cesena (FC), Italy
[4] IEIIT-BO-CNR, Viale Risorgimento, 2, I-40136 Bologna, Italy
{gmoro,csartori}@deis.unibo.it

1 Introduction

The Peer-to-Peer (P2P) paradigm offers an intuitive approach for resource discovery and sharing, often without the necessity of a central authority or server. At present, the emphasis is mainly on sharing information and computing power, but other kind of services could be considered. P2P systems are intended for applications requiring high level of cooperation and communication, and the goal is to efficiently leverage the available computing power, bandwidth and other services among the peers.

The notion of agent has been introduced with a two-fold purpose: i) a new paradigm for the modeling and implementation of complex software systems and ii) a way to include in a computational abstraction some behaviors which are usually associated with "living beings", such as the capability to take autonomous actions in a specific context/environment in response to other agents' activities and/or based on design objectives [1,2].

The agent paradigm and P2P computing are complementary concepts in that cooperation and communication between peers can be driven by the agents that reside in each peer. Agents may initiate tasks on behalf of peers. For instance, intelligent agents can be used to prioritize tasks on a network, change traffic flow, search for files locally, determine anomalous behavior and then take appropriate action, exchange services and compete for them, negotiate and finally cooperate to achieve a specific goal.

In this paper, we point out some major research issues in P2P systems emphasizing the analogies and complementarities between P2P and the agent paradigm. In particular, in Sect. 2 we define and list the desired characteristics of P2P in Sect. 3 we describe the major P2P application classes; in Sect. 4 we review the analogies between P2P paradigm and the agent paradigm; in Sect. 5 we elaborate on some research perspectives in this area, and then we finally conclude on the potential short-term developments in this area of research.

G. Moro and M. Koubarakis (Eds.): AP2PC 2002, LNAI 2530, pp. 1–14, 2003.
© Springer-Verlag Berlin Heidelberg 2003

2   Peer-to-Peer Computing

A wide variety of definitions of P2P computing have been proposed in the literature. The following are two representative ones:

- *P2P* refers to a class of systems and applications that employ distributed resources to perform a critical function in a decentralized manner. The resources encompass computing power, data (storage and content), network bandwidth, and presence (computers, human, and other resources) [3];
- *P2P computing* is a network-based computing model for applications where computers share resources and services via direct exchange.

In a client/server model, the client makes requests of the server with which it is networked. The server, typically an unattended system, responds to the requests and acts on them. With P2P computing, on the other hand, each participating computer, referred to as a peer, functions as a client with a layer of server functionality. This allows the peer to act both as a client and as a server within the context of a given application.

P2P applications build up functions such as storage, computations, messaging, security, and file distribution, through direct exchanges between peers. A peer can initiate requests, and it can respond to requests from other peers in the network. The ability to make direct exchanges with other users liberates P2P users from the traditional dependence on central servers. Users have a higher degree of autonomy and control over the services they utilize.

The following subsections highlight possible benefits of P2P paradigm and describe the kind of P2P architectures and its properties.

2.1   Benefits of P2P

Several benefits ensue from P2P networking, including:

- *Cost sharing/reduction*: centralized systems serve many clients but the bulk of the cost in resources is born entirely by the central system. This may be prohibitive. P2P architectures may provide an approach to spread the cost over all the peers. For example, the Napster system enables the cost sharing of file storage. Because of this, P2P has impacts on business-to-business as well as business-to-customer interactions. Productivity is increased and costs are reduced through the tapping of resources that previously were unused;
- *Resource aggregation and interoperability*: a decentralized approach lends itself naturally to a framework which supports the aggregation of resources. Each node in the P2P system contributes additional resources such as computing power or storage space. Aggregated resources particularly benefit those applications requiring for example, computer-intensive simulations or large distributed file systems. The potential for benefits from aggregation is enormous, but this presupposes the enabling of interoperability between the various hardware and software platforms;

- *Autonomy*: for control or security reasons, users may mandate that all data and processing on their behalf be performed locally. P2P systems support this level of autonomy;
- *Privacy*: users may also want to preserve their privacy and remain anonymous to service providers. It is difficult to ensure anonymity in a centralized architecture as the server typically is able to identify the client, at least through the Internet address. P2P architectures enable users to keep their information local because all activities are local. FreeNet is a prime example of how anonymity can be built into a P2P application;
- *Dynamism*: P2P systems assume that the computing environment is highly dynamic, which in turn implies that resources enter and leave the system continuously. This environment fits particularly those distributed applications where the scale and the variations of the resources required are not predictable. In Instant Messaging, for example, the so-called "buddy lists" are used to inform users when persons with whom they wish to communicate become available. Without this support, users would be required to "poll" for chat partners by sending periodic messages to them. Likewise, distributed computing applications such as distributed.net and SETI@Home [5] must adapt to changing participants.

2.2   P2P Architectures

Experts distinguish between pure P2P and hybrid P2P depending on whether all the participating computers are indeed peers [6,7]. We also distinguish two types of architectures: decentralized vs. semi-centralized. A *pure P2P architecture* or decentralized is one that does not contain any central point of control or focus. Peers are regarded as being of equal standing and autonomous (i.e. independent, intelligent, etc). Data and computation may spread over all the peers, and peers can communicate directly with each other, and hence, are constantly aware of each other, or they may communicate indirectly through other peers. In the latter case, the organization of peers may either have a regular structure, such as a hierarchy, or be totally unstructured. An indirect unstructured architecture removes the need for any form of management to enforce a specific network configuration; however the emphasis and the workload is shifted to the discovery service as changes to the network can happen without the awareness of all the peers. FreeNet is an example of a system used for distributing files. It is built using an indirect unstructured architecture.

A *hybrid P2P architecture* or semi-centralized is one that contains at least one central point of control or focus. The purpose of the control peers can range from the maintenance of strict control over the whole network to simply acting as a central reference point for the remaining peers. In single centralized index server, there exists a single peer that can act as a lookup repository for all the other peers within the network. This peer may be utilized to maintain an index or a catalog for the available data or processing capabilities on the network. Such a central index node removes the need for a discovery service. When a peer connects to the network it is required to inform the index peer of its location. Napster is a typical example. All the peers other than the central server may be either totally autonomous or without autonomy. In the latter case, the peers are essentially controlled by the central node, as in the example of SETI@home. Architectures with multiple server peers may also be contemplated. These may have several advantages including, improvement of systems reliability by removing a potential single point of failure, and performance by distributing the load. If the nodes happen to be physically quite spread out having multiple central nodes could help tackle any loss in Quality-of-Service.

2.3   Properties of P2P

The appropriate P2P architecture is always application-dependent. Its selection is determined by the extent to which the properties of the architecture match those required by the applications. A list of the main properties follows:

- *Reliability* is arguably the most important characteristic of almost all software systems. Users expectations of quality do no longer tolerate software failures on a regular basis. Unreliable software can be costly to end-users and can result in loss of reputation for the software developers. A precise definition of reliability has however remained elusive. The distributed nature of P2P systems exarcerbates the problems caused by low reliability. A P2P system is particularly prone to network failures and so mechanisms are needed to reduce their impact on the system.
- *Scalability* is the ability of a system to operate without a noticeable drop in performance despite variability in its overall operational size. For example, would a system originally intended for 10 users operate satisfactorily for a thousand users? Scalability within P2P systems is measured along several dimensions, including for example the number of users using the system and the number of nodes within the system. Therefore scalability should play a significant role when designing a P2P system.
- *Security* represents the ability level of a system to protect itself against accidental or deliberate intrusion. Ensuring security within P2P systems is more difficult than with standard centralized server systems. There is always a trade-off between on the one hand, authenticating your communication partners and sharing information only with the people you trust, and on the other, supporting the anonymity of users.
- *Data Integrity* means that data should become neither corrupt nor invalid due to issues such as concurrency or network problems. Should such a data integrity problem occur, it could result in systems failures or incorrect business decisions. Maintaining data integrity is more difficult with P2P systems due to the frequent exchange of data between peers. Data is particularly susceptible to corruption during transfer, and because of the autonomy property, multiple inconsistent data versions may coexist in the system. Decision mechanisms are needed to figure out the correct version.
- *Anonymity* in P2P applications is the ability to hide a user's identity, but without compromising authentication. The anonymity property may extend

to the data. To hide a user's identity, pseudonyms rather than IP addresses can be used to identify users. Another approach is to map data communications through disinterested and trusted third party proxies.

- *Load Balancing* refers to the property which ensures that peers in the system are not overworked or underused. The goal obviously is to achieve an efficient use of the resources in the system. For example, in a network system composed of several servers to handle requests, the assigned load is as evenly distributed as is possible among the servers.
- *Peer Discovery* is an important property of a P2P system concerning its ability to discover the other peers in the network and their available services. Systems that are based on semi-centralized architectures can rely to a large extent on the central index peer to provide the addresses of other peers in the network. With decentralized architectures the discovery task is typically spread across all peers. Each peer maintains its own local cache of known peer addresses. Discovery consists in sending messages from one peer to the next until the required peer is found.

3   P2P Applications

P2P applications may be classified into five broad categories, including file sharing, collaboration, edge services, and finally distributed computing. We shall discuss below representative examples in each category.

3.1   File Sharing

The three most popular file sharing applications are described below. They span the spectrum between pure P2P and hybrid P2P depending on the role the servers play in the architecture.

Napster. Napster is a phenomenon that drew a lot of discussion into P2P computing. It a software tool that allows direct swapping of MP3 files and other add-on services, such as instant messaging. Napster is an example of a centralized P2P architecture, where a group of servers perform the lookup function needed by the other peers. A peer must first establish an account with the Napster server and provide the list of music files it has available. Subsequently, it can send search requests to the Napster server and receive a list of peers who offer the desired music file. Then the requester can select any of these peers to directly download the file. [8].

Gnutella. It is an example of a pure p2p application i.e. there are no central servers involved [9]. Gnutella allows any-type file sharing, provides complete anonymity, is fault-tolerant towards failures of peers thus the reliability is significantly enhanced, and adapts well to dynamically changing configurations of peers. The Gnutella protocol basically allows the subscribers to form a virtual network. The subscription is established by connecting to some known Gnutella host, provided by specialized servers. Starting from the initiator, the messages are routed to a set of peers using a constrained broadcast mechanism in a breadth-first fashion which limits the number of hops between peers. If the message received by a peer is a search request for a specific file, then the peer checks its local store and responds through the same path as the one followed by the request if there is a hit.

Freenet. The goal is to provide a P2P network designed to allow the distribution of information over the Internet in an efficient manner and without censorship [10]. Freenet is an example of a completely decentralized architecture. A computer on the Internet becomes *peer* of the freenet network by simply running a piece of software called the *Freenet Server* or *Freenet Daemon*. As peers interact, they accumulate knowledge about other peers, and this knowledge is then leveraged in the discovery process. However, no peer at any point has knowledge about the entire system, and all peers are treated equally.

Besides the above popular systems, a plethora of others have been developed based on the P2P paradigm. We list some of them here without discussion: Akamai, FastTrack, iMesh, OceanStore [11], Pastry [12], Chord [13], CAN [14], JXTA [15], Gridella [16], P-Grid [17], Random Walker, Farsite, etc.

3.2 Collaboration

P2P computing empowers individuals and teams to create and administer real-time collaborative applications. Collaboration tools in this case mean that teams have access to the most up-to-date data, and thereby improving productivity by decreasing the time for multiple reviews by project participants and teams in different geographic areas. The stringent requirements of this application pose a formidable challenge in achieving security and integrity. Pioneers of collaborative environments include Groove Networks, Endeavors, and Eugenia [6]. As with file sharing, collaboration can decrease network traffic by eliminating e-mail and server storage needs by storing the project locally. The following are some areas of communication that have been largely affected by P2P:

– Communication: ICQ, IRC, Aimster – Instant Messaging;
– Content delivery: deliver enterprise content to desktops;
– Internet Search: OpenCOLA (http://www.opencola.com/) –
  Personal Knowledge Manager.

3.3 Edge Services

One form of P2P computing, known as edge services, pushes content towards peers whose clients may find the content relevant, freeing thus storage space on servers, balancing the load on those servers, and easing the network traffic to critical centralized systems. As a result, total storage space available is increased while server maintenance and bandwidth expenses are decreased. This has also a positive impact on employee productivity, as files and content are delivered faster. An example of edge services is Intel Share and Learn Software (SLS) [20].

3.4   Distributed Computing

P2P computing can help businesses or scientific applications with large-scale computer processing needs. Using a network of computers, P2P technology can use idle CPU MIPS and disk space, allowing businesses and organizations to distribute large computational jobs across multiple computers. In addition, results can be shared directly between participating peers. The combined power of previously untapped computational resources can easily surpass the normal available power of an enterprise system without distributed computing. The results are faster completion times and lower cost because the technology takes advantage of power available on client systems. Examples of distributed applications are described in SETI@home [5].

4   Agents: A Well-Suited Paradigm for Peers

An agent model for P2P systems enables the description of complex systems with a higher level of abstraction [21], that is by means of metaphors which better capture high level features of real world situations. These tools in turn allow a better comprehension of P2P systems and also the extension of their functionalities.

Though there is no accepted definition on what is an agent, there is instead a set of characteristics which are commonly recognized by the community as endowing agents. There is a strong agreement that the following three characteristics form a common kernel of fundamental features of agents:

- *autonomy*, agents can operate without any direct human or any outside program intervention, and incorporate some control over their actions and internal state
- *reactivity*, agents perceive the environment and its changes, and react to it as required by their goals
- *social ability*, agents interact with other agents (and, possibly, with humans) by means of a communication language (either with the goal of *cooperation* and/or *competition*), giving rise to multi-Agent systems or community systems.

Other useful characteristics have also been described in the literature. However, their relevance is domain-dependent. For instance, adaptation and learning are most appropriate in the context of intelligent agents. These characteristics are listed below:

- *pro-activity*: agents, in addition to the ability to react to the changing conditions in their environment, can also initiate actions in order to reach a specific goal
- *adaptation/learning*: agents learn by adapting their behaviors after a set of experiences for the purpose of improving the efficiency and efficacy of a given task and/or of performing new tasks which were hereto beyond their capabilities

- *mobility*: agents have the ability to move from one to another node in a network.

These characteristics are also desired for peers. A peer should be able to *autonomously* decide when to enter into or to exit from the network, when to satisfy a service request, whether to ask for a payment for a rendered service and so on.

Reactivity can be useful, for instance, to ensure that the P2P system is brought to an optimal state after the startup or ending of a peer.

Social ability can bring to peers new features, such as *trust, reputation*, emergent behaviors from cooperation/competition on given social tasks.

Pro-activity can be useful for peers which can advise users, on the basis of their interests, of new events/opportunities on the network.

Adaptation and Mobility could allow a peer to implement a learning algorithm, such as crawling the network, discovering links and resources, in order to improve global performances.

In addition, P2P systems have some relevant limitations:

- *expressiveness of messages*, message languages are at present very simple and can communicate only well defined pieces of data or objects, rather than information with more complex semantics
- *data models*, exchanged information is based only on the simple model of file and directory
- *data integration/transformation*, peers environment is uniform and does not take into account heterogeneity, inconsistency and other similar problems which are likely to occur in distributed environments
- *routing*, routing protocols are very critical, mostly in pure P2P networks where servers are not present.

The superimposition of the agent paradigm on peer architectures allows to transcend the above limits: the agent paradigm through which expressing messages to be exchanged, usually deal with heterogeneous environments, complex data models, and can possibly move across a network. In the following, we will discuss some key issues in this merge of concepts from two different research areas.

4.1   Issues for Agent-Based Peers

Trusting a Peer. Nodes of a P2P network provide services and references to services. When a node issues a service request it does not know *if* the service will be provided, by virtue of the autonomy property. Therefore the concepts of *trust* and *reputation*, which are well known for agents, are well suited for the definition of the *social behavior* of peers [22,23,24]. The notion of trust is complementary to that of *hard security*, usually provided by passwords, cryptography, etc. Hard security allows knowing the identity of an agent, but does not ensure that it will act as expected or it will provide a good service.

The major challenges to deal with trust in multi–agent systems are the following:

- how an agent can decide when it should reveal its reputation
- how an agent can find thrustworthy agents if it did not have any contact with them
- speed up the propagation of information through the social network.

The mechanism described by Yu and Singh [24] establishes prizes and penalisations. When a service request query is issued, an agent will answer only if it is reasonably confident of being able to match the query. A proposed answer is evaluated on the basis of direct experience, of evaluations given by neighbours and of trust on neighbors. In this sense, the approach is said to be *social* and trust information can propagate. Cooperation with another agent or desertion will generate positive or negative evaluations, respectively. In order to discourage bad behavior, a good reputation is built slowly, but rapidly destroyed.

Architectural Issues of a Peer. We try here to sketch the main components of an agent-based peer.

- *Assistant*, the assistant deals with user interests and keeps a dynamic profile; user queries are converted into a proper communication language and passed to the Contract Net Agent.
- *Contract Net Agent*, it deals with queries, checking if they can be answered locally or on the network; in the latter case it will query the Yellow Pages or, if it will not find anything specific enough, it will broadcast a query or send it according to a given efficient routing algorithm [25,13]
- *Yellow Pages*, they keep track of the resources which could be used to answer queries, including a description of the general interests of nodes.
- *Search Agent*, it is started by the Contract Net Agent to materially execute a query; it can "learn" to improve its search performance and can update interests descriptions in the Yellow Pages.

Communication between Peers. Agent communication languages (ACL), which derive from a linguistic theory called *Speech Act Theory*, try to mimick human communication with natural language by considering the sentences for their effect on the world. Speech acts, which are acts carried out using a language, are classified in categories/types, for instance requests, declarations, suggestions, queries and so on. Agent communication languages use messages to carry speech act from an agent to another. Each message has a sender and a receiver, a type and a content, therefore to allow two agents to understand each other it is needed a common description of the world and an interaction protocol which specifies which conversation patterns are legal.

In the standard FIPA [26] the ACL is based on the assumption that two agents, who wish to converse, share a common ontology for the domain of discourse. It ensures that the agents ascribe the same meaning to the symbols used in the message. For a given domain, designers may decide to use ontologies that are explicit, declaratively represented (and stored somewhere) or, alternatively, ontologies that are implicitly encoded with the actual software implementation of the agent themselves and thus are not formally published to an ontology service.

According to [27] an ontology should describe *actions, predicates and entities*. For instance by examining the life cycle of a peer one can determine the following main actions independently on the application domain:

- join: a peer ask another one permission to join the network;
- disjoin: a peer ask another one permission to disjoin from the network; in this way, rather than simply disconnecting, its behaviour is more respectful w.r.t the other nodes and can increase its reputation because the P2P network can also re-organize its structure;
- look up: a peer issues a query to find something by means of its Search Agent;
- update: a peer inform another one about some changes in its local data
- request: a peer asks something to another one, for instance to use some service.

As far as the interaction protocol is concerned FIPA provides elementary protocols directly induced by the semantics of the single communicative acts (fipa-request, fipa-query, etc.) and more sophisticated negotiation protocols (fipa-contract-net, fipa-auction-dutch, etc.).

4.2   P2P Agent-Based Applications

In a forthcoming future peers will be not only individuals but also companies which will give rise to business networks where their agents will negotiate, trade, cooperate and compete as in a big virtual society. Security, together with laws and legal issues extended to agents, will become more and more relevant in order to make this arena a safe and profitable environment for business. Companies will be able not only to share information but also cooperative tasks, let us think for instance to banks or insurances interested in cooperating to discover frauds or user profiles but without compromising customer privacy. The knowledge discovery could occur by means of P2P data mining agents which negotiate strategies to exploit as much as possible data, but without gathering data in a single repository and/or without exchanging huge amount of information in the network.

P2P Wireless Networks. The relevance of P2P short range wireless communications by means of transmission protocols such as Bluetooth, WiFi and so on will rapidly increase for two main reasons: (i) cellular phones, PDA and analogous devices, which are more pervasive than computers, are incorporating such communication protocols together with environments able to execute more and more sophisticated applications (ii) P2P communications through such protocols and devices will be free of charge and therefore we will have self-organizing wireless networks (e.g. ad-hoc metropolitan networks) made up by the people themselves.

Even if at present most P2P applications deal with file exchange, they will rapidly evolve to provide new services thanks mainly to the absence of any central authority which leads naturally users and applications to self-organization. For example, consider how many useful information services related to vehicles can be built on P2P short range wireless communications; centralized architectures like the one based on communications via satellite are not suitable for high numbers of interactive communications, in fact they offer mainly one-way broadcasting because of cost reasons and severe limits to scalability, instead inter-vehicle agent-based interaction could provide scalable, dynamic, interactive services. On the other hand, a possible risk deriving by the freedom offered by these open and highly dynamic P2P networks is anarchy and wasting of resources, therefore safe policies, protocol, trust mechanisms should help in avoiding this.

Intelligent Agent Services. As a distributed computing technology, P2P has enormous impact on the search capabilities on the Internet. Intelligent Agents or *bots* (short for robots) are P2P software tools that can perform search in an exponential fashion to find information that you need [18,19]. Two applications where bots have great potential are healthcare knowledge discovery and data mining. In Healthcare Knowledge Discovery, P2P technology is combined with the latest improvements in artificial intelligence based classification and indexing to deliver complete healthcare ontology desired by healthcare professionals. Data mining often requires a series of search steps; hence bots can save labor as they persist in a search, refining it in the process. Bots can make decisions based on past experiences, which will then become an important tool for data miners trying to perfect complex searches that delve into billions of data points.

5   Research Challenges

We list below some of the many open problems in P2P research, we believe that borrowing ideas from the paradigm of agents can ease the solution of some of them.

- *Robustness.* The ability to handle failures (of any kind) is particularly difficult in the case of P2P as the control is completely and autonomously distributed. While much work has been done on making distributed data structures in general robust to failure, there are several important remaining issues [28], including the investigation of fault tolerance through replication, on-line monitoring and repairing, and protocols for correctness verification.
- *Robustness in Dynamic Systems.* With a large number of nodes participating in a distributed data structures even in a modestly dynamic environment, the system may never be stable, i.e., quiescent. Instead, the network will always be in changing, with nodes constantly arriving and departing. Reasoning about such dynamic systems and their robustness represents a particularly challenging research issue.
- *Robustness and Reliability of Participants.* In an environment where the nodes are autonomous and may belong to different administrative domains and probably different design objectives, the reliability of the information about and from nodes may not be completely trustworthy. The fact that

nodes may not fully trust each other implies the need for new approaches to levels of reliability. This area requires extensive research spanning engineering, social and economic issues.

– *Network Performance.* The performance of search, update and interaction operations on a data structure depends in a great part on the characteristics of the underlying network, such as the bandwidth, number of users, amount and type of transferred data, and so on. This is generally hidden from the distributed data structure abstraction. The awareness about these characteristics provides research opportunities to design both cooperative and/or noncooperative policies to improve the overall performance of the network.

– *Semantics Issues.* The usability of a P2P systems requires the design of simple and standard abstractions to communicate between the peers and to request services. General-purpose APIs must be identified that satisfy a broad range of applications yet remains simple and easy to support. To increase the applicability of P2P systems users should be able to issue complex queries, but this requires metadata describing the resources managed by these peers, which is easy for specialized cases but not for general purpose applications, mostly if queries can involve two or more peers. Semantic routing of querying is also important to efficiently discover data and services in P2P networks; in fact locating efficiently right peers allows one to explore a wider portion of the network guaranteeing more accurate results with a minor number of repetitive queries to retrieve the same data.

– *Coordination Issues.* In pure P2P large networks with a high number of participants, where the control is totally decentralized and no global shared resource is available, the coordination approaches based on shared tuple centers (for instance JavaSpaces, TSpaces, Manifold, MARS, Lime) are not suited: (i) for scalability reasons and (ii) because coordination tasks, which are inherently distributed among peers, cannot be described/managed in a centralized system/blackboard. A possible alternative is to think each coordination activity as an emergent behaviour itself from P2P interactions, therefore an issue is how to define, verify and guarantee a desired coordination task, or more generally a given social task, by means of self-organization mechanisms in these open and highly dynamic environments.

6   Conclusion

P2P personal information-sharing services will see explosive growth, reaching 35% of all online users by 2006. Once personal P2P applications are common and the infrastructure supports them, computing will change. Developers of Web-based applications will realize that adding P2P functionality makes their apps come alive –user communication is the secret sauce for enhancing client-server applications.

Main companies has already started to release frameworks for the development of P2P applications [15,29] and by 2006, P2P services will come bundled in premium broadband fees and personal information-sharing applications from

Adobe, Palm, and AOL. As P2P technology matures, it will infect traditional client-server applications like the Web. Consumers will engage in conversations while doing almost any interactive task. By 2006, it is likely that 10 percent of business interactions will occur via P2P-enabled platforms.

P2P is a methodology that will enable machine-to-machine and client-to-client interaction via the Web services model. The intersection of these two worlds with the agent paradigm will extend the challenges of global-class computing, such as multi-owned and multi-operated transactions, to Internet-connected client devices. Enterprises should be familiar with emerging P2P platforms and the concept of peer spaces as they develop their global-class computing strategies.

References

1. Klusch, M.: Information agent technology for the internet: A survey. Data and Knowledge Engineering, Special Issue on Intelligent Information Integration. Elsevier Science **36** (2001) 337–372
2. Wooldridge, M.: Intelligent agents: The key concepts. In Marík, V., Stepánková, O., Krautwurmova, H., Luck, M., eds.: Multi-Agent-Systems and Applications. Volume 2322 of LNCS., Springer-Verlag (2002) 3–43
3. Melville, L., Walkerdine, J., Sommerville, I.: Ensuring dependability of P2P applications at architectural level. Technical Report IST-2001-32708, Lancaster University, http://polo.lancs.ac.uk/p2p/Documents/PropertiesDeliverable.pdf (2002)
4. Milojicic, D.S., Kalogeraki, V., Lukose, R., Nagaraja, K., Pruyne, J., Richard, B., Rollins, S., Xu, Z.: Peer-to-peer computing. Technical Report HPL-2002-57, HP Laboratories Palo Alto, http://www.hpl.hp.com/techreports/2002/HPL-2002-57.pdf (2002)
5. qwe: qwe (2000) http://setiathome.ssl.berkeley.edu.
6. Barkai, D.: Peer-to-Peer Computing: Technologies for Sharing and Collaborating on the Net. Intel Press (2002)
7. Yang, B., Garcia-Molina, H.: Comparing hybrid peer-to-peer systems. In: Proceedings of the 27th Int'l Conf. on Very Large Databases (VLDB). (2001)
8. Napster: protocol specification (2002) http://opennap.sourceforge.net/napster.txt.
9. Gnutella: (Development home page) http://gnutella.wego.com/.
10. Clarke, I., Sandberg, O., Wiley, B., Hong, T.: Freenet: A distributed anonymous information storage and retrieval system. In: In Proceedings of the Workshop on Design Issues in Anonymity and Unobservability. (2000) http://freenet.sourceforge.com.
11. Kubiatowicz, J., Bindel, D., Chen, Y., Eaton, P., Geels, D., Gummadi, R., Rhea, S., Weatherspoon, H., Weimer, W., Wells, C., Zhao, B.: Oceanstore: An architecture for global-scale persistent storage. In: Proceedings of ACM ASPLOS. Volume 35., ACM (2000) 190–201
12. Rowstron, A., Druschel, P.: Pastry: Scalable, decentralized object location, and routing for large-scale peer-to-peer systems. Lecture Notes in Computer Science **2218** (2001) 329–340
13. Stoica, I., Morris, R., Karger, D., Kaashoek, F., Balakrishnan, H.: Chord: A scalable Peer-To-Peer lookup service for internet applications. In: Proceedings of the 2001 ACM SIGCOMM Conference. (2001) 149–160

14. Ratnasamy, S., Francis, P., Handley, M., Karp, R., Shenker, S.: A scalable content addressable network. In: Proceedings of ACM SIGCOMM 2001. (2001) 161–172
15. Gong, L.: Industry report: Jxta: A network programming environment. IEEE Internet Computing **5** (2001) 88–97
16. Aberer, K., Punceva, M., Hauswirth, M., Schmidt, R.: Improving data access in p2p systems. IEEE Internet Computing **6** (2002) 58–67
17. Aberer, K.: P-grid: A self-organizing access structure for p2p information systems. In et al., C.B., ed.: In Proceedings of International Conference on Cooperative Information Systems. Volume 2172 of Lecture Notes in Computer Science., Springer (2001) 179–194
18. Ouksel, A.M.: A framework for a scalable agent architecture of cooperating heterogeneous knowledge sources. In Klusch, M., ed.: Intelligent Information Agents: Agent-Based Information Discovery and Management on the Internet. Lecture Notes in Computer Science, Springer (1999) 100–121
19. Sycara, K.: In-context information management through adaptive collaboration of intelligent agents. In Klusch, M., ed.: Intelligent Information Agents: Agent-Based Information Discovery and Management on the Internet. Lecture Notes in Computer Science, Springer (1999) 78–99
20. Intel Ltd: Peer to peer computing, p2p file-sharing at work in the enterprise.   Technical report, Intel Ltd, http://www.intel.com/eBusiness/pdf/prod/ peertopeer/p2p_edgesvcs.pdf (2001)
21. Bonsma, E., Hoile, C.: A distributed implementation of the SWAN peer–to–peer look–up system using mobile agents. [30]
22. Yolum, P., Sing, M.P.: An agent–based approach for trustworthy service location. [30]
23. Despotovic, Z., Aberer, K.: Trust-aware delivery of composite goods. [30]
24. Yu, B., Singh, M.P.: A social mechanism of reputation management in electronic commerce. In: CIA 2000. (2000) 154–165
25. Pandurangan, G., Raghavan, P., Upfal, E.: Building low-diameter p2p networks. In: IEEE Symposium on Foundations of Computer Science. (2001) 492–499
26. FIPA: Foundation for intelligent physical agents (2000) http://www.fipa.org/.
27. FIPA: Ontology service specification (2000) http://www.fipa.org/specs/fipa00086/XC00086D.html#_Toc505571322.
28. Ratnasamy, S., Shenker, S., Stoica, I.: Routing algorithms for dhts: Some open questions. In: In Proceedings. of 1st International Workshop on Peer-to-Peer Systems. (2002)
29. Microsoft: (Microsoft windows xp peer-to-peer software development kit) http://msdn.microsoft.com/library/default.asp?url=/downloads/ list/winxppeer.asp.
30. Moro, G., Koubarakis, M., eds.: International Workshop on Agents and Peer-to-Peer Computing (AP2PC'2002). Volume 2530 of LNCS., Bologna, Italy, Springer-Verlag (2003)

Peer-to-Peer Computing for Information Systems*

Munindar P. Singh

Department of Computer Science
North Carolina State University
Raleigh, NC 27695-7535, USA
singh@ncsu.edu

Abstract. Peer-to-peer (P2P) computing is clearly valuable in modern computational environments, which are best described as *open*, emphasizing the autonomy and heterogeneity of their constituents. However, conventional P2P approaches fail to realize the full potential of P2P computing. However, when we take an agent-based view of P2P – with the agents acting as peers and modeling, communicating, and learning about each other – P2P offers a powerful architecture for large-scale information systems.

The agent-based P2P approach easily addresses the challenges of service discovery, location, composition, execution, and monitoring, which are key to modern information systems. It also promises to provide a natural means for applying the participants' context in helping them find and use information and services. Further, the agent-based P2P approach offers a conceptually well-founded basis for structuring information systems, which can be thought of as a dynamic, context-sensitive analog of link analysis on today's static Web.

1 Introduction

Distributed, open information systems have been around for a while, but their importance has been increasing rapidly with the spread of networked applications [1]. It is helpful to take a services stance in understanding such systems. Here, we think of *service composition* in a broad sense. Intuitively, we can claim that an open information system relies upon trustworthy service composition for its successful functioning. A simple example of service composition is putting information together from multiple sources; a richer example is supply-chain management involving multiple parties carrying out complex transactions.

There is a fundamental synergy between P2P computing and information systems. P2P needs flexible protocols and a principled way of modeling computations over P2P infrastructure, both of which can be provided by information systems concepts. At the same time, information systems need support for trustworthy service composition, and ideally without central authorities and without preconfiguration. These are capabilities that P2P approaches can readily provide.

However, current instantiations of both fields tend to be limited. P2P systems merely spread computation without regard to information semantics or the context of the appli-

---

* I would like to thank the other panelists and my students for useful discussions. This research was supported by the National Science Foundation under grant ITR-0081742.

G. Moro and M. Koubarakis (Eds.): AP2PC 2002, LNAI 2530, pp. 15–20, 2003.

cations in which the information is used. Current information systems assume a logical closed world with configuration preceding execution.

This position paper presents our views on where some of the most interesting research questions arise. We submit that a fruitful area of research is emerging where semantics and context are applied over a P2P architecture to enable flexible description, discovery, configuration, execution, monitoring, and compliance. This area lies at the confluence of agents and P2P approaches, specifically an approach that involves referrals among agents serving as peers in a P2P architecture.

2   Challenges for Information Systems

In our broader understanding of services, we taken them not merely as remotely invoked methods but as potentially involving rich interactions [6,8]. Likewise, service composition is more than just chaining several methods, but includes approaches for service discovery, location, planning and execution, engagement (participative execution), monitoring, and compliance. Consequently, the success of modern information systems presupposes solutions to the above problems.

Below, we present some questions that must be addressed in order to develop information systems of the sort introduced above.

– *Planning and Execution.*
  How should agents act so as to plan and execute different tasks effectively and efficiently? One way is by designing policies, which can, for example, provide a basis for choices made by agents in ignoring or responding to others' communications and providing or not providing services. This leads to the next question of how can we model applications so that they can be linked to appropriate policies.
– *Engagement.*
  The engagement of services can be thought as proceeding through particular interaction protocols, which specify how two or more parties may interact. The purpose of these interactions is so one or more providers can render services for one or more consumers. How can protocols be modeled and the right ones mutually selected so that suitable interactions may be obtained in a distributed system?
– *Discovery and Location.*
  This involves finding the right service providers. How do we discover the best providers without causing bottlenecks or making parties reveal too much information? There may be central authorities, but how do we decide whether to trust them? Specifically, we might choose between two main doctrines of service discovery and location. We may emphasize either (1) *authority*, giving importance to a provider's ability to provide the requested service or (2) *familiarity*, giving importance to a provider's understanding of the service consumer's needs. We conjecture that authority (which corresponds to Web search engines) is superior for widely-presented services and familiarity is superior for narrowly-focused services.
– *Monitoring and Compliance.*
  This is required for our information systems, because their components are heterogeneous and autonomous. How do we achieve this without injecting central bottlenecks or violating the autonomy of the participants?

Traditional work on information systems has tended to be centralized; in modern practice too, we see distribution at the infrastructure level, but still with logical centralization. We claim that P2P approaches can provide superior solutions for the above requirements, but don't. Agents can help by enabling newer ways of structuring computations. Service discovery, location, composition, execution, and monitoring are all major tasks for distributed information management systems. Under assumptions of openness, each of these tasks can be performed better in a P2P framework than in centralized approaches.

3   Referrals

The idea of a referral is simple [2,4,9]. A referral is no more than a link from one party to another in a distributed system. However, a referral is not merely static, but is given by one party to another in a certain context, typically in response to a request but possibly without an explicit request.

Imagine that we are given a P2P system consisting of several peers who can perform tasks for one another and can keep track of some of their peers. In this framework, our protocol for referrals is quite simple. Upon receiving a request, a peer may do one of the following:

- Ignore it.
- Perform the requested task locally.
- Perform the requested task by forwarding requests to other peers on own authority or original requester's authority.
- Return a referral to another peer (typically as an endorsement).

Conversely, upon receiving a referral, a peer may do one of the following:

- Ignore it.
- Follow it, later possibly evaluating service providers and the agents who gave referrals leading to them.

Note that, in the above, the peers can always ignore messages from others, and that they can proceed without referrals should that somehow be desirable. Capturing referrals in this manner has two main advantages. Referrals

- Preserve peer autonomy and heterogeneity. Referrals decouple discovery of a peer from the decision to engage that peer. The requester can take advice without being forced to (in effect) initiate computations at other peers, which is what happens when, e.g., a computation is passed along in a wave.
- Enable sophisticated representation and reasoning about when and what referrals to give to whom. These can include considerations of (1) context reasoning to understand peer requests, (2) social mechanisms for cooperation, e.g., reciprocity, and (3) incentives and economic mechanisms.

Specifically, referrals among agents can be viewed as a key organizing principle for distributed systems, which addresses how a computation may spread while enabling learning by the participants regarding other participants. Referrals provide a natural way to cooperate with a requester without impinging on the autonomy of the requester or potentially wasting resources by starting computation waves. Current time-to-live approaches inherently assume that all parties follow a similar protocol.

However, using referrals opens up challenges of how and when referrals should be given. Referrals potentially address the dual challenges of getting work done in an open system, while also engendering trust among the participants. Our recent work has addressed service location, flexible caching, and Web structure.

3.1   Comparison with P2P

We claim that P2P is an architecture style or pattern, rather than a specific technology [7]. Just as the well-known layered architecture style is not restricted to operating systems or applications, so is not P2P restricted to systems or to applications. In fact, there is a lot to be gained by applying a P2P architecture at a higher level than in traditional P2P approaches.

Conventional P2P approaches are limited in two major ways, which restrict their applicability to information systems. In particular, existing P2P approaches

- Apply primarily at the systems level and often involve limited and rigid protocols.
- Either have significant centralized components or require manual configuration or presuppose rigid behavior.

For example, one of the main means for a P2P system to distribute a computation is through waves wherein a peer can forward the request from one peer to other peers. P2P computation waves unnecessarily couple service discovery, execution, monitoring, and (engagement) protocols.

3.2   Context

Referrals provide an interesting locus for accommodating context. Consider the case of a Web page. It provides the same information, including links to other pages, to all readers. By contrast, a referrals-based approach enables the peers to supply information (specifically links) based on the specific query. They can potentially model each other's needs, carry out long-lived conversations, and infer each other's context. Thus context can be more readily accommodated than through static information alone.

3.3   Structure

Understanding the structure of an evolving system is important for understanding its functioning and important properties such as its reliability. In our case, the structure relates closely to how trust is engendered among the interacting parties. An important analogy is with Web structure, which helps determine authoritative sources on the Web [5]. However, the structure of today's Web is based primarily on hand-generated links. When the structure is used to infer the authority of a Web page, this inference is based on an implicit assumption of rationality on part of the people who place links – each link is interpreted as a kind of an endorsement.

How would the structure of a system be if generated by autonomous agents, e.g., via referrals, under different agent policies? Could referrals take the place of link annotations by being highly contextualized to specific queries by specific askers at specific times?

We conjecture that referrals can induce a well-founded structure that is more predictive of trust than current link analysis approaches. A true P2P, referrals-oriented Web would have links that were explicitly generated by agents, potentially for narrowly specified topics. Thus the structure would be more precise. Further, there would be an explicit evaluation of referrals. Thus a richer structure would be induced on the Web leading to more precise judgments of authority and trust.

4   Conclusions

As a way to summarize the above discussion, let us consider how the above requirements for services are satisfied by different implementations, but how they are satisfied can differ a lot. Let us consider centralized, traditional distributed, and P2P architectures (with the latter augmented with referrals as described above).

- *Centralized*. Discovery is trivial: via setting environment variables to point to class libraries; endorsement is by the programmer who binds the right classes; and monitoring and compliance checking is performed by no one.
- *Traditional distributed*. Discovery is via central registries; there is an implied endorsement by the registry (and an endorsement by the programmer in selecting a particular registry); and monitoring and compliance checking is performed by service consumer.
- *P2P (with referrals)*. Discovery is via cooperative lookup; endorsement is through community and rational interaction; and monitoring and compliance is through checking by the community.

There are two main claims here. One, without agent-based referrals, P2P systems will remain inadequate for addressing the challenges of information systems: requiring manual configuration (leaving much complexity for application designers) or being inherently limited to the low-level infrastructure. Two, equipped with referrals, P2P systems can address many of the challenges facing information systems.

References

1. R. Bayardo, W. Bohrer, R. Brice, A. Chichocki, G. Fowler, A. Helal, V. Kashyap, T. Ksiezyk, G. Martin, M. Nodine, M. Rashid, M. Rusinkiewicz, R. Shea, C. Unnikrishnan, A. Unruh, and D. Woelk. InfoSleuth: Semantic integration of information in open and dynamic environments. In *[3]*, pages 205–216. 1998. (Reprinted from *Proceedings of the ACM SIGMOD Conference, 1997*).
2. Michael N. Huhns, Uttam Mukhopadhyay, Larry M. Stephens, and Ronald D. Bonnell. DAI for document retrieval: The MINDS project. In Michael N. Huhns, editor, *Distributed Artificial Intelligence*, pages 249–283. Pitman/Morgan Kaufmann, London, 1987.
3. Michael N. Huhns and Munindar P. Singh, editors. *Readings in Agents*. Morgan Kaufmann, San Francisco, 1998.

4. Henry Kautz, Bart Selman, and Mehul Shah. ReferralWeb: Combining social networks and collaborative filtering. *Communications of the ACM*, 40(3):63–65, March 1997.

5. Jon Kleinberg and Steve Lawrence. The structure of the Web. *Science*, 294:1849–1850, November 2001.

6. Munindar P. Singh. The service Web. *IEEE Internet Computing*, 4(4):4–5, July 2000. Instance of the column *Being Interactive*.

7. Munindar P. Singh. Peering at peer-to-peer computing. *IEEE Internet Computing*, 5(1):4–5, January 2001. Instance of the column *Being Interactive*.

8. Munindar P. Singh. Physics of service composition. *IEEE Internet Computing*, 5(3):6–7, June 2001. Instance of the column *Being Interactive*.

9. Munindar P. Singh, Bin Yu, and Mahadevan Venkatraman. Community-based service location. *Communications of the ACM*, 44(4):49–54, April 2001.

Peer Services: From Description to Invocation

Manuel Oriol

University of Geneva
24, rue Général Dufour
1204 Genève, Suisse
oriol@cui.unige.ch

Abstract. In this article, we describe our work on peer services and
their description to allow an invocation of them in a distributed environment. The basic idea is that service publication and service invocation
are made using *descriptions* of what is available and what is requested,
respectively. There is no prior agreement between services, their descriptions are built independently. Service publications and service requests
are sent to a coordinating element of the architecture responsible for
matching publications and requests descriptions.

1   Introduction

A range of very different and promising concepts arose in the past few years: peer-
to-peer (P2P) techniques. Being massively successful for end-users with exchange
files architectures, researchers have focused in the peer-to-peer development in
order to provide new specific technologies adapted to peer-to-peer programming.

A P2P architecture consists in building a set of peers that share a certain
number of resources. Schematically, the main characteristics of a P2P system
are the following. It is *decentralised*. A P2P architecture does not need to have a
central software component to manage interactions between its peers. In order to
facilitate communications, semi-centralised approaches have arisen (e.g. JXTA
Search) but the fundamental distributed nature of P2P systems is still very
present. It is *potentially large*. Successful examples of P2P systems show that they
are particularly scalable. Typically, at 17:00 GMT it is not rare to have more than
200 peers connected at the same time to the Gnutella network providing an access
to more than 200 gigabytes of data [1]. It is *very dynamic*. A P2P network is made
of peers that have no constraints on their behaviour. For instance, a peer may
disconnect anytime, it is then impossible to know *a priori* if a request will succeed
or not. It is *heterogeneous*. A P2P network may be made of many different
programs (programmed by different people on different platforms) disposing of
many various connectivity grouped by a P2P interaction protocol. It *provides
(distributed) services*. One of the main point in P2P architectures is that peers
provide and use services in parallel. Being a peer contractually implies that
you may use services from other peers and that they may use your services. In

---

[1] Measure made in April 2002.

G. Moro and M. Koubarakis (Eds.): AP2PC 2002, LNAI 2530, pp. 21–32, 2003.
© Springer-Verlag Berlin Heidelberg 2003

this article we propose an architecture that allows programmers to implement service invocations asynchronously, using an extreme associative naming and late binding. This architecture is based on the fact that the service invocation and service description are both a "formal" description of what is requested and what is offered respectively.

In Sect. 2, is given an overview of our motivations and of the general architecture, in Sect. 3, are described implementations for P2P networks, in Sect. 4, we show how we describe services and how we match them, in Sect. 5, we show related work, and we finally conclude in Sect. 6.

2   Motivations and Conceptual Architecture Overview

2.1   Motivations

In this article we advocate the fact that peers providing services need to be fundamentally different from other traditional middleware approaches.

Middleware approaches are made of two different families of systems: remote invocation mechanisms (like CORBA, DCOM and RMI) and information storing through repositories (Linda-like systems [1]).

The first family usually considers components that allow programs to invoke remotely methods on components that may be considered statically bound during the discovery and use states. This family of systems provides also a complete infrastructure that allows programmers to find components in order to build some sort of reference to be able to invoke methods. P2P networks are very dynamic and a particularity is that peers may leave and come back at any time with different accessibility and computing power capabilities. Such dynamic behaviour is not considered as a normal feature and then cannot be adapted to P2P networks.

The second family of middleware approaches considers that information should be exchanged asynchronously through a repository. The problem with such an approach applied to P2P networks is that huge amount of data may be exchanged and any repository downtime may provoke major problems due to such message centralising.

According to these facts, we advocate for a new type of communication infrastructure based on three different concepts:

Extreme Associative Naming. We provide a mechanism based on anonymity. This means that a calling peer will not know *a priori* which peer will answer the service invocation or by which entry point it will pass; but, in fact, it does not matter as long as we know that the task to achieve is correctly effected. Further there is no direct reference on other peers code (anonymity).

Late Binding. Because of anonymity, any peer asking for an invocation cannot know for sure which code will be executed. To achieve this, programmers must specify the *kind of action* their peers invoke and also the *kind of action* their peers provide. In our opinion, it is most important to qualify a service and be sure of the task it will perform rather than simply reference its name without any assurance on its behaviour as it is the case with approaches like CORBA, DCOM or RMI.

Asynchronous Communications. All invocations will be one-way. This means that calling peers do not wait for an answer. Invocations are asynchronous: a service invocation returns immediately, the calling peer continues its execution. The answer will possibly arrive later, once a corresponding service has been found and evaluated. As a consequence, in case of missing answers, peers will not know if the action has been considered by the contacted peer.

In the following subsection, we describe the conceptual architecture that results from these ideas.

2.2   Conceptual Architecture

The proposed architecture we describe is based on peer and services (left part of Fig. 1). A peer is a software composed of data and services. A service is a piece of code coupled with its formal description (see Sect. 4.1 for more details).

Applications are an aggregate of peers that may need to request services from other peers. Programmers do not know in advance the description of available services. Executing entities wishing to invoke a service do not search for available services. They simply build the "description" of the needed service and send an asynchronous request (i.e. service description requests) to the Peer Network Service Manager (right part of Fig. 1) that is in charge of finding an adequate service to invoke.

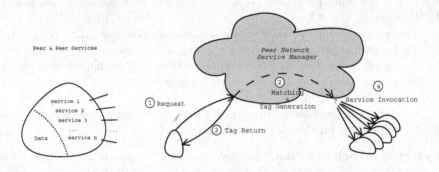

Fig. 1. Entity presentation and services invocation

The invocation process is decomposed in the following steps (Fig. 1):

1. Request a service to the Service Manager. The message includes the arguments, a description of the requested service, and a value quantifying the minimal point the called service has to match.

2. The Service Manager performs a matching and generates a unique tag assigned to the request.
3. The Service Manager sends immediately the tag to the caller. The tag could be used later to receive the answer.
4. The Service Manager invokes immediately the callee with arguments and a description of how the service matched.

To be more precise, we show here how to write an invocation of service in a Java-like language:

Tag T = Invoke(*Description of service*, *Minimal Matching*); where "Description of service" consists in a collection of labels that have to match, and "minimal matching" is the minimal adequacy between the desired service and the service that will be effectively invoked.

As seen in the invocation process, the call is extremely associative because the calling peer requests a service by its description, and not by naming it explicitly or naming it at all. It is also asynchronous because the service invocation returns immediately. Finally, the binding of methods is made lately because the choice of the code is made dynamically through a matching process (see Sect. 4.2 for more details).

The generation of a tag for each message may seem at first inappropriate, but these tags provide several features: provide the caller a way of receiving an answer, re-establish a communication channel in either way and delegate answer collection to other peers (e.g. to newer versions).

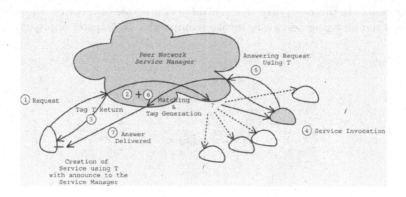

Fig. 2. Service invocation and answering

To understand better how answers are given and how the returned tag allows asynchronous service satisfaction, we show here a small example where there is a call of service that waits for an answer. In Fig. 2 the four first steps are the same steps already presented in Fig. 1. We detail now the three other steps needed for the answer, that correspond to a mirrored version of the steps necessary for the invocation:

5. In this scheme, the initial caller creates a service for collecting the answer and uses the tag T in the description of this service. When answering, the initial callee uses the tag T, received at the invocation, in order to call the service built on it (this part of the step is similar to step 1).
6. The matching of the service related to the tag, and a new tag generation process are achieved (similar to step 2).
7. The answer is delivered to the initial calling peer (this step is similar to step 4).

This model is a conceptual one. Applying it to a P2P architecture means that we need to find a way to build an infrastructure that keeps the principles we described above valid.

3   Distributed Service Invocation

In this section we propose three possibilities of architectures for services invocation implementing the concept of the Peer Network Service Manager we described in Sect. 2: a centralised approach, a semi-centralised approach and a decentralised approach.

For each of these possibilities, we describe informally how to implement our conceptual architecture, show how requests are passed from peer to peer and evoke advantages and drawbacks.

3.1   Centralised Approach

Description. In this case, (Fig. 3) a central peer processes all service requests and chooses the best peer service to invoke (comparable to Napster approach [2]).

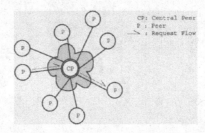

Fig. 3. Centralised approach

It constitutes an approach similar to the conceptual description shown previously because the central peer acts as a unique peer network service manager matching invocations and requests descriptions.

Request Flow. A request for service is made to the central peer that chooses the peer to which it should be passed. The invocation is then made to the desired peer and a tag is generated and passed to the requesting peer.

Advantages. Being very similar to our model it is easy to verify that it corresponds to what we described. The fact that the central server may be trusted, because it is the only way to communicate, implies that protection domains are implementable. This also means that the provider of the architecture is able to make it evolve using an upward compatibility and thus let programmers make their clients evolve. The request is passed through only one peer, before being effectively made, which may result to be very fast.

Drawbacks. The main drawbacks are mainly concerned with accessibility to the central server. If a peer cannot access directly to the peer server, it cannot use the architecture. If the peer server has a downtime, no peer can work. If the provider of the peer server makes incompatible changes, other peers should make their peer clients evolve. Finally, if the load of the application increases to the point where the central peer server is down, the complete system does not work at all.

3.2 Semi-centralised Approach

Description. In this approach (Fig. 4) we consider a hybrid topology, where several central peers interact very strongly while other peers rely on one of the central peers. It constitutes an approach comparable to JXTA Search [3] and Gnutella [4] approaches.

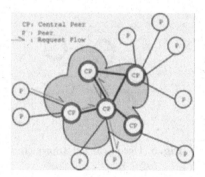

Fig. 4. Semi-centralized approach

The fact that there could be many central peers does not mean that this is a centralised approach as central peers may be built and controlled by different people. The general functioning considered is a peer willing to connect to the system, it finds a central peer through a yellow page service and connects to it. The list of these yellow page services may be fixed in advance and then extended when linking to the peer network.

Calls for services may then be coded using a separation of concerns dynamically evolving, which means that central peers should dispose of a repartition protocol for request types.

Request Flow. When a request is made, it is sent to the central peer to which the peer is connected. It is then passed through the central peers until the one in charge of this type of requests is found. Once it has been found, the central peer in charge of this type of requests passes the request to the peer it selected, satisfying the request. Finally, it returns a tag to the calling peer.

Advantages. Such an approach allows the peer application designers to share the load of computing power required to treat requests indirection between a more restrained and reliable subnetwork of peers. It is also very simple for peers to connect and propose services to the application. It is well adapted to huge systems that are very dynamic as the part needed for communicating is very heavy.

Drawbacks. This approach does not fit for *ad-hoc* networks where there is not necessarily a central peer able to redirect requests. If connectivity falls between central peers, the system may slow down considerably as there may not be just one indirection for requests but several.

3.3   Decentralized Approach

Description This approach (Fig. 5) consists in having in each peer a part that manages some of the requests (comparable to BlueTooth *ad-hoc* networks approach).

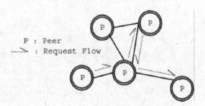

Fig. 5. Decentralized approach

We imagine such a system as a self organised architecture concerning the repartition of requests. This means that there is a P2P protocol that ensures that all services are still referenced even if peers leave the peer network.

Request Flow. This approach is fundamentally similar to the semi-centralised one except that each peer may pass requests to others and thus all the peers are usable as central peers.

Advantages. This approach is very much adapted to *ad-hoc* networks since in such networks we cannot consider that there is a distinction between central peers and other peers and it would even be difficult to decide that they may not behave in the same way.

Drawbacks. This approach does not seem very adapted to enormous peer networks as many messages pass from peer to peer and it is not considered that some peers may assume different roles depending on their connectivity or the computing power they have.

4 Service Description and Matching

The previous parts of this paper presents the general architecture of a service-oriented architecture for P2P networks. In this part we show the concepts of the service description and its associated matching in an informal way.

The main principle of our description and matching is that each service is described using tree-like structures. The matching is then built on trees describing functionality, behaviour and quality of service.

4.1 Service Description

In this work, the service description is probably one of the most important features of the architecture along with the matching (that uses it actively). Because of anonymity, calling peers must have a way to describe the service they request. **There is no way to name either a peer or a service** and this is why descriptions are needed to characterise services without naming them.

In this context, we need to know *what* kind of service we want, *how* the answering peer satisfies the service, and *how well* it satisfies it. Informally, services may then be described in three parts answering these three questions respectively:

Functionality. This is the semantic part of the message, describing the functionality of a service by characterising its kind. An analogy with traditional object programming could be the different names present in a method signature. Another analogy made with sorting would be the fact that it is a sorting algorithm. In this analogy, because there are so many possible sorting algorithm services and that they may be specified, we say that the functionality may be described by a list of labels going from the most general to the most precise. For example, a service doing a Bubble Sort has the following functionality: Functionality: "Sort": "BubbleSort". This syntax expresses the fact that we are characterising a service functionality of the kind sort and more precisely: a BubbleSort.

Behaviour. This is the information that will guarantee the compliance of the functional check. Basically it contains arguments that propose to the service to realise its task and the way the service should work (e.g. gives an answer, and if so, does it answer through a particular service or a service built with the message tag...). An analogy with traditional object programming could be the types of a method and its arguments. Another analogy with sorting would be that it takes in parameter a table of integers, it returns a result and sends back the result using the tag. This behaviour is expressed as follows: Behavior: argument: int a[]: return: int[].

Quality of Service. This is the part of the message that allows to select a service from a group of corresponding services in order to match most exactly the quality of service desired with the quality of service proposed. There is no analogy with traditional programming since the choice between methods does not concern the programmers except that the method may be `local` or in a protection domain. For the sorting example it would eventually indicate computational complexity. Similarly to previous parts we express the quality of service as follows: `QoS: "local": "Complexity": "Nlog(N)".`

We can already notice on these small examples that for each of these categories it is not sufficient to entirely describe the desired service and this is why we will now argue for a more complex structure. We advocate that using only one word or a flat structure to qualify one of the parts is not sufficient for describing a service request, particularly when faced with unanticipated modifications in the structure of an application.

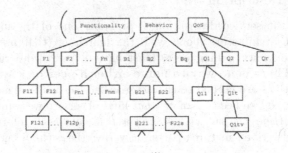

Fig. 6. Description of services

Each field of this description is defined as a tree (Fig. 6). Therefore, two branches going out from a node correspond to an **OR** between the two subtrees, and a branch corresponds to an **AND** between the upper level and the subtree associated. The tree A in Fig. 7 is then translated as follows:

$$QoS \wedge ((Q1 \wedge (Q11 \vee (Q12 \wedge (Q121 \wedge Q1211)))) \vee Q2).$$

Even though the functionality describes the service using well-known names, such as "sort", it is important to note that it is not necessarily the actual name of the service that will answer the request. It is simply a way of qualifying the kind of service. In pseudo-code, announcing the BubbleSort service working on integers and characters may be:

```
Announce(Functionality: "Sort": "BubbleSort",
         Behavior: argument: (int a[]: return int[],
                              char a[]: return char[]),
         QoS: "local": "Complexity": "Nlog(N)")[2,4,2];
```

This means that we announce the service that sorts integer or characters and that it should at least correspond to a sort request. The behaviour is then fixed (takes integers and returns integers, or takes characters and returns characters), and should be a local invocation.

The next subsection shows how to build relations that may allow us to match a service description, published in the Service Manager, with a service description used to make requests.

4.2   Matching Mechanism

The matching mechanism constitutes the main solution both for dynamic choice of code and for anonymity of services. The point we want to present is the ability to match trees and make this matching process as intuitive as possible, given the informal translation we expressed previously for trees.

We say that two trees match at a given depth when the depth is the length of the longest branch departing from the root that exists in common in the two trees.

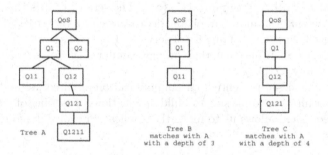

Fig. 7. Tree matching

In this approach we build a matching mechanism between trees that is not syntactically equivalent, it is semantically equivalent and at this point we foresee to use ontologies [5] to ensure that descriptions match. As an example, in Fig. 7, tree B matches with tree A at depth 3 and tree C matches with tree A at a depth of 4.

A problem with this approach is that it is impossible to specify the fact that we would prefer a shorter branch if the matching occurs at a certain point. It is also impossible to match a branch until a certain point, and to stop consider the matching after that point. That explains the reason why we define the following 5 operators:

- ? means that there is a node and that this node may have any label.
- * means a potentially infinite sequence of nodes.
- ⊥ means that the branch stops at the node where this label is attached: if the branch to match has instead a node at this place, the matching for the whole branch has a depth of 0.
- ∅ adds 1 to the depth of the branch where it is attached given that it matches.
- ∅* adds ∞ to the depth of the branch where it is attached.

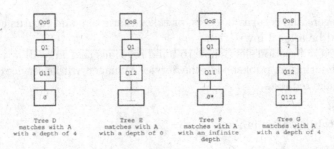

Fig. 8. Extended tree matching

Figure 8 shows examples of such matching.

In this way, we can quantify the quality of matching between a requested service S_r and a proposed service S_p. In this case, we say that S_p matches the functionality requested, the behaviour requested or the quality of service requested at a depth belonging to $\mathbb{N} \cup \{\infty\}$. The service that is then invoked is the service having the most important depth matching (by order of preference functionality, behaviour and quality of service). If several services have the same matching depth, it means that they provide similar services and one of them is chosen randomly.

In this section, we presented our communication architecture and its principles. This architecture allows us to build applications consisting of disconnected software peers, and allows us to make the application evolve dynamically.

5   Related Work

The JXTA service architecture [6,7] also has a way to define services and to invoke them. The main difference with the system we propose consists in two facts: JXTA services are described using a flat structure that only allows wild cards for matching strings between them. In addition, the JXTA services have to be discovered before being used which constitutes a potentially long-term agreement.

WSDL [8] is a norm for describing web services. The description is constituted by a document that binds some parts to other documents (like protocols description). The goal of WSDL is mainly to allow programmers to describe services. Once found, active components have to decide if the described service corresponds to a valid possibility or not. Comparing to what we describe, there is no service manager infrastructure that manages the matching between services although we easily imagine integrating our infrastructure with WSDL descriptions in order to automate the matching. UDDI [9] allows to fill the gap between describing and finding a service. It constitutes a phone-book used to find services. Services described using WSDL can be published and retrieved through UDDI [10]. Adding WSCL to the whole system [11] allows to describe future interactions. The main difference with what we propose resides in the fact that it is the programmer's role to choose between services matching the description. This also means that services match or do not match: there is no way to quantify the quality of matching. Software components also know each other, which makes answer delegation difficult as it could hardly be described using inter-peer conversations descriptions.

6   Conclusion

In this paper we advocate that there is a strong need for a new concept for programming very dynamic and distributed applications (like P2P applications): invoking services using only a description of them. Our main idea is to automate the concept of service discovery/invocation, searching the most suitable service for each invocation in order to fulfil a given request at best. In this paper, we described possible implementation infrastructures applicable to P2P architectures. As we showed, P2P distributed services architecture may be implemented in several ways depending on the P2P target application. We are currently implementing a prototype of the communication infrastructure and would like to implement a prototype on top of JXTA in the future.

References

1. Carriero, N., Gelernter, D.: Applications experience with Linda. ACM Sympos. on Parallel Programming (1985)
2. Napster, I.: Napster. http://www.napster.com (2001)
3. Waterhouse, S.: JXTA search: Distributed search for distributed networks. http://spec.jxta.org/v1.0/docbook/JXTAProtocols.html (2001)
4. Gnutella.com: Gnutella. http://www.gnutella.com (2002)
5. Gruber, T.R.: Toward principles for the design of ontologies used for knowledge sharing. International Journal of Human-Computer Studies **43** (1995) 907–928
6. On, R.T.: Project JXTA: An open, innovative collaboration. http://www.jxta.org/project/www/docs/OpenInnovative.pdf (2001)
7. Traversat, B., Abdelaziz, M., Duigou, M., Hugly, J.C., Pouyoul, E., Yeager, B.: Project JXTA: Virtual network. http://www.jxta.org/project/www/docs/JXTAprotocols.pdf (2001)
8. Christensen, E., Curbera, F., Meredith, G., Weerawarana, S.: Web services description language (WSDL) 1.1. http://www.w3.org/TR/2001/NOTE-wsdl-20010315 (2001)
9. uddi.org: UDDI technical white paper (2000)
10. Curbera, F., Ehnebuske, D., Rogers, D.: Using WSDL in a UDDI registry 1.05. UDDI Working Draft Best Practices Document, http://www.uddi.org/pubs/wsdlbestpractices-V1.05-Open-20010625.pdf (2001)
11. Beringer, D., Kuno, H., Lemon, M.: Using WSCL in a UDDI registry 1.02. http://www.uddi.org/pubs/wsclBPforUDDI_5_16_011.doc (2001)

Execution Environment of Peer-to-Peer Services in a Mobile Environment

Tadashige Iwao[1], Makoto Okada[1], Kazuya Kawashima[2], Satoko Matsumura[2], Hajime Kanda[2], Susumu Sakamoto[2], Tatsuya Kainuma[2], and Makoto Amamiya[3]

[1] Service Management Laboratory, Fujitsu Laboratories Ltd.
4-1-1 Kamikodanaka, Nakahara-ku, 211-8588 Kawasaki, Japan
{iwao,okadamkt}@flab.fujitsu.co.jp
[2] 2nd Development Division, Fujitsu Prime Software Technologies Ltd.
1-16-38 Aoi, Higashi-ku, 461-0004 Nagoya, Japan
{kawashima,matsumura,h-kanda,susumu,kainuma}@pst.fujitsu.com
[3] Faculty of Information Science and Electrical Engineering
Kyushu University
6-1 Kasuga-Koen, Kasuga, 816 Fukuoka, Japan
amamiya@is.kyushu-u.ac.jp

Abstract. This paper describes an execution environment for peer-to-peer services in a mobile environment. These days, mobile devices such as PDAs and mobile telephones have the power and the capability to support a variety of services independently. In the near future, peer-to-peer services will become commonplace for mobile devices in a mobile environment. However, at present, it is difficult for these devices to provide peer-to-peer services such as file sharing and the access of CPU power since the performance of these devices is not comparable to those of PCs. Therefore, suitable peer-to-peer services and their execution environment in a mobile environment are required for use on mobile devices. Hence, we propose execution environment for suitable peer-to-peer services in a mobile environment. A large-scale experiment, with six hundred participants, was conducted using a practical application of the proposed framework. This paper also contains the results and discussions of this experiment.

1   Introduction

Recently, the performance of mobile devices, such as PDAs and mobile phones, has increased enough to provide a wide variety of services independently. An individual can provide services to others using their mobile devices. Such services are called peer-to-peer services. In the near future, peer-to-peer services will become commonplace for mobile devices. The peer-to-peer services on these devices will enable people to use them in a mobile environment. However, the performance of these devices is not comparable to those of PCs. In a mobile environment with low power devices, one possible basic service is information browsing. Therefore, one possible peer-to-peer service is the simple exchange of

G. Moro and M. Koubarakis (Eds.): AP2PC 2002, LNAI 2530, pp. 33–44, 2003.

information among peers in a mobile environment. In addition, information that depends on physical locations will be of use in a mobile environment. In such a situation, the location-dependent information may change according to users. For example, permitting only registered members to view flight information from local airports. It is, therefore, required that the information, in peer-to-peer services in a mobile environment, manages itself according to the location and the users.

Current major peer-to-peer systems such as Gnutella[1], Napster[2], Magi[3], Groove[4] and SETI@home[5] focus on PCs, and do not provide services for the mobile environment. These systems are popular on the Internet, and have thousands of users. Gnutella and Napster provide file sharing in a peer-to-peer format. Magi and Groove are groupware systems which provide file sharing with secure and instant messages. Users of these systems find other peers who have the files they desire. These systems focus on PCs because of the large data storage requirements. SETI@home is a project that performs calculations to find signals of extra-terrestrial origin by using PCs, in which the owners of the Internet-connected PCs give consent to participate in the project. The software that performs these calculations operates as a screen saver, since the calculation places a heavy load on the PC during use. These kinds of applications need high CPU performance, and are not suitable for mobile devices such as PDAs and mobile telephones. It is difficult for mobile users to use applications which sap the performance of PDAs and mobile telephones. Thus, file sharing and accessing of computing power are not suitable for the mobile environment. Cybiko[6] is a mobile terminal device that enables users to communicate with each other using RF transmissions, and provides chat, e-mail, and share images. Cybiko, however, does not provide a framework, in which services depend on the users and location. Hence, a study must be conducted to determine what kinds of services are suitable for peer-to-peer services in a mobile environment. We also need an execution environment for the peer-to-peer services in a mobile environment such as location and user dependent services.

We propose an execution environment for peer-to-peer services in a mobile environment, called *Virtual Private Community* (VPC)[7,8], that makes information an agent that controls itself, and interact with other agents autonomously. The peer-to-peer services are defined as *policy packages* that consist of rules to activate agents, agent definitions called *roles*, and contents for the services. VPC is carried out by VPC platforms(VPC-Ps) which manage user attributes, and decide which agents to activate according to the rules in the policy package, and the attributes of the users. VPC-Ps operate on the mobile devices of the users. VPC allows services to be provided according to location and the users, and to propagate among users in a mobile environment. Large-scale experiments were conducted with practical applications using VPC for a period of two weeks. About six hundred people participated in this experiment.

Section 2 discusses suitable services of peer-to-peer services and their execution environment in a mobile environment. Section 3 describes details of VPC. Section 4 shows the practical application, in a large-scale experiment, of a VPC prototype system to provide peer-to-peer services.

2 Execution Environment for Peer-to-Peer Services in a Mobile Environment

The exchange of information among peers is the most important feature in peer-to-peer services. Information is provided by, and used by, the peers in a peer-to-peer environment. There are two phases in treating the information; the propagation, and the utilization of information. The propagation of information is performed by the transfer of information from one peer to another. In the utilization of information phase, there are two modes; a stand-alone mode and an interaction mode. A stand-alone mode involves the use information off-line, such as playing music files. This mode does not require interaction with other peers. An interaction mode involves the interaction among peers to use applications such as chat, network games, and groupware. The number of peers involved in the interaction may be small or large, and the interaction should be conducted in a peer-to-peer manner.

Also, location dependency of information is important in a mobile environment. Information also has dependence on location, time, users, context, and so on. Services are affected by information dependency, and are provided using information. There are services with information dependent on physical location since users move around in a mobile environment. For instance, one of the services is an explanation service of displays in front of users in a museum. Moreover, user dependency of information makes services exclusive. Only the users on which information depends can receive the services with the information. Thus, information dependencies affect services, and should be also considered in peer-to-peer services in a mobile environment. Execution environments for peer-to-peer services have not only to support the two phases and two modes, but also to support information dependencies.

One methodology is to make the information an agent that decides its own behavior among the peers in the propagation and utilization phases. The agents are also able to control information dependencies. The agent propagates among the peers, and authenticates users in the users' own mobile devices. The agent also interacts with other propagated agents that work with other peers. The agent may change itself according to peers by the result of authentication, and copyright information. In order to make this a reality, we need a framework for the agent.

3 Virtual Private Community (VPC)

Our framework, called *Virtual Private Community* (VPC), enables information in peer-to-peer services to act as an agent. VPC provides a mechanism that defines an agent behavior, authenticate users, and executes agents. Necessary agents for a peer-to-peer service are defined in a policy package that consists of a condition rule to decide active agents according to users, a set of agents(called *roles*), and necessary information(contents) for the service. Agents communicate with each other through communities that are created by agents who have accepted the policy packages. Services are offered by interaction among agents in

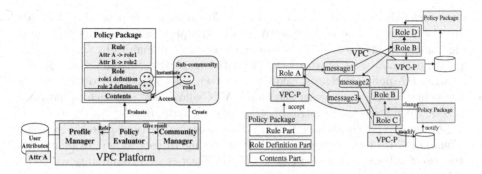

Fig. 1. Basic model of VPC   **Fig. 2.** VPC communication overview

communities. For example, in a music retail service, a policy package contains two agents, an authorized agent which can play the complete music file, and a trial agent which can play only part of the music file. Users who have purchased the music file can listen to the music through authorized agents.

Dependencies of information in VPC are separated into attributes of entities such as users and location, and activation rules of information (agents). Entities have their own attributes. Activation rules are described in each service (policy package). The dependencies of information are deduced by a set of attributes of entities and activation rules.

3.1 VPC Basic Model

Figure 1 shows a basic model of VPC. In the basic model, a policy package defines the agents, condition of activation for each agent, and information that is treated by the agents. Agents are activated by *VPC platforms* (VPC-Ps) that manage user attributes, evaluate policy packages according to the user attributes, decide appropriate roles, and create the community. The agents access contents in the policy packages, in which the agents are defined.

Main parts of a VPC-P are a profile manager, a policy evaluator, and community manager. A profile manager manages the user profile in anti-tamper devices such as Java Card [9]. A policy evaluator decides roles depending on the user attributes. A community manager creates a corresponding sub-community with a policy package, and connects the sub-community with a VPC-P who provides the policy package when the policy package indicates an interaction mode. The sub-communities form a network which is referred to as a virtual community. A community manager also executes selected agents in the sub-community. VPC supports both phases of propagation and utilization, and also supports both the stand-alone and interaction mode in the utilization phase. In the stand-alone mode, the community manager does not connect with the others, even if others have the same community.

Figure 2 shows the overview of the communication process of VPC. VPC-Ps are able to exchange policy packages among themselves, and to communicate with each other using the policy packages. Communities are created by VPC-Ps that accept the same policy packages. VPC-Ps provide services by collaboration among themselves. VPC-Ps can join existing communities by accepting the policy packages used by the VPC-Ps in the respective communities. VPC-Ps analyze the policy packages, deduce their own roles according to the rules of the policy packages, and user attributes. VPC allows any role such as database access, calculation, and control of other existing systems.

A community consists of VPC-Ps that accept a particular policy package. Thus, VPC-Ps form communities by connecting to each other. Communities consist of sub-communities on each VPC-P. Entities of a community reside on distributed VPC-Ps that connect the community.

In the basic model of VPC, participants in a community should be kept anonymous. Knowing the identities of the participants in a community means disclosure of the participants' attributes. The disclosure of participants' attributes in a community creates security problem and therefore, the anonymity of the participants must be maintained.

3.2 Policy Package

Figure 3 depicts a structure of policy packages. A policy package consists of a set of rules as a condition table, a set of roles as agents, and a set of contents. A rule consists of a condition and role names. A condition is described with logical expressions using attributes. An attribute consists of a database name, a variable name, and the value of the variable. A role consists of a role name, a program name, and an initialization method. A content consists of a content name, and content path that locates the real content data. Content includes program codes that implements roles. A policy package is written in XML.

Policy packages are encoded by S/MIME [10]. S/MIME enables VPC to detect falsification of policy packages by checking hash codes of policy packages. When VPC detects falsification of policy packages, the VPC discards the policy packages.

3.3 User Profiles

A profile manager has access interfaces for roles. User profiles are stored as a variable and its value, or as digital certificates of PKI[11]. Roles and a policy evaluator are able to access data through a profile manager by specifying the variable name.

A profile manager evaluates expressions of variables and values. A profile management part has corresponding evaluation modules for each database. It evaluates given expressions using the evaluation modules. Therefore, the profile management part allows evaluation of expressions that use types.

3.4 Evaluation of Rules in Policy Packages

A policy evaluator deduces roles by evaluating rules in policy packages according to users' attributes. A policy evaluator refers to conditions of rules in policy

```
<policy package>  ::= <rules> <roles> <contents>
<rules>           ::= <rule> | <rule> <rules>
<rule>            ::= <condition> <role names>
<role names>      ::= <role name> | <role name> <role names>
<condition>       ::= "TRUE"
                    | "and" <condition> <condition>
                    | "not" <condition>
                    | "eq" <attribute> | "<" <attribute>
<attribute>       ::= <variable name> <value>
<roles>           ::= <role> | <role> <roles>
<role>            ::= <role name> <program name> <init description>
<contents>        ::= <content> | <content> <contents>
<content>         ::= <content name> <content path>
```

Fig. 3. Structure of policy packages

packages, evaluates each term of each condition with a profile manager, and decides appropriate roles for the user. Then, it compares a list of current active roles and deduced roles, installs necessary roles that are not currently active into sub-communities, and removes unnecessary roles from the sub-communities.

A policy evaluator requests evaluation of each term of conditions in a rule, of a policy package to a profile manager. The profile manager accesses the specified variables in a term, and obtains a value for the specified variables. It then evaluates the term with the value, and returns TRUE or FALSE as a result. The policy evaluator combines the results, and decides the validity of the condition. The policy evaluator deduces appropriate role names by evaluating all conditions in the rule according to user profiles.

The policy evaluator obtains role programs with deduced role names from the policy package. Role programs are Java objects in VPC-Ps. The role assignment part creates instances of role programs with initialization according to "init description" in the policy package, and adds them into the corresponding communities.

User has a set of attributes $A = \{a_1, ..., a_n\}$. The rule part of a policy is a set of activation rule $W = \{c_1 \rightarrow r_1, ..., c_i \rightarrow r_i\}$. An activation rule consists of a pair of conditions, which is the combination of attributes ($c_k = a_{k_1} \wedge ... \wedge a_{k_n}$), and a role r_k to activate. An evaluator $E(A, W) = \{r_k | c_k \rightarrow r_k \in W, c_k \vdash A\}$ is a function that determines a set of roles according to user attributes and activation rules. A predicate $c_k \vdash A$ means $\forall a_{k_i} \in elements(c_k) \wedge a_{k_i} \in A$. The function $elements(c_k)$ returns a set of attributes used in c_k. Roles that are assigned for users are given by the evaluator E with activation rules.

3.5   Interaction among Roles in Communities

Collaboration among agents in communities is performed by message passing and the messages have to be accepted by appropriate roles in order to enable the collaboration. Our framework adopts the mechanism of collaboration among roles developed by Field Reactor Model [12] that is a coordination model [13] based on Dataflow Computing [14]. The Field Reactor Model (FRM) provides a method of flexible collaboration among agents by employing pattern matching.

VPC-P provides pattern invocation that is based on FRM. The patterns in VPC-P correspond to patterns in FRM and pattern invocation provides a method of invoking functions of roles without signatures of functions and addresses of roles. When a message of a pattern is sent into a community, VPC-P automatically invokes the appropriate functions. As well, values returned from the functions are put into the community as messages. Collaboration among roles is constructed as a chain of message passing, and the roles do not require the specification of addresses of roles to invoke. VPC-P allows the users to define patterns and roles.

Role calculation is performed according to the following; a set of patterns that are used in a community C is $P = \{p_1, \ldots, p_m\}$. There are roles $R_1, \ldots, R_n$ in community $C(C = \{R_1, \ldots, R_n\})$ and a role R_k is expressed as $R_k =< I_k, f_k, O_k >$. f_k is a function that has pattern $I_k (\in P)$ as an argument and returns pattern $O_k (\in P)$. The pattern matcher $M(m)$ checks whether a message m matches the pattern of function f_k, and if there is success, then it invokes function f_k. Then the function f_k returns messages as its values with this process being described by $M(m) = \{\cup_{i=1}^{n} O_k | I_k = m\}$. Thus the computation between roles in the community C proceeds as $M(m), \forall m_n \in M(m_{n-1})$. The community C repeats this process until complete collaboration among roles is created. This method of collaboration is similar to the coordination model such as Linda [15].

Patterns of roles are object types. A VPC-P allows any Java objects as roles and messages. VPC-Ps provide type match invocation, a method, in which methods of objects are invoked when the same type of messages as an argument of the methods are placed in the communities. Return values of the methods are placed back into the communities when the return values are not null. The methods of roles are merely declared as normal methods.

3.6   Peer-to-Peer Services with VPC

VPC makes information agents act as roles in a policy package. Authorized users that have certificates can see and use the information through assigned roles. In addition, VPC supports location dependent services; Fig. 4 shows the overview of location dependent services. In VPC, location dependent services are also described as policy packages. The policy packages contain roles for browsing a list of services that are provided at the location, and for downloading the policy packages. A policy package manages several policy packages through roles. Roles to obtain policy packages act as gate keepers of each policy packages. Only users with appropriate certificates can reach the inner part of policy packages. This mechanism allows adaptation of services not only depending on location, but also depending on time, context in a service, and so on.

VPC-Ps that have policy packages dependant on the corresponding location, broadcast an URL of a policy package that distributes location dependent policy packages. When users move into certain locations such as a hotspot, the VPC-Ps

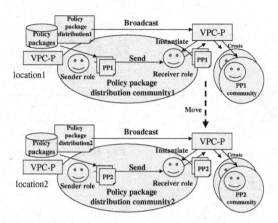

Fig. 4. Location dependent services

of the users receive the URL, obtain the policy package, distribution package, and then evaluate it. Then, a receiver role is assigned to VPC-Ps of the users, and the corresponding policy packages for the location is obtained. Once the receiver role has evaluated the received policy packages, the users may see information according to their user attributes.

In order to provide services depending on time, context in a service and so on, attributes that are managed by VPC-Ps include parameters such as time and context in a service. The parameters switch roles according to rules in policy packages. Also, the roles can change the parameters. By switching roles by parameters and modifying parameters by roles, services depending on time and context can be provided. In this case, rules in policy packages should be defined including such parameters.

4   Experiment with Practical Application

A large-scale experiment on VPC was conducted in an underground shopping center in Nagoya city (Japan) for a period of two weeks. The aim of the experiment was to ensure the effectiveness of a new peer-to-peer (p2p) service and a p2p medium using VPC in a stand-alone mode.

In the experiment, each user has a PDA running WindowsCE, and the users receive information, such as special bargain from shops around the user, depending on the user location, through a wireless LAN. The information of the service is provided as a policy package with VPC. Users can see the information that matches the user attributes. For example, the information in a drug store has two contents, cosmetics for ladies and shaving lotions for men. When the user is a woman, she sees the cosmetics information. A bingo game interface was employed in order to make the experiment more attractive to the users. A bingo card for each user is given during registration. Each set of information includes its own ID that is a bingo number. Users can exchange given information (policy

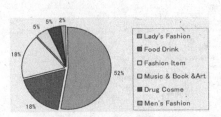

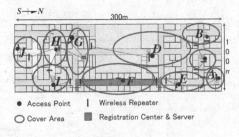

Fig. 5. Categories of shops   **Fig. 6.** Overview of the shopping center

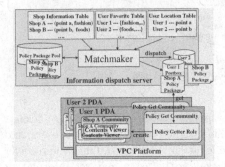

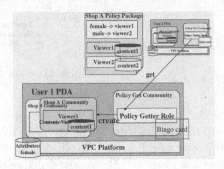

Fig. 7. System overview   **Fig. 8.** Exchange information among peers

packages) among themselves. When users win the game, they receive a coupon that is only able to be used in the shopping center.

Categories of shops in the shopping center are shown in Fig. 5. This experiment was broadcast by TV media and FM radio stations, as well as receiving newspapers. About six hundred people participated in this event, thanks to the media.

4.1 System Overview

Figure 6 shows an overview of the shopping center and location of wireless LAN access points. The size of the shopping center is approximately 300m x 100m. There are 107 shops. 802.11b for wireless LAN was used. Ten access points were set in this area. Each access point was connected by wireless LAN repeaters (twenty repeaters were used in total). Each access point covered an area containing approximately ten shops, and managed MAC addresses of PDA terminals. Channels of the access points were different from that of the neighborhood in order to avoid interference. Users were registered at the registration center when they began the game.

A system overview is shown in Fig. 7. The system consists of a server, which sends information to each user, and VPC that works on the user PDA terminals. PCs or PDAs for each access point could not be prepared because of the expense, and also because of the fire prevention laws in Japan. Therefore, it was decided to use a server and multiplex it. The server has policy packages of all the shops and the three tables; shop information table, user favorite table, and user location table. The user location table maintains connections between PDAs and access points. The user favorite table has a set of the users' favorite categories, and is created for each individual user during registration. The shop information table has pairs of shop locations and the categories for each shop. The main module is a matchmaker that decides which policy packages to send to each user, matching user's location and preferences with shop information. The server has a postbox for each user, and dispatches corresponding information within the area, in which users exist, to the users' postboxes. Users' VPC-Ps receives policy packages and evaluate them.

Figure 8 shows the diagram of exchange of information among peers. Information is exchanged among peers through a "policy get" community. A "policy get" community that has a "policy getter" role exchanges information among the peers and to obtain information from the server, and is always activated on the PDA terminals. The role also inquires other peers by broadcasting messages periodically. When the user wants information and other peers indicate willingness to give the information, the two "policy getter" roles on both users' VPC-Ps, exchange the information with each other. The "policy getter" role also checks the user postbox periodically. The "policy getter" role creates shopping communities, when it receives policy packages from the postbox or other peers. A "viewer" role that enables a user to see its contents (HTML) is activated. The "viewer" role is changed according to user attributes.

4.2   Results and Discussion

About six houndred users participated in the experiment. Figure 9a shows the numbers of persons per generation. Figure 9b shows the change in the numbers of players per day. It also shows the total numbers of information exchanges, and the numbers of repeat players of the game. The increase in the number of repeat players was especially remarkable.

The following user comments were received: 1) It is a lot of fun as a game. 2) I am interested in the time services. 3) I want to exchange information more. 4) I need to pinpoint information by location more exactly.

The following comments were received from shop owners: 1) P2P services may become a new advertising medium. 2) We want to use these services as a new marketing tool to focus on specific customers. 3) PDAs are not popular among ordinary people. We require these services for mobile phones. 4) Please perform this event for a year.

The answer to question "ordinary people use or require p2p services?" is yes. The customers need a medium through which they can discover the goods or services that they require, in order to get them with efficiently. On the other hand, shop owners want to advertise goods or services to customers who are interested in their products. There is sufficient potential for p2p services to become such a medium. The p2p services in VPC especially, enables users to access information according to location, time, service context, and so on.

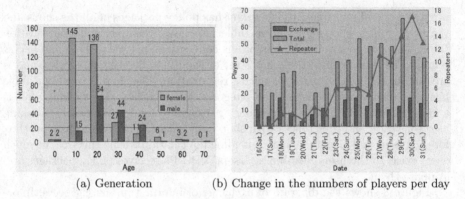

(a) Generation   (b) Change in the numbers of players per day

Fig. 9. Results

5   Conclusion

This paper proposed the framework for peer-to-peer services in a mobile environment using mobile devices such as PDAs and mobile telephones. Limited resources of most mobile devices make them unsuitable for file sharing and the commandeering of CPU power. In a mobile environment, information browsing is the most basic service. The information may also change according to the location and the particular user. Moreover, as the copyright of information needs to be protected, a framework, called a Virtual Private Community, is provided to make information an agent that manages access rights, and to interact with other agents autonomously. The peer-to-peer services are defined as policy packages that consist of the rules to activate agents, agent (role) definitions, and contents. VPC is carried out by VPC platforms (VPC-Ps) that manage user attributes and decide which agents to activate according to rules in the policy package and the attributes of the users. A large-scale experiment with a practical application using VPC was conducted, involving six hundred people who thoroughly enjoyed the experience. In the experiment, young women (teens-20s) in particular, returned to participate repeatedly, and enjoyed this peer-to-peer service with their friends. The word of this experiment spread fast among the people in this age group. They also frequently exchanged information among themselves. In Japan, the use of the i-mode web browser for mobile telephones (created by DoCoMo Ltd.) has increased explosively among the people in this age group, and now has thirty million users. There is a strong possibility that peer-to-peer services will also become very popular due to the influence of the people in this age group.

Acknowledgments. The authors would like to thank Dr. Yamasaki, Mr. Shiouchi, and Mr. Wada for influencing comments in developing the VPC basic model. This work was conducted under a grant for the "Research on Management of Security Policies in Mutual Connection" from Telecommunications Advancement Organization (TAO) of Japan.

References

1. Fernando Bordignon and Gabriel Tolosa, Gnutella: Distributed System for Information Storage and Searching Model Description,
   http://www.gnutella.co.uk/library/pdf/paper_final_gnutella_english.pdf (2000)
2. Napster: http://www.napster.com. (1998)
3. Magi: http://www.endeavors.com/solutions.html (2002)
4. Groove: http://www.groove.net/ (2000)
5. By Eric Korpela, Dan Werthimer, David Anderson, Jeff Cobb, and Matt Lebofsky:SETI@Home: Massively Distributed Computing for SETI. Computing in science & engineering, January/February 2001 (Vol. 3, No. 1), pp. 78–83, http://www.computer.org/cise/articles/seti.htm, IEEE (2001)
6. Cybiko: http://www.cybikoxtreme.com/index.asp (1999)
7. T. Iwao, Y. Wada, S. Yamasaki, M.Shiouchi, M. Okada, and M. Amamiya, "A Framework for the Next Generation of E-Commerce by Peer-to-Peer Contact: Virtual Private Community", WETICE2001, pp. 340-341, IEEE (2001)
8. T. Iwao, Y. Wada, S. Yamasaki, M. Shiouchi, M. Okada, and M. Amamiya, "Collaboration among Agents in Logical Network of Peer-To-Peer Services, SAINT2002, pp. 6-7, IEEE (2002)
9. Sun Microsystems, "Java Card 2.1.1 Platform", http://www.java.sun.com/products/javacard/javacard21.html,
10. B. Ramsdell, Editor, "S/MIME Version 3 Message Specification", http://www.faqs.org/rfcs/rfc2633.html, 1999
11. Stephen Kent, and Tim Polk, "Public-Key Infrastructure", http://www.ietf.org/html.charters/pkix-charter.html, 2000
12. Tadashige Iwao, Makoto Okada, Yuji Takada and Makoto Amamiya, "Flexible Multi-Agent Collaboration using Pattern Directed Message Collaboration of Field Reactor Model", LNAI 1733 pp.1–16, PRIMA'99
13. G.A. Papadopoulos and F. Arbab, "Coordination Models and Languages", Advances in Computers Vol. 46, pp 329–400, 1998
14. Amamiya, M., Hasegawa, R.: Dataflow Computing and Eager and Lazy Evaluation, New Generation Computing, 2, pp.105–129, OHMSHA and Springer-Verlag (1984).
15. Carriero, N. and Gelernter, D, "Linda in Context", Communications of the ACM Vol. 32–4, pp 444–458, 1989

An Agent-Based Approach for Trustworthy Service Location*

Pınar Yolum and Munindar P. Singh

Department of Computer Science
North Carolina State University
Raleigh, NC 27695-7535, USA
{pyolum,mpsingh}@eos.ncsu.edu

Abstract. We view the Internet as supporting a peer-to-peer information system whose components provide services to one another. The services could involve serving static pages, processing queries, or carrying out transactions. We model service providers and consumers as autonomous agents. Centralized indexes of the web are replaced by individual indexes kept by the agents. The agents can cooperate with one another. An agent may provide a service to another agent or give a referral that leads it in the right direction. Importantly, the agents can judge the quality of a service obtained and adaptively select their neighbors in order to improve their local performance.

Our approach enables us to address two important challenges. One, in contrast with traditional systems, finding trustworthy parties is nontrivial in open systems. Through referrals, agents can help one another find trustworthy parties. Two, recent work has studied the structure of the web as it happens to have emerged mostly through links on human-generated, static pages. Whereas existing work takes an after-the-fact look at web structure, we can study the emerging structure of an adaptive P2P system as it relates to the policies of the members.

1 Introduction

Peer-to-peer (P2P) systems can provide a natural basis for large-scale, decentralized information systems architectures. The two functions of information systems, querying and modifying information, are broadened in their scopes when we move to open environments. For querying, instead of looking for correct or relevant results, we look for authoritative (more generally, trustworthy) resources who can provide correct and relevant results, even though a unique correct result may not be defined. For transactions, instead of precise or relaxed consistency, we look for trustworthy resources who can deliver consistent performance with respect to suitable (e.g., economic or contractual) criteria. In both cases, there is an increased emphasis on *locating* trustworthy resources, who are willing and able to provide the *services* needed.

* This research was supported by the National Science Foundation under grant ITR-0081742. Any opinions, findings, and conclusions or recommendations expressed in this material are those of the authors and do not reflect the views of the National Science Foundation. We thank the anonymous reviewers for helpful comments.

Traditional mechanisms for locating services are based on search engines and registries. However, many niche providers will be invisible to traditional search engines, thereby yielding low recall. Because user needs are personalized, identifying the right services from a registry is nontrivial, thereby yielding low precision. Lastly, a registry or certificate authority cannot determine trustworthiness, especially for specific tasks.

By contrast, a P2P approach is natural. Some peers would be service providers, possibly catering to a niche clientele. Other peers would learn about and use the above peers and help others find them. When peers mutually help each other, they can potentially develop into communities of interest and practice where the reputations of different providers can be made and broken. Some peers may take on specialized functions similar to service registries, but others will still have to establish that these specialized peers make trustworthy service recommendations.

Referrals are essential for locating services in decentralized systems. Referrals have been used in specific applications (see Sect. 4). However, we propose that referrals form the key organizing principle for large-scale systems. Links over which parties request or give referrals and the referrals they give induce a natural structure on a system, leading to two important consequences. One, major application classes can be modeled via different structures. Two, the structure evolves in interesting ways based on the policies followed by the different parties during the referral process.

Organization.   Section 2 introduces our model of adaptive agent-based P2P systems. Section 3 describes our experimental setup, key hypotheses, and results. Section 4 discusses the relevant literature and motivates directions for further work.

2   Technical Framework

We now introduce our basic model. We model a system as consisting of *principals*, who provide and consume *services*. The principals could be people or businesses. They offer varying levels of trustworthiness and are potentially interested in knowing if other principals are trustworthy. Our notion of services is broad, but we discuss two main kinds of services below. These correspond to knowledge management and e-commerce, respectively.

The principals can track each other's trustworthiness and can give and receive *referrals* to services. Referrals are common in distributed systems, e.g., in the domain name system (DNS), but are usually given and followed in a rigid manner. By contrast, our referrals are flexible – reminiscent of referrals in human dealings. Importantly, by giving and taking referrals, principals can help one another find trustworthy parties with whom to interact. Notice that trust applies both to the ultimate service provider and to the principals who contribute to referrals to that provider.

The principals are autonomous. That is, we do not require that a principal respond to another principal by providing a service or a referral. When they do respond, there are no guarantees about the quality of the service or the suitability of a referral. However, constraints on autonomy, e.g., due to dependencies and obligations for reciprocity, are easily incorporated. Likewise, we do not assume that any principal should necessarily be trusted by others: a principal unilaterally decides how to rate another principal.

The above properties of principals match them ideally with the notion of *agents*: persistent computations that can perceive, reason, act, and communicate. Agents can represent different principals and mediate in their interactions. That is, principals are seen in the computational environment only through their agents. The agents can be thought of carrying out the book-keeping necessary for a principal to track its ratings of other principals. Moreover, the agents can interact with one another to help their principal find trustworthy peers.

In abstract terms, the principals and agents act in accordance with the following protocol. Either when a principal desires a service or when its agent anticipates the need for a service, the agent begins to look for a trustworthy provider for the specified service. The agent queries some other agents from among its *neighbors*. A queried agent may offer its principal to perform the specified service or, based on its *referral policy*, may give referrals to agents of other principals. The querying agent may accept a service offer, if any, and may pursue referrals, if any.

Each agent maintains models of its acquaintances, which describe their *expertise* (i.e., quality of the services they provide), and *sociability* (i.e., quality of the referrals they provide). Both of these elements are adapted based on service ratings from its principal. Using these models, an agent applies its *neighbor selection policy* to decide on which of its acquaintances to keep as neighbors. Key factors include the quality of the service received from a given provider, and the resulting value that can be placed on a series of referrals that led to that provider. In other words, the referring agents are rated as well. An agent's own requests go to some of its neighbors. Likewise, an agent's referrals in response to requests by others are also given to some of its neighbors, if any match. This, in a nutshell, is our basic social mechanism for locating services.

The above framework accommodates the following important properties of open information systems. One, the peers can be *heterogeneous*. The peers can offer services or follow policies distinct from all others. Two, each peer operates *autonomously* based on its local policies. Three, the peers can *adapt*. Each peer can arbitrarily modify its offerings and their quality, its policies, and its choice of neighbors.

Together, the neighborhood relations among the agents induce the structure of the given society. In general, as described above, the structure is adapted through the decisions of the different agents. Although the decisions are autonomous, they are influenced by various policies.

2.1 Applicable Domains

The above framework enables us to represent different application domains naturally. In a typical commerce setting, the service providers are distinct from the service consumers. The service consumers lack the expertise in the services that they consume and their expertise doesn't get any better over time. However, the consumers are able to judge the quality of the services provided by others. For instance, you might be a consumer for auto repair services and never learn enough to provide such a service yourself, yet you would be competent to judge if an auto mechanic did his job well. Similarly, the consumers can generate difficult queries without having high expertise. For example, a consumer can request a complicated auto-repair service without having knowledge of the domain.

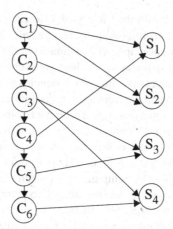

Fig. 1. A schematic configuration for e-commerce

The commerce setting contrasts with the knowledge management setting where the idea for "consuming" knowledge services might be to acquire expertise in the given domain. Yet the consumer might lack the ability to evaluate the knowledge provided by someone who has greater expertise. However, agents would improve their knowledge by asking questions; thus their expertise would increase over time. Following the same intuition, the questions an agent generates would also depend on its expertise to ensure that the agent doesn't ask a question whose answer it already knows.

Figure 1 is an example configuration of service consumers and providers that corresponds to a commerce setting. The nodes labeled C denote consumers and the nodes labeled S denote service providers. Consumers are connected to each other as well as to the service providers. These links are essentially paths that lead to service providers with different expertise. In this model, the service providers are dead ends: they don't have outgoing edges because they don't initiate queries or give referrals. Thus their sociability stays low. Their true and modeled expertise may of course be high. Section 3.3 considers some other characterizations of structure that influence and are influenced by different elements of our approach.

2.2 Evaluation Methodology

We have implemented a distributed platform using which adaptive P2P systems can be built. However, since large-scale systems of services don't yet exist, we investigate the properties of interest over a simulation, which gives us the necessary controls to adjust various policies and parameters. The simulation involves n agents, a large fraction of whom are service consumers looking for providers. Consumers have high *interest* in getting different types of services, but they have low expertise, since they don't offer services themselves. Providers have high expertise but low sociability. The interests and expertise of the agents are represented as term vectors from the vector space model (VSM) [1], each term corresponding to a different domain.

Each agent is initialized with the same model for each neighbor; this model being rigged to encourage the agents to both query and generate referrals to their neighbors. Since we do not have actual principals (i.e., humans) in the evaluation, the queries and the answers are generated by the system. More precisely, an agent generates a query by slightly perturbing its interest vector, which denotes that the agent asks a question similar to its interests. An agent answers a question if its expertise matches a question. If the expertise matches the question, then the answer is the perturbed expertise vector of the agent. When an agent gets an answer to its question, it evaluates it by again comparing the answer to the question. When an agent does not answer a question, it uses its *referral policy* to choose some of its neighbors to refer. After an agent receives an answer, it evaluates the answer by computing how much the answer matches the query. Thus, implicitly, the agents with high expertise end up giving the correct answers. After the answers are evaluated, the agent uses its *learning policy* to update the models of its neighbors. In the default learning policy, when a good answer comes in, the modeled expertise of the answering agent and the sociability of the agents that helped locate the answerer (through referrals) are increased. Similarly, when a bad answer comes in, these values are decreased. At certain intervals during the simulation, each agent has a chance to choose new neighbors from among its acquaintances based on its *neighbor selection policy*. Usually the number of neighbors is limited, so if an agent adds some neighbors it might have to drop some neighbors as well. Section 3 studies the referral policies and the neighbor selection policies in more detail.

2.3   Evaluation Metrics

The relevant global properties of the system that we study here are formally characterized by some metrics, usually involving vector operations.

Qualifications.   Two variants of a provider's expertise for a desired service are introduced. To capture the *similarity* between an agent and a query, we seek a formula that is commutative, i.e., a vector i is as similar to j as is j to i. A common similarity measure is the cosine of the angle between two vectors, but measuring the similarity of two vectors using the cosine of the angle between them does not capture the effect of the length of the vectors. Since the two vectors will always be in the first quadrant, we choose a formula that does not consider the angle between the two vectors explicitly. The following formula captures the Euclidean distance between two vectors and normalizes it to get a result between 0 and 1. It also applies in measuring the similarity of the members in a group based on their interests and expertise. (n is the number of dimensions I and J have.)

$$I \oplus J = \frac{e^{-\|I-J\|^2} - e^{-n}}{1 - e^{-n}}. \tag{1}$$

The *capability* of an agent for a query measures how similar and how strong the expertise of the agent is for a given query [2]. Capability resembles cosine similarity but also takes into account the magnitude of the expertise vector. What this means is that expertise vectors with greater magnitude turn out to be more capable for the query vector. In (2), Q refers to a query vector and E refers to an expertise vector.

$$Q \otimes E = \frac{\sum_{t=1}^{n} (q_t e_t)}{\sqrt{n \sum_{t=1}^{n} q_t^2}} \tag{2}$$

Quality. The quality of a system measures how easily agents find useful providers. Quality is the basis upon which different policies are evaluated. We define quality as obtained by an agent and then average it over all agents.

The *direct quality* viewed by an agent reflects, via (2), the usefulness of the neighbors of the agent, given its interest and their expertise. That is, we estimate the likelihood of the neighbors themselves giving good answers to the questions and ignoring the other agents.

Next, we take into account an agent's neighbors and other agents. Here, we measure how well the agent's interest matches the expertise of all other agents in the system, scaled down with the number of agents it has to pass to get to the agent. That is, the farther away the good agents from the agent, the less their contribution to the quality seen by the agent. The contribution of j to i's quality is given by:

$$\frac{I_i \otimes E_j}{path(i, j)} \tag{3}$$

where the shortest path length is used in the denominator. This metric is optimistic, since a provider may not respond and peers may not produce helpful referrals.

n**th Best.**   For a small population, it is reasonable to assume that each agent can potentially reach all other agents to which it is connected. But in large populations, an agent will be able to reach only a small fraction of the population. For this reason, instead of averaging over all agents, we take the nth best measure. That is, we measure the quality obtained by a peer by its nth best connection in the network. The choice for n is tricky. If n is too big, each peer's quality is equally bad. On the other hand, if n is too small, the quality will reflect the neighbors quality as in the direct quality metric. For the results reported below, we take n to be twice the number of neighbors of an agent.

3   Locating Service Providers

The neighborhood relations among the agents define the structure of the society. More precisely, a directed graph $G(V, E)$ is constructed, in which each node $v \in V$ in the graph represents an agent and each edge $(u, v) \in E$ between two nodes u and v denotes that v is a neighbor of u. Since the whole society can be viewed as a graph, the search for a service provider is essentially a search starting from a consumer node, which may terminate at a provider node. In this respect, the search might look trivial and could be performed with any standard search algorithm. However, there are two major challenges. One, each agent in the system has a partial view of the graph. For example, in Fig. 1, C_2 knows that C_3 and S_2 are its neighbors, but may not know that S_4 is C_3's neighbor. Two, each agent in the graph is autonomous and can well have different policies to take care of different operations like answering a question or referring a neighbor. Thus, getting at a node closer to a target provider does not guarantee that the search is progressing. For example, C_2 may ask C_3 but if C_3 is not responsive, then the search path becomes a dead-end.

With only incomplete information and possible non-cooperative peers, what is a good strategy to follow in order to find the desired service providers? We approach this question from several angles. In Sects. 3.1 and 3.2, we study referral and neighbor selection policies that can be used in different populations. We evaluate the performance of these policies and suggest when they can be used. In Sect. 3.3, we study particular topologies of networks and show why some topologies are undesirable.

3.1 Referral Policies

A referral policy specifies to whom to refer. We consider some important referral policies. We tune the simulation so that an agent answers a query only when it is sure of the answer. This ensures that only the providers answer any questions, and the consumers generate referrals to find the providers.

1. *Refer all matching neighbors.* The referring agent calculates how capable each neighbor will be in answering the given query (based on the neighbor's modeled expertise). Only neighbors scoring above a given capability threshold are referred.
2. *Refer all neighbors.* Agents refer all of their neighbors. This is a special case of the matching policy with the capability threshold set to zero. This resembles Gnutella's search process where each servent forwards an incoming query to all of its neighbors if it doesn't already have the requested file [3].
3. *Refer the best neighbor:* Refer the best matching neighbor. This is similar to Freenet's routing of request messages, where each Freenet client forwards the request to a peer that it thinks is likeliest to have the requested information [4].

We test the performance of different policies by varying the capability threshold. Figure 2 plots this threshold versus the ratio of number of good answers received to the number of peers contacted for different policies. We plot different populations on this graph varying the percentage of experts in the population. There are three populations, each with 400 agents but with 10%, 20%, and 25% experts in them. Each agent generates

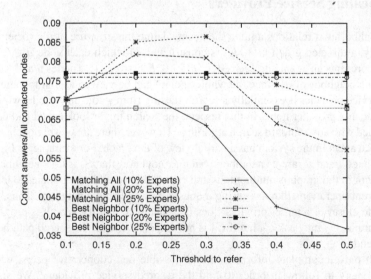

Fig. 2. Performance of referral policies

eight queries during a simulation run, resulting in 3200 queries all together. Each agent is neighbors with two percent of the population, which in this case is eight agents. Each agent sends its query to its neighbors. The neighbors then apply the selected referral policy. Thus, based on the referral policy, each query results in different number of agents being contacted. We limit the length of the referral chains to five – similar to Gnutella's time-to-live value. In Fig. 2, the lines marked *Matching All* show *Refer all matching* policy for varying thresholds on the x axis. The lines marked *BestNeighbor* plot the *Best Neighbor* policy, which is independent of the threshold.

Result 1. Among these referral policies *Refer all matching* finds providers with the highest ratio, where the best threshold increases with the percentage of experts in the society.

3.2   Neighbor Selection Policies

At certain intervals during the simulation, each agent has a chance to choose new neighbors from among its acquaintances. Usually the number of neighbors is limited so if an agent adds some neighbors it might have to drop some neighbors as well. A neighbor selection policy governs how neighbors are added and dropped. Such policies can strongly influence the structure of the resulting graph.

What would happen if each agent chose the best service providers as neighbors? Or is it better to choose agents with higher sociability rather than higher expertise? At one extreme, if each agent chooses the best providers it knows as neighbors, then the graph would acquire several stars each centered on an agent who is the best provider for the agents whose neighbor it is. On the other hand, if everybody becomes neighbors with agents that have slightly more expertise than themselves the structure will tend to be a tree, similar to an organizational hierarchy. To evaluate how the neighbor selection policies affect the structure, we compare three policies using which an agent selects the best m of its acquaintances to become its neighbors.

- *Providers*. Sort acquaintances by how their expertise matches the agent's interests.
- *Sociables*. Sort acquaintances in terms of sociability.
- *Weighted average*. Sort acquaintances in terms of a weighted average of sociability and how their expertise matches the agent's interests.

We measure the performance of different neighbor selection policies. Figure 3 plots direct quality metric versus the quality metric for different neighbor selection policies. W denotes the weight of the sociability in choosing a neighbor. When W is set to 0, the Providers policy, and when W is set to 1, the Sociables policy is in effect. Other values of W measure weighted averages of the sociability and expertise. In our simulation, each agent selects neighbors after every two queries. Thus, each policy is executed four times during the simulation run. The four points on the plot lines correspond to these.

Result 2. When all agents apply the same neighbor selection policy, *Providers* yields the highest direct quality.

Notice that *Providers* might not perform as well if each agent can exercise a different policy. The benefit of this policy is that by trying to get close to the providers, each

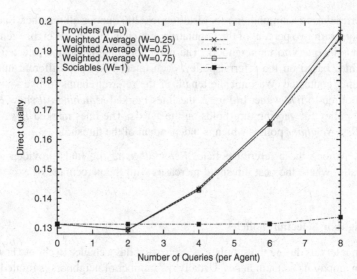

Fig. 3. Performance of neighbor selection policies

consumer maximizes the probability that it will be neighbors with at least one service provider.

While *Providers* ensures the proximity of consumers and providers, *Sociables* makes it impossible for the consumers to find the providers. Sociability corresponds to the likelihood of referring agents with high expertise. Since none of the agents have experts as neighbors, they cannot refer the experts. Interestingly, this policy results in the minimum number of neighbor changes. The sociability of the agents only increases during the first few questions, when there are still a few consumers who are still neighbors with providers. After that, those consumers who have providers as neighbors prefer more sociable consumers as neighbors.

3.3 Structure

Recall that each agent chooses its neighbors based on local information only, without knowing which neighbors other agents are choosing. Even though each agent is doing the best for itself, the resulting graph may be undesirable. Consider a bipartite graph. A graph G is bipartite if it consists of two independent sets, i.e., two sets of pairwise nonadjacent vertices. When the simulation is started, we know that there is one independent set, the group of service providers. Since these do not have outgoing edges, no two service providers can have an edge between them. Thus the providers form an independent set. Now, if the consumers also form an independent set, then the graph will be bipartite. Essentially, the consumers' forming an independent set means that all the neighbors of all the consumers are service providers. Notice that if this is the case, then the consumers will not be able exchange referrals. If the graph becomes bipartite, the system loses all the power of referrals and all consumers begin operating on the sole basis of their local knowledge. We observe that the quality of a bipartite graph is stable and non-optimal. Since the service providers do not have outgoing edges, they will not refer any new agents. Thus, the consumers will not get to know new agents, and will not be able to change their neighbors, making the graph stable. However, for each agent there will be many other agents that it cannot reach. Configurations that allow reachability to these agents will have better quality. Thus, the quality of the bipartite graph is not optimal.

Even if the graph is not bipartite, the structure could be very close to a bipartite graph. Let's say that the graph would be bipartite if we took out a few edges from the graph. This is still dangerous, since the graph might quickly evolve into a bipartite graph. The number of edges needed to be removed is a metric for determining the structural quality of the graph.

Obviously, we need to prevent the graph from turning into a bipartite graph. The only way to do so is if the agents choose their neighbors in a certain manner so as to ensure that these structures are not realized. Accordingly, we study the neighbor selection policies to see if they can cause the graph to turn into a bipartite graph.

Result 3. In a population where each agent exercises the *Providers* policy, if there are more providers than the number of neighbors an agent can have, then the graph converges to a bipartite graph.

Convergence to a bipartite graph is unavoidable when each agent discovers the service providers in the society. A partial solution is to try to obstruct this discovery by keeping the length of the referral graph short. With a short referral graph, each agent can discover only a small number of new agents. Thus, it is likely for a consumer to find a couple of service providers but unlikely that it will find all of them.

A weakly connected component of a graph is a maximal subgraph that would be connected when the edges are treated as undirected [5]. Thus different components have disjoint vertices and are mutually disconnected. Consequently, consumers can at best find service providers in their own components: We observer that if there is more than one weakly connected component in a graph, then there is at least one consumer that will not be able to find at least one service provider.

Result 4. In a population where each agent exercises the *Sociables* policy, the graph ends up a with a number of weakly connected components. Since the consumers are the only sociable agents, consumers link up with other consumers only. This results in the providers being totally isolated from the consumers.

3.4 Clustering

We define a clustering coefficient that measures how similar the neighbors of an agent are. Our coefficient is similar in motivation to Watts' coefficient [6]. However, we also take into account how similar the agent itself is to its neighbors. The average of all the agents' clustering coefficients constitutes the clustering coefficient of the graph. The reflexive interest clustering $\gamma(i)$ measures how similar the interest vectors of an agent i's neighbors (including i itself) are to each other. The reflexive interest clustering of graph G is the average of $\gamma(i)$ for all nodes in G. Below, N_i denotes the set consisting of node i and all its neighbors. E_i denotes all the edges between the nodes in N_i.

$$\gamma(i) = \frac{\sum_{(i,j)\in E_i} I_i \oplus I_j}{|N_i|(|N_i| - 1)} \tag{4}$$

Result 5. Reflexive interest clustering decreases with an increase in quality. An increase in quality shows that some consumers are getting closer to the qualified service providers. This decreases the reflexive interest clustering since now all those clustered consumers can get to the service provider through referrals and no longer need to be neighbors with other similar consumers. Consider a group of travelers who are not aware of a qualifier travel agent. As soon as one of them discovers it, the quality of the network will increase. Further, it will refer this new travel agent to its neighbors when asked for, affecting the neighbors to eventually point to the travel agent. This will decrease the interest clustering of that particular group of travelers.

4 Discussion

Our approach takes an adaptive, agent-based stance on peer-to-peer computing. This enables us to study the emergent structure of peer-to-peer networks as they are employed to help participants jointly discover and evaluate services. Below, we discuss some related approaches and then consider the greater goals of our work and the directions in which it might expand.

Directory Services. WHOIS++ uses a centroid-based indexing scheme which resembles an inverted index. Each WHOIS server maintains a centroid for itself. It is free to pass its centroid to other servers. Since the servers do not model each other, they send their centroids to arbitrary servers. Lightweight Directory Access Protocol (LDAP) allows clients to access directories on different servers, which are arranged in a hierarchy. Some LDAP servers can give referrals to other servers, but as for DNS, the referrals in LDAP are given rigidly.

Referral Networks. These are a natural way for people to go about seeking information [7]. One reason to believe that referral systems would be useful is that referrals capture the manner in which people normally help each other find trustworthy authorities. MINDS, based on the documents used by each user, was the earliest agent-based referral system [8]. Kautz *et al.* model social networks statically as graphs and study some properties of these graphs, e.g., how the accuracy of a referral to a specified individual relates to the distance of the referrer from that individual [9]. Yu presents a more extensive literature survey [10].

Service Location. Gibbins and Hall study the techniques for query routing in mediator-based resource discovery systems [11]. They represent the queries and resources through a description logic and determine the relevance of a query to a resource by subsumption or unification. Our approach is closer to what Gibbins and Hall term the disordered mediator networks, where the mediators are not forced into a particular network topology but choose who to contact as they see fit.

Recently, several peer-to-peer network architectures have been proposed, e.g., [12, 13,14]. Essentially, these systems model the network as a distributed hash table where a deterministic protocol maps keys to peers. The peers in these systems are not autonomous: the peers don't choose the keys that are assigned to them. Each peer has a table that aids the search when the item being searched does not reside at this peer. This is similar to our neighbors concept. However, in our approach, each peer can change its neighbors as it sees fit. Current systems lack this adaptability. First, the peers in the tables are defined deterministically. Second, peers cannot change their neighbors, unless the neighbors get off-line.

Directions. Our framework provides additional opportunities for research. One, probe deeper into the characteristics of the application domain, such as the services being offered, the demand for them, payment mechanisms in place, and so on. Two, explore the relationships between various policies and performance further, especially in the context of the structural assumptions of different applications. Three, model richer properties underlying the connectivity among the peers, e.g., communication cost and available bandwidth. This work will bring us closer to our long-term research goal of developing principles that can be cast in practical algorithms for producing robust, efficient, and trustworthy adaptive peer-to-peer information systems.

References

1. Salton, G., McGill, M.J.: An Introduction to Modern Information Retrieval. McGraw-Hill, New York (1983)
2. Singh, M.P., Yu, B., Venkatraman, M.: Community-based service location. Communications of the ACM **44** (2001) 49–54
3. Kan, G.: Gnutella. In: [15]. (2001) 94–122
4. Langley, A.: Freenet. In: [15]. (2001) 123–132
5. West, D.B.: Introduction to Graph Theory. 2nd edn. Prentice Hall, NJ (2001)
6. Watts, D.J.: Small Worlds: The Dynamics of Networks Between Order and Randomness. Princeton Studies in Complexity. Princeton University Press, Princeton (1999)
7. Nardi, B.A., Whittaker, S., Schwarz, H.: It's not what you know, it's who you know: work in the information age. First Monday **5** (2000)
8. Bonnell, R., Huhns, M., Stephens, L., Mukhopadhyay, U.: MINDS: Multiple intelligent node document servers. In: Proc. of the 1st IEEE Int. Conf. on Office Automation. (1984) 125–136
9. Kautz, H., Selman, B., Shah, M.: ReferralWeb: Combining social networks and collaborative filtering. Communications of the ACM **40** (1997) 63–65
10. Yu, B.: Emergence and Evolution of Agent-based Referral Networks. PhD thesis, Department of Computer Science, North Carolina State University (2001)
11. Gibbins, N., Hall, W.: Scalability issues for query routing service discovery. In: Proceedings of the Second Workshop on Infrastructure for Agents, MAS and Scalable MAS. (2001)
12. Stoica, I., Morris, R., Karger, D., Kaashoek, M.F., Balakrishnan, H.: Chord: A scalable peer-to-peer lookup service for Internet applications. In: Proceedings of the ACM SIGCOMM Conference on Applications, Technologies, Architectures, and Protocols for Computer Communication, ACM (2001) 149–160
13. Ratnasamy, S., Francis, P., Handley, M., Karp, R., Shenker, S.: A scalable content-addressable network. In: Proceedings of the ACM SIGCOMM Conference on Applications, Technologies, Architectures, and Protocols for Computer Communication. (2001) 161–172
14. Aberer, K.: P-Grid: A self-organizing access structure for P2P information systems. In: Proceedings of Cooperative Information Systems (CoopIS). (2001) 179–194
15. Oram, A., ed.: Peer-to-Peer: Harnessing the Benefits of a Disruptive Technology. O'Reilly & Associates, Sebastopol, CA (2001)

Trust-Aware Delivery of Composite Goods

Zoran Despotovic and Karl Aberer

Department of Communication Systems
Swiss Federal Institute of Technology (EPFL)
1015 Lausanne, Switzerland
{zoran.despotovic,karl.aberer}@epfl.ch

Abstract. The vast majority of the interactions in typical online communities nowadays is between complete strangers. In such settings reputation reporting and trust management models play a crucial role for proper functioning of those communities. A lot of work has been done on the issues of collecting and spreading reputations and subsequent computation of trust. The application of such data for decision making, however, is far less explored. In this paper we present a solution for scheduling exchanges among participants of an online community which takes into account their trustworthiness. In this way we can enable exchanges that would otherwise not be taking place. Thus this work also demonstrates that trust can in fact increase economic activity.

Keywords. reputation reporting, trust management, safe exchange

1   Introduction – Reputation and Trust

The rapid growth of the Internet and accompanying computing and networking technologies have made it possible for any computer around the globe to participate in a collaborative scenario such as e-commerce, teamwork, Peer-To-Peer file sharing, etc. As a result, online communities with highly autonomous members are emerging. This autonomy does not stem only from recently developed technological innovations in the area of distributed computing (P2P in particular) but also from the fact that today's typical online environments span the globe making the enforcement of the common law among their members impossible or intolerably expensive. In such a situation reputation reporting and trust assessment mechanisms play a crucial role for deterring opportunistic behaviour and encouraging trusting interactions in those environments enabling thus their proper functioning (e.g., in the area of e-commerce we refer to [7] for a detailed analysis of the importance of eBay's reputation management scheme, Feedback Forum, for the success of eBay).

Numerous works on reputation and trust management in online communities have appeared recently [1,5,7]. In our opinion, an inter-disciplinary approach taking into account works on the trust issues from the areas of sociology, psychology, and economics is needed here. Figure 1 shows the common reference model that most approaches apply. The reputation management module is responsible for collecting information about the past behavior of the members of

G. Moro and M. Koubarakis (Eds.): AP2PC 2002, LNAI 2530, pp. 57–68, 2003.
© Springer-Verlag Berlin Heidelberg 2003

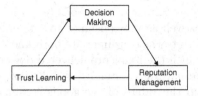

Fig. 1. Reputation and trust management reference model

the community under consideration as well as making this information available for others to use. Once the data about past interactions of potential partners has been collected, the trust management module comes into play by calculating predictions of their future behavior. Finally, the decision making module, analysing the performance of those predictions in the interaction that is about to happen and having the risk averseness related inputs from the user, makes decision whether to interact or not. The results of the interactions are then fed back into the reputation management module for the future use.

At the moment research focuses on how to organize reputation reporting models and, subsequently, compute the trustworthiness of potential exchange partners. What is missing in the literature is the analysis of whether and under what conditions to interact after the trust assessments have been made. In other words, the question how to use trust data to select optimal strategies in interactions is not addressed. In a typical example of exchanges of goods for money, a seller may require an insufficiently trustworthy buyer to deliver the payment before the delivery of the goods. On the other hand, this may be unacceptable to the buyer because of the seller's bad reputation and the buyer may as well require the seller to deliver the goods before the money is delivered. In most cases the reputation records of the two partners will suggest, however, that it is not necessary to go into these two extremes and that the deliveries of the goods and the payments can be arranged in such a way that the partners' expectations are met with high probability. For this purpose a closer analysis of the quality of the exchange strategies with respect to the trustworthiness of the partners is needed. This is where our approach comes into play. It represents a trust-related decision making scheme that can be used in many online exchange scenarios.

2   The Setting – Safe Exchange

[8] presents the basis for our work. We consider exchanges between two participants in an e-commerce scenario. The starting assumption is that one of the two participants (the "supplier") is supplying and selling a set of "goods" $C = \{c_1, \ldots, c_n\}$ to the other partner (the "consumer"). We further assume that they agreed about the overall price the consumer will have to pay for the goods (P^{contr}) as well as that the consumer may deliver the payments in arbitrarily sized chunks. The set of goods C consists of a number of items and it is assumed that the supplier's value function $V_s(x)$, describing the supplier's cost for gen-

erating and delivering any item x of the goods (expressed in monetary units or on a different scale), as well as the consumer's value function $V_c(x)$, describing what the good x is worth to the consumer are both known to the both partners. As well, the order in which the items are delivered does not matter, so that the above functions can be naturally extended to all subsets of the original set of items - by summing up the values of the goods contained in the subsets. (Or precisely, for any $A = \{c_1, \ldots, c_k\} \subset C$, we have $V_s(A) = V_s(c_1) + \cdots + V_s(c_k)$ and $V_c(A) = V_c(c_1) + \cdots + V_c(c_k)$).

In this setting, the main problem can be now stated as follows: how to combine the deliveries of the goods and the payments in such a way that, at any point during the exchange, future gains of both partners are greater than their gains from the instant defection. With such an exchange strategy the partners have no rational incentive to break the exchange at any point before its end. Therefore, an exchange sequence that meets these conditions is called *safe* (exchange) sequence. Note that the term rational exchange is also used in the literature [3].

As far as the existence of a safe exchange sequence is concerned, the main result of [8] can be described in the following way. Assuming that the supplier delivers the goods in the order $c_{i_1}, \ldots, c_{i_n}$ $(n = |C|)$ then this order is safe if and only if the payments and the goods are delivered in such a way that the gains of the both partners at any point k $(1 \le k \le n)$ in the exchange lie between these two bounds:

$$P^{min}(k) = V_c(\{c_{i_1}, \ldots, c_{i_k}\}) + P^{contr} - V_c(C)$$

and

$$P^{max}(k) = V_s(\{c_{i_1}, \ldots, c_{i_k}\}) + P^{contr} - V_s(C)$$

where P^{contr} is the overall payment to be delivered.[1] The line $P^{min}(k)$ defines the lower bound and the seller must deliver the goods in such a way that this bound is not crossed. Similarly, the consumer has to deliver the payments without crossing the upper bound $P^{max}(k)$.

With these two functions defined the main theorem states that a safe (exchange) sequence exists if and only if there exists an order $c_{i_1}, \ldots, c_{i_n}$ such that, for any $1 \le k < n$:

$$P^{min}(k+1) \le P^{max}(k).$$

But, this result is rather negative for isolated exchanges. Because $P^{min}(n) = P^{max}(n) = P^{contr}$ whichever of the two partners is supposed to make the last delivery he is better off by leaving the exchange at the penultimate step. Therefore, a mechanism for moving apart the $P^{min}(n)$ and $P^{max}(n)$ is needed and, assuming that the participants will be engaged in repeated exchanges (possibly with different partners), reputation effects (modeled through "defection costs") are suggested as one such mechanism. A more detailed discussion on this view on

---

[1] For a given order, such as $c_{i_1}, \ldots, c_{i_n}$, to make the notations more compact we write $P^{min}(k)$ instead of $P^{min}(\{c_{i_1}, \ldots, c_{i_k}\})$. Similar notations will be used for $P^{max}(k)$, $V_s(k)$ and $V_c(k)$. $V_s(n)$ and $V_c(n)$ will be denoted by V_s and V_c.

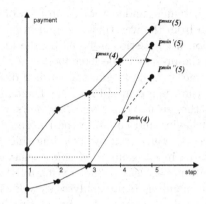

Fig. 2. Safe exchange example

the notion of reputation is given in the next section. Figure 2 presents an example. Here, the solid line (from $P^{min}(4)$ to $P^{min}\,'(5)$) shows a situation in which a safe exchange does not exist. In this case we have that $P^{max}(4) < P^{min}\,'(5)$, which is not acceptable. At the point $k = 4$, if the supplier delivers the next item, then the consumer should immediately defect because his utility at the next point would be higher than his utility at the end of the exchange. On the other hand, the dashed line shows an example in which a safe sequence exists $(P^{max}(4) > P^{min}\,''(5))$.

3 Trust Aware Safe Exchange

The results described in the previous section can be applied in many different settings. The necessary condition for the applicability of the approach is that the good being sold is divisible into a set of chunks whereby the valuations of these chunks are known to the both partners (or, a number of independent items must be collected and sold together). The condition can be met in many practical situations such as trades in eBay's auctions, exchanges of MP3 files for money in a P2P system or trades of services in a teamwork environment. But, a serious practical problem associated with the original approach is that a fully safe exchange sequence for the deliveries of the chunks of goods and the payments may not exist in many cases. Assuming that interactions in the mentioned systems are backed by underlying reputation and trust management models, a trust aware extension of the above results is required as it may help schedule exchanges between (sufficiently) honest partners in these cases.

We mentioned in the previous section that [8] suggests reputation effects modeled through "defection costs" as a mechanism that may enable the existence of a safe exchange sequence of the deliveries of goods and payments. The question how to compute these costs was not answered. In the following we sketch the reasoning behind this statement and introduce our view on reputations and trust by differentiating them from the way they are used in [8].

Namely, the mentioned suggestion is based on the idea that it may not be beneficial to defect in the present if the likelihood of having interactions in the future is sufficiently large (e.g., [2] presents a detailed discussion on the importance of this parameter in the repeated Prisoner's Dilemma game). In principle, it should be possible, though not easy, to assess one's view on this likelihood based on their past behavior and compute the threshold whether defecting is beneficial (defection costs). But, even by including this "shadow of future" in the model we still remain in the domain of *safe* exchanges, i.e, as long as the partners are acting rationally, risks do not exist and that trust per-se is not necessary. On the other hand, as many analyses as well as common sense show, people *do* take risks and *do* use trust while interacting with strangers. In this work, we provide a mechanism that, having the levels of risk averseness the two participants of the previously described scenario are willing to accept, finds an exchange strategy satisfying these levels.

Every set of goods that the supplier wants to sell to the consumer and their valuations, $V_s(x)$ and $V_c(x)$, have associated gains of the two partners. The seller's gain is the difference between the overall price of the goods and the seller's costs caused by generating and delivering the goods ($P^{contr} - V_s(C)$). Similarly, the consumer's gain is the difference between his valuations of the goods and the price he has to pay ($V_c(C) - P^{contr}$). If the exchange can be carried out in the safe manner these gains are guaranteed, but, in situations when a fully safe exchange sequence does not exist (due to the mentioned valuations) these gains cannot be achieved. Yet, if their opponents are sufficiently trustworthy, the partners can accept even unsafe exchanges. But in this case an adaptation of the original approach that takes into account the expectations of the two partners is needed. Therefore, we proceed in the following way: We assume that the two parties can compute probabilistic estimates of a specific (in the simplest case honest and dishonest) behavior of the other side. This is the task of the underlying trust computation module. [5] presents a theoretically well-founded solution for this problem. [1] is a practical approach that can be used in P2P environments. Now, we expect the partners to refine their expectations from the exchange by decreasing the expected gains. The question of how much to decrease the expected gains is left to the partners themselves. Obviously, these decreases will be based on the risk averseness of the two parties and the trustworthiness of the other side. Without elaborating further on that, note that these expectations easily translate into two bounds representing the values that the partners accept to be indebted. Having these new, decreased, expected gains we provide a provably correct quadratic-time algorithm that finds an exchange sequence, if one exists, that satisfies these expectations.

4   Algorithms

In this section we give a detailed description of the algorithm for scheduling exchanges between two partners taking into account their trustworthiness.

Let us assume that the seller delivers the goods $C = \{c_1, \ldots, c_n\}$ in the order $c_{j_1}, \ldots, c_{j_n}$ ($\{j_1, \ldots, j_n\}$ is a permutation on the set $\{1, \ldots, n\}$). Assume as well that the seller has specified that he wants his expected utility (with respect to the trustworthiness of the consumer) to be higher than U_s^{given}:

$$U_s^{exp} \geq U_s^{given}$$

On the other hand, whenever the seller delivers an item causing the lower bound P^{min} to be crossed he exposes himself to the risk that the consumer will leave the exchange. But the consumer's rationality implies that this will happen only at the step i for which the difference $P^{min}(i) - P^{max}(i-1)$ is maximal. Therefore, the seller's expected utility becomes:

$$U_s^{exp} = p_c^H [P^{contr} - V_s] + (1 - p_c^H)[P^{max}(i-1) - V_s(i)],$$

where i is the step during the exchange that achieves the maximum of $P^{min}(i) - P^{max}(i-1)$ ($P^{min}(i) > P^{max}(i-1)$) and p_c^H is the probability of the consumer's honest behavior and we are assuming that it can be obtained from the underlying trust model.
Further, because

$$P^{max}(i-1) - V_s(i) = P^{max}(i-1) - V_s(i-1) - V_s(c_{j_i})$$

and, for any i,

$$P^{max}(i-1) - V_s(i-1) = P^{contr} - V_s = G_s$$

is a constant independent of i (the seller's gain from the exchange) we have:

$$p_c^H G_s - (1 - p_c^H)[V_s(c_{j_i}) - G_s] \geq U_s^{given},$$

which leads to the following inequality:

$$V_s(c_{j_i}) \leq C_s,$$

where

$$C_s = \frac{G_s - U_s^{given}}{1 - p_c^H}.$$

Thus, whenever the seller has to cross the boundary P^{min} and deliver an item c then the value of the goods c must satisfy:

$$V_s(c) \leq C_s. \tag{1}$$

The following algorithm finds an ordering of the items (if one exists) with the property that whenever the seller goes below the lower bound P^{min} the item being delivered at that step satisfies: $V_s(c) \leq C_s$.

Algorithm 1.
Input: the set of goods C, for each $c \in C$ the consumer's and supplier's values of the good c: $V_c(c)$ and $V_s(c)$, the seller's parameter C_s, $P_{init}^{max} = P - V_s(C) = G_s$ and $P_{init}^{min} = P - V_c(C) = -G_c$

1. Divide C into two sets POS and NEG s.t.
   $POS = \{c \in C \mid V_s(c) - V_c(c) \geq 0\}$ and
   $NEG = \{c \in C \mid V_s(c) - V_c(c) < 0\}$
2. $P^{max} = P_{init}^{max}$, $P^{min} = P_{init}^{min}$, $p = |POS|$, $n = |NEG|$
3. For $i = 1$ to p {
   $F = \{c \in POS \mid P^{min} + V_c(c) \leq P^{max}\}$
   If $F = \emptyset$ then
        $F = \{c \in POS \mid V_s(c) \leq C_s\}$
   If $F = \emptyset$ then return $NO\ SOLUTION$
   $c^* = argmax_{c \in F}(V_s(c) - V_c(c))$
   $chunk[i] = c^*$
   $P^{max} = P^{max} + V_s(c^*)$, $P^{min} = P^{min} + V_c(c^*)$
   $POS = POS - \{c^*\}$ }
4. For every c in NEG: $P^{max} = P^{max} + V_s(c)$, $P^{min} = P^{min} + V_c(c)$
5. For $i = n + p$ down to $p + 1$ {
   $F = \{c \in NEG \mid P^{min} \leq P^{max} - V_s(c)\}$
   If $F = \emptyset$ then
        $F = \{c \in NEG \mid V_s(c) \leq C_s\}$
   If $F = \emptyset$ then return $NO\ SOLUTION$
   $c^* = argmax_{c \in F}(V_c(c) - V_s(c))$
   $chunk[i] = c^*$
   $P^{max} = P^{max} - V_s(c^*)$, $P^{min} = P^{min} - V_c(c^*)$
   $NEG = NEG - \{c^*\}$ }
6. Return the vector $chunk$.

The algorithm first divides the set of goods into two groups, one containing the goods with the values that move apart P^{min} and P^{max} ($V_s(c) - V_c(c) \geq 0$) and the other one consisting of the goods that make P^{min} and P^{max} closer ($V_s(c) - V_c(c) < 0$). Then, it makes a forward pass (step 3) selecting an item c satisfying the condition $V_s(c) \leq C_s$ and, at the same time, maximizing the difference $V_s(c) - V_c(c) \geq 0$. Obviously, this makes more room for items with large $V_c(c)$ that are pushed towards the end of this part of the sequence. Step 5 presents a backward pass adopting the same idea as step 3. The algorithm runs in $O(|C|^2)$ time. For the complete proof of the correctness of the algorithm we refer to [4].

The problem of the non-existence of a safe sequence of the deliveries can be overcome by the consumer's reaction as well. At any point k such that $P^{max}(k) < P^{min}(k+1)$ the consumer may deliver $P^{min}(k+1) - P^{max}(k)$ more money and thus enable the exchange to reach its end. But any such action from the consumer's side is unavoidably related to a certain level of risk due to the supplier's eventual dishonesty. Let us take a closer look at what the consumer may expect from the exchange in this case.

For a given order of deliveries $c_{i_1}, \ldots, c_{i_n}$ such that $P^{max}(k) < P^{min}(k+1)$ the consumer's expected utility can be expressed as:

$$U_c^{exp} = p_s^H [V_c - P^{contr}] + (1 - p_s^H)[V_c(k) - P^{min}(k) - V_c(c_{i_{k+1}})]$$

As $V_c - P^{contr} = V_c(k) - P^{min}(k) = G_c$ (the consumer's gain from the exchange) we have:

$$U_c^{exp} = G_c - (1 - p_s^H)V_c(c_{i_{k+1}})$$

Then the requirement that this expected value satisfies $U_c^{exp} \geq U_c^{given}$ is equivalent to:

$$V_c(c_{i_{k+1}}) \leq C_c$$

where $C_c = \frac{G_c - U_c^{given}}{1 - p_s^H}$.

Given C_c an algorithm that finds an ordering of the deliveries such that $V_c(c_{i_{k+1}}) \leq C_c$ whenever $P^{max}(k) < P^{min}(k+1)$ can be constructed by following the same line of reasoning as in the Algorithm 1. The only change is that when no safe step can be found we select the items c satisfying $V_c(c) \leq C_c$.

Assume now that, for a given set of goods C and the consumer's and seller's valuations of these goods, $V_c(c)$ and $V_s(c)$ $(c \in C)$, not only that there exists no fully safe sequence, but moreover, let us assume that due to the 'peculiar' values $V_c(c)$ and $V_s(c)$ $(c \in C)$ and/or too high expected thresholds U_s^{given} and U_c^{given}, it is impossible to get over all 'unsafe" cases $(P^{max}(i) < P^{min}(i+1))$ by the exclusive reaction of either the seller or the consumer. What is left to check in this case is whether these problems can be overcome by a cooperative action of the both partners.

The situation we are facing now is shown in Figure 3. Splitting the interval $x = P^{min}(i+1) - P^{max}(i)$ as shown in this figure the consumer would reach a point higher than $P^{max}(i)$ (x_c higher) and the seller would reach a point x_s units lower than $P^{min}(i+1)$.

Now, applying the same reasoning on the partners' expectations as before, we can see the requirements that $U_s^{exp} \geq U_s^{given}$ and $U_c^{exp} \geq U_c^{given}$ are equivalent to:

$$V_s(c_{j_{i+1}}) \leq x_c + C_s \text{ and } V_c(c_{j_{i+1}}) \leq x_s + C_c \tag{2}$$

where C_s and C_c have the same meaning as before. It is important to note here that if $V_s(c_{j_{i+1}})$ and C_s have such values that the condition $V_s(c_{j_{i+1}}) \leq x_c + C_s$ is met only with $x_c > x$ then the seller can relax this requirement by letting $x_c = x$ because he does not take any risk for $x_c \geq x$.

The following algorithm finds a sequence that satisfies these two conditions.

Algorithm 2.
Input: the set of goods C, for each $c \in C$ the consumer's and supplier's values of the good c: $V_c(c)$ and $V_s(c)$, the seller's parameter C_s, $P_{init}^{max} = P - V_s(C) = G_s$ and $P_{init}^{min} = P - V_c(C) = -G_c$

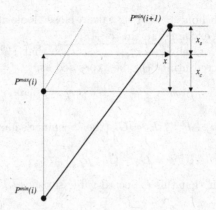

Fig. 3. Joint Overcoming of an Unsafe Step

1. Divide C into two sets POS and NEG s.t.
$$POS = \{c \in C \mid V_s(c) - V_c(c) \geq 0\} \text{ and}$$
$$NEG = \{c \in C \mid V_s(c) - V_c(c) < 0\}$$
2. $P^{max} = P^{max}_{init}$, $P^{min} = P^{min}_{init}$, $p = |POS|$, $n = |NEG|$
3. For $i = 1$ to p {
$\qquad F = \{c \in POS \mid P^{min} + V_c(c) \leq P^{max}\}$
$\qquad$ If $F = \emptyset$ then
$\qquad\qquad$ For every c in POS
$\qquad\qquad\qquad x = P^{min} + V_c(c) - P^{max}$
$\qquad\qquad\qquad x_c = V_s(c) - C_s$
$\qquad\qquad\qquad$ If $x_c > x$ then $x_c = x$
$\qquad\qquad\qquad x_s = x - x_c$
$\qquad\qquad\qquad$ If $V_c(c) \leq x_s + C_c$ then
$\qquad\qquad\qquad\qquad F = F \cup \{c\}$
$\qquad$ If $F = \emptyset$ then return $NO\ SOLUTION$
$\qquad c^* = argmax_{c \in F}(V_s(c) - V_c(c))$
$\qquad chunk[i] = c^*$
$\qquad P^{max} = P^{max} + V_s(c^*)$, $P^{min} = P^{min} + V_c(c^*)$
$\qquad POS = POS - \{c^*\}$
4. For every c in NEG: $P^{max} = P^{max} + V_s(c)$, $P^{min} = P^{min} + V_c(c)$
5. For $i = n + p$ down to $p + 1$ {
$\qquad F = \{c \in NEG \mid P^{min} \leq P^{max} - V_s(c)\}$
$\qquad$ If $F = \emptyset$ then
$\qquad\qquad$ For every c in NEG
$\qquad\qquad\qquad x = P^{min} - P^{max} + V_s(c)$
$\qquad\qquad\qquad x_c = V_s(c) - C_s$
$\qquad\qquad\qquad$ If $x_c > x$ then $x_c = x$
$\qquad\qquad\qquad x_s = x - x_c$

$$\text{If } V_c(c) \leq x_s + C_c \text{ then}$$
$$F = F \cup \{c\}$$
If $F = \emptyset$ then return $NO\ SOLUTION$
$c^* = argmax_{c \in F}(V_c(c) - V_s(c))$
$chunk[i] = c^*$
$P^{max} = P^{max} - V_s(c^*),\ \ P^{min} = P^{min} - V_c(c^*)$
$NEG = NEG - \{c^*\}$
6. Return the vector $chunk$.

In the above algorithm, it cannot be determined how the "unsafe interval" has been split (or equivalently, what x_c and x_s satisfying the conditions (2) have been actually chosen) because of the two greedy steps that choose chunks maximizing the differences $V_s(c) - V_c(c)$ and $V_c(c) - V_s(c)$ respectively. But this potential drawback can be easily overcome by constraining the content of the feasible set F. Essentially, what we are facing here is a bargaining problem and depending on the sort of the bargaining solution we want to have (maximal overall net utility is a good example) we can derive new conditions that further constrain the set of acceptable chunks. These constraints can be easily integrated into the algorithm without affecting its main properties, its greedy nature and the complexity in particular.

But, this reasoning may prompt the reader to ask the following question: how will the shown interval be split in an actual exchange when there is no third party to impose a particular splitting strategy? To answer it we recall our starting assumption that does not require the expected utilities of the two partners to be maximal but just above given thresholds. It is this assumption that makes room for the acceptability of more than one strategy, which can be clearly seen on the mentioned problem. Therefore an agreement between the partners is necessary here. A game theoretic setting in which maximal expected utilities are required by the partners will be the subject of future work.

5   Discussion on Potential Limitations

In this section we elaborate on the potentially limiting factors of the setting introduced in Sect. 2 and our trust aware extension presented in the Sects. 3 and 4. We first mention the most important factors that may limit the usability of the approach in practice and then comment on each of them:

- The goods must be divisible;
- The ordering of the items does not matter;
- Valuations of the items as seen by the two partners must be known to both of them;

Divisibility of the Goods. It should be clear from the previous discussion that the practical usability of the approach is highly dependent on the possibility to divide the goods into a number of chunks. While this is certainly not possible in most of exchanges of material (tangible) goods (we cannot deliver the sleeves, buttons and the rest of a shirt separately), it is feasible with electronic goods, which can be split arbitrarily and assembled upon reception without any effort. As far as this kind of exchanges is concerned, a typical scenario for application of the approach is exchanges of movie or music files for money. A movie file can be divided into a number of segments each of them having the value of its own. But the fact that the whole movie has been delivered has an additional value that is not present among the values of the isolated segments. This situation can be easily overcome by introducing a fictitious chunk that must be left for the end of the exchange. Note that a modification of the above algorithms that checks the satisfiability of this last chunk is necessary in this case.

We also remark that there is one more interesting possibility to model this sort of exchanges in which one fictitious chunk would come after each delivery of a really existing chunk. But the above algorithms cannot be normally applied in this case, unless the values associated with fictive chunks are all equal independently of their positions. What is necessary in this case is an order constraint based extension of the algorithms.

Ordering. The fact that the ordering of the items does not matter practically means that the supplier's and the consumer's current utilities are additive and change with a delivery of an item only for the partners' corresponding valuations of the item being delivered. This assumption leads to the low complexity of our algorithms. If it was removed a backtracking step to check the previously delivered items would be necessary at each delivery. This would lead to an increased (if not exponential) complexity of the algorithms. Fortunately, with the extension described above (a fictitious chunk at the end of the exchange) this does not present a major problem in the most typical scenario of electronic exchanges.

Known Valuations of the Goods. The partners must know the two bounds (P^{max} and P^{min}) in order to be able to perform only acceptably safe steps. As the value functions (V_s and V_c) are explicitly present in these two bounds it is clear that the partners must know each other's valuations of the goods. In practice, they will hardly ever be able to know these values exactly. On the other hand, we believe that close assessments of the valuations can be made. On the sellers' side these utilities are related to the price a seller can obtain on a market, considering additional factors such as the expected time needed to sell the good. On the consumers' side these utilities could for example be related to the popularity of the goods, taking into account specific characteristics of the consumer, e.g. being part of a specific consumer group.

6   Conclusions and Future Work

In this paper we propose a mechanism for scheduling exchanges of goods for money that is aware of the trustworthiness of the exchange participants. It is based on the risk averseness related inputs from the two exchange partners. The main contribution of the work is that it provides the theoretical foundations that enable sufficiently trustworthy partners carry out exchanges in cases when they cannot proceed in a completely safe manner.

Further, we elaborated on the practical usability of the approach giving some clues for how to overcome potentially limiting factors for its applicability in practice. These problems will be explored in more detail in our future work. As well, what is left to be checked is how the model behaves on real data from typical online settings. A particularly important question we must answer here is that of the relationship between the granularity levels of the partitioned goods, on the one hand, and the fraction of the cases in which our algorithms will find a sufficiently safe sequence, on the other hand, given different values of the trustworthiness of the participants as a parameter. Having this question answered we will be able to present closer assessments of the practical usability of the approach.

Finally, a game-theoretic extension of this work arising when the partners are interested in maximizing their expected gains from the exchanges will be considered in the future work. In particular, we will address the problem of the uniqueness of the optimal strategies available to the exchange partners under this assumption.

References

1. Aberer, K., Despotovic, Z.: Managing Trust in a Peer-2-Peer Information System. Ninth International Conference on Information and Knowledge Management (CIKM 2001), Atlanta, USA (2001)
2. Axelrod, R.: The Evolution of Cooperation. Basic Books, New York (1984)
3. Buttyan, L.: Building Blocks for Secure Services: Authenticated Key Transport and Rational Exchange Protocols. Ph.D. Thesis No. 2511 (2001), Swiss Federal Institute of Technology, Lausanne (EPFL) (2001)
4. Despotovic, Z., Aberer, K.: Trust-Aware Delivery of Composite Goods. Swiss Federal Institute of Technology, (EPFL), Technical Report, April (2002)
5. Mui, L., Mohtashemi, M., Halberstadt, A.: A Computational Model of Trust and Reputation. 35th Hawaii International Conference on System Science (HICSS) (2002)
6. Myerson, R.B.: Game Theory: Analysis of Conflict. Harvard University Press, Cambridge, MA (1991)
7. Resnick, P., Zeckhauser, R.: Trust Among Strangers in Internet Transactions: Empirical Analysis of eBay's Reputation System. Working Paper for the NBER workshop on empirical studies of electronic commerce (2001)
8. Sandholm, T.W.: Negotiation Among Self-Interested Computationally Limited Agents. PhD Thesis, University of Massachusetts, Amherst (1996)
9. Sandholm, T., Ferrandon, V.: Safe Exchange Planner. International Conference on Multi-Agent Systems (ICMAS), Boston, MA (2000)
10. Tesch, T., Aberer, K.: Scheduling Non-Enforceable Contracts among Autonomous Agents. Third IFCIS Int. Conference on Cooperative Information Systems, New York, USA (1998)

Engineering an Agent-Based Peer-to-Peer Resource Discovery System

Andrew Smithson and Luc Moreau*

Department of Electronics and Computer Science
University of Southampton
Southampton SO17 1BJ UK
{ans199,L.Moreau}@ecs.soton.ac.uk

Abstract. We have designed an agent-based peer-to-peer resource discovery system, which combines a set of original features. We distinguish synchronous and asynchronous searches, and structure them in terms of speech acts in an agent communication language. We rely on a distributed reference counting counting mechanism to detect the termination of asynchronous distributed searches. Ontologies are used to define resource descriptors in an extensible and open manner, as well as queries over such resources. A graphical user interface dynamically constructed from available resource descriptors is proposed. The system has been fully implemented in SoFAR, the Southampton Framework for Agent Research.

1 Introduction

Resource discovery is a critical activity in large scale distributed systems such as Grid environments [1]. However, these environments tend to be constituted by the confederation of multiple domains [2] or the aggregation of multiple Virtual Organisations [3], and therefore they do not naturally support a central point of control that could be used as a repository for resource descriptors.

In practice, when applications run in a large scale distributed system, opportunistic temporary associations tend to be created (e.g. as virtual organisations or even virtual private networks) to reflect the social or organisational structure of the institutions involved in such computations. Such opportunistic and ad-hoc associations are by excellence the type of associations supported by peer-to-peer computing. Consequently, we have undertaken the design of an agent-based peer-to-peer search system for resources in a large scale distributed environment. Peer-to-peer computing and agent-based systems are well suited for this task, as we now explain.

Our first main design decision was to make the system follow the peer-to-peer model of networking as opposed to the traditional client-server model. It avoids a central point of failure, which is a major weakness in large scale distributed

---

* This research is funded in part by EPSRC myGrid project (reference GR/R67743/01).

G. Moro and M. Koubarakis (Eds.): AP2PC 2002, LNAI 2530, pp. 69–80, 2003.

systems; this also means that the system cannot be shut down by removing a central node, as illustrated in the recent court decisions against the Napster music sharing service [4].

In a peer-to-peer system, search protocols need to be developed to use the network topology in the most efficient manner. It is not feasible for each peer to know of every other peer on the network; so, if every peer knows of a subset of all the peers, then it can communicate with them, and then each of those peers can then pass on the request to the set of peers that they know about, and so on. In this way, the request fans out from the originator and can reach many hosts in an exponential manner. For example, if each peer knows about five peers and the request is forwarded just four times, then the request will eventually reach up to $5 + 5^2 + 5^3 + 5^4 = 780$ peers. Obviously, there will be peers that know about the same peers, so this number may be slightly smaller.

Agent-based computing [5] offers the desired characteristics to implement a peer-to-peer system. Indeed, from a design viewpoint [6], agents are the right abstraction to represent peers, because of their autonomous and social natures [7]. In such a peer-to-peer context, their complex interactions can be the basis of a cooperative multi-agent system. Additionally, from an engineering viewpoint, agents systems [8] support ontologies able to provide extensible descriptions of resources, which is a fundamental property for building open systems.

A number of non trivial issues need to be investigated in order to build an agent-based peer-to-peer search system.

1. Nature of the search and how results get propagated;
2. Detection of a search termination, and cyclic search prevention;
3. Extensible and open descriptors for resources, and associated querying.

Our focus in this paper is on the *engineering* of an open and extensible peer-to-peer system. We describe our solutions to these issues, and present our design of the system we have implemented in SoFAR, the Southampton Framework for Agent Research [8]. First, we overview the key issues we address (Sect. 2), we then present the overall architecture (Sect. 3), which we follow by some design details (Sect. 4). We then talk about specific implementation aspects (Sect. 5).

2   Key Issues Overview

In this section, we overview the key issues related to building an agent-based peer-to-peer search system.

2.1   Types of Search

Two methods are available to return search results. Either results can be returned along the path the search request took, as in the Gnutella system [9], or they can be returned directly to the search originator. We can regard the former approach as *synchronous*: peers have to wait until their neighbour peers have returned their results, to which they can add their own results, before propagating them back

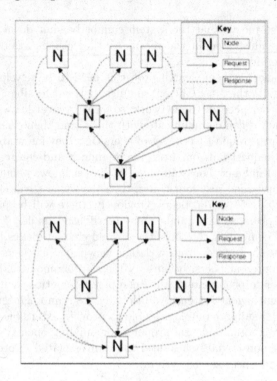

Fig. 1. Synchronous (top picture) and asynchronous (bottom picture) searches

to the previous peers that issued the requests (cf. Fig. 1). The latter approach is more *asynchronous*, as each peer can return the results directly to the originator as soon as they are available (cf. Fig. 1).

With the synchronous method, all results are returned to the originator at once, which also marks the end of the search, whereas the asynchronous method returns results to the originator as soon as available, but another mechanism is necessary so that the system can indicate the end of the search.

The synchronous search provides some anonymity to the search, as peers do not know who the request originator is, nor does the originator know where the results came from. With the asynchronous search, the anonymity of the originator is lost as each peer needs to know who to send the results to.

2.2   Distributed Termination

Asynchronous search has some interesting properties: as soon as a search result is found, it can be returned to the originator. From the originator's viewpoint, results are streamed, which allows users to have an early access to information, or which allows further processing to be pipelined with the ongoing search. As far as the functionality of a search system is concerned, it is also important to notify the user that all results have been produced, so that the user knows that there is no need to wait further. Such a facility requires an extra mechanism to indicate when all results have been delivered. This is the role of a *termination detector*, which is able to notify the originator that the following three conditions are satisfied in the whole system: *(i)* there is no peer left that has to process a request, *(ii)* there is no message in transit containing a request, *(iii)* there is no message in transit containing a result.

As we do not want the same peers forwarding the same request round a loop in the network, each search query will need to contain a mechanism by which each peer can decide if it has previously seen this request.

2.3 Descriptor and Query Language

Resources need to be described in such a way that they can be queried by each of the agents performing the search. To this end, we use *ontologies* to construct an "explicit specification of a conceptualisation [10]". Ontologies are created for each aspect of a resource that needs to be described. These descriptions can then be grouped together and "attached" to resources.

We expect descriptions to be extensible and users to be able to create their own descriptions. The system should be able to support such new descriptions, as they come on line, without the need to change the search procedure, and without having to re-compile or re-deploy the system.

Describing resources is only one facet of resource discovery. There is also a need for a query language able to operate over resource descriptions. We expect this language to be simple enough to be usable by any user. A graphical user interface is desirable as it can help users who are not computer literate. The difficulty here is to define such an interface supporting the definition of queries over a description language that is extensible.

3   Overall Architecture

The agents for the system fall into two categories, those that send and receive the search requests and those that service them against the resources and their ontology descriptions.

Initially, there is an agent that sends out the created search request, marked as 'ResultsAgent' in Fig. 2, and that is defined as the endpoint for the results being returned, as either an array of results or individual result from the peers hosting the resources. A search agent receives requests and passes them onto the peers it knows about, while at the same time performing the search on all the agents for each of the resources being shared on that peer. These are marked as 'SearchAgent' in Fig. 2, and communicate both with other peers on the network and other agents running on the local peer.

The other agents found in the system, marked as 'Resource SearchAgent' in Fig. 2, are designed and built to match any search query to the resources they know about, whether that is a set of files on the system or other resources available to users. The results are passed back to the SearchAgent on the same

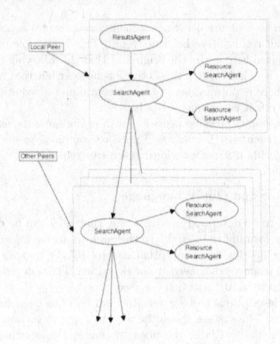

Fig. 2. Overall architecture

peer, which then get passed on back to the originator in the case of the synchronous search or sent back to the originator's ResultsAgent in the case of the asynchronous protocol.

4   Design Details

The purpose of this section is to provide some details about our design, focusing in particular on the ontology for descriptors, the specification of queries, and the detection of distributed termination.

4.1   Descriptor Ontology

In order to be discovered, resources need to be described. To maintain some uniformity in the system, we introduce the idea of an abstract concept called a *Descriptor*. Any kind of description mechanism has to extend (in the object-oriented sense) the abstract concept Descriptor. These Descriptors can then be bundled together in order to form a resource description.

One of the resources currently available for sharing within the system is a file stored on a user's computer or file store. The descriptors currently available can describe: filenames, authors, MIME types, copyright details, and the contents of a file. For bibliographic resources, we propose to use the Dublin Core metadata format. For Web services, WSDL descriptions of their interfaces can be used (http://www.w3.org/TR/wsdl).

Symmetrically, a search query can be derived from the ontology of descriptors. The SoFAR agent framework provides an ontology-based query language, which can be used by users to specify the resources they are interested in. Such a query language is based on pattern matching over ontological terms and constraints resolution. Section 5.2 describes the user interface that helps users compose queries based on such a language.

4.2   Query Specification

Both synchronous and asynchronous searches require a search query, a time-to-live argument and a unique identifier, whose roles are successively defined below.

The query is expressed in the ontology-based query language and specifies the set of descriptor patterns and constraints that resource descriptors must match. Queries are not restricted to a single pre-defined ontology; they can operate over descriptors defined at run-time provided that they express constraints over a subclass of Descriptor.

The time-to-live argument is defined as an integer and is used to control the depth of the search. A search starts off with a time-to-live value. Every time a peer forwards a query, it decrements the value of the time-to-live parameter. Once a peer receives a query with a zero time-to-live parameter, the peer no longer forwards the query. In the synchronous search, it is at this point that the results are being returned back to the search originator.

The purpose of the unique identifier is to avoid cyclic searches during which a search request would be repeatedly forwarded (within the predefined time to live) in a cycle of peers. The identifier needs to be unique across all peers in the system. For every incoming query, a SearchAgent decides if the query has been seen before; if it has not processed it before, it stores the identifier and undertakes the query.

These three parameters are all that is required for a synchronous search. For an asynchronous search, two further parameters are required, respectively to identify the query originator and a search termination detector. The first extra parameter specifies where the results should be returned to directly; this parameter typically identifies the agent that sends out the request to ensure that the results get back to the same place. The second extra parameter is used to detect the termination of an asynchronous search, which we describe in the next subsection.

The results of a search contain the set of Descriptors of each discovered resource, and the location of the resource, expressed as a URL, which can then be used to access the resource.

4.3   Distributed Termination

The problem of distributed termination detection is formulated as follows. Let us consider an asynchronous distributed system, where nodes only communicate by exchange of messages. A computation is said to be in a *terminated state* if each node has completed its local computation and if there is no message in transit. Termination detection is defined as the ability to assert that the system has reached a terminated state.

We use a well-known result [11] in distributed systems, according to which deciding whether a distributed computation is terminated can be implemented by distributed reference counting. For an asynchronous search, the originator creates a *token*, which is a newly created object that is reference counted; on the originator, a method is associated with the token, which is triggered when the token's reference counter reaches zero. When the originator initiates the query, it includes the token as part of the query; every hosts that forwards the query is also required to include the same token. When a peer terminates its search locally, it is required to "lose" its reference to the token, which in effect decrements the counter associated with it on the originator. The token's reference counter reaches the value zero when no other peer contains a reference to the token and no request with that token is in transit. Many algorithms can be used for distributed reference counting, and we are currently investigating which one would be most suitable to a peer to peer context.

An action can then be activated when the counter reaches zero, i.e., when the search has completed. An obvious application is to alert the user of the search's completion; another kind of processing on the results would be to forward results to another agent.

5   Implementation

In this section, we describe how the system was implemented in SoFAR, the Southampton Framework for Agent Research [8]. SoFAR defines an agent as an entity implementing a set of speech acts, representing common basic communication patterns. In addition to asynchronous performatives as prescribed by FIPA and KQML agent communication languages, SoFAR also supports synchronous performatives because they are useful for querying data- and knowledge- bases or for integrating with Web Services [12].

5.1   Agents Implementation

The SearchAgent is designed to receive requests from other peers, process them locally and pass them onto the other peers it knows about. The two types of searches are supported by different performatives. A synchronous search is implemented by the performative `query_ref`, which returns the array of descriptors that match the search. Asynchronous search is supported by the performative `request`, which does not return any result.

A peer maintains a collection of proxies to agents that are running on the local system and to other peers the agent knows about. When a search query comes in, the agent starts two threads to pass the request onto the agents stored in both collections. In the synchronous search, the agent blocks until both threads

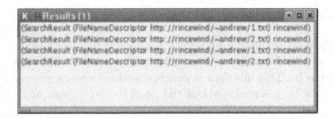

Fig. 3. Results

have completed at which time all the results are returned back along the search chain. The asynchronous search just lets the two threads run since once they are running the main agent has no further part to play in the execution. The SearchAgent also allows other resource agents to be added to or removed from the system dynamically, through a mechanism of registration.

The FileSearchAgent is an example of an agent managing file resources. The FileSearchAgent accepts incoming search requests, checks if it knows about any files that match the search query, and returns the information to the originator along the specified route. The agent holds a persistent database mapping filenames onto resource descriptions. A database entry successfully matches a query if the descriptions contained in the entry satisfy each of the query conjuncts.

The returned result is a FileNameDescriptor which contains the name of the file that matched the query and a URL from which it can be accessed, for instance using RMI, or downloaded, for instance, using HTTP or FTP. We can therefore see that the agent framework is only used for discovering resources, while more specialised protocols are used for accessing the resource itself.

Results are returned finally to a ResultsAgent which deals with them as specified by the user. It makes use of a ResultsProcessor implementing the following three methods:

```
void add(Predicate[] results)
void add(Predicate result)
void alert()
```

The add methods are called when results are returned to the ResultsAgent, while the alert method is called when the asynchronous search is completed. Currently, there are two implemented ResultsProcessors within the system. The first one prints the results to the standard output stream. The second processor, after creating a scrolling window, prints the results in the window and generates an alert window when the asynchronous search completes.

When results are printed in the window (cf. Fig. 3), the user has the ability to select them by double clicking on them. An action can be programmed with the selection, and can be parameterised by the type of the selected data (through a visitor pattern). When a file result is selected, the user is presented with a dialog box to choose a location where the file can be saved; then, the file is transferred from the hosting peer's computer to the user's computer.

5.2   Graphical User Interface

The main purpose of the graphical user interface is to allow a user to set up the parameters of search queries to send off into the network while waiting for the results to come in. This interface is programmed as an open system so that new descriptors can be inserted without the need to re-program or re-compile the interface.

Descriptor Creation. When users have to define a new instance of a Descriptor, a window allows them to instantiate the fields of the Descriptor. The window acts as an input form whose layout is based on the definition of the Descriptor, which can be gained from the ontological definition of the Descriptor. (Reflexive methods are provided by the SoFAR framework to that effect.)

In the ontological definition of a concept, a field defined as a primitive type, e.g. string or integer, is represented as a text box in which the user can type the value they want, and which is converted into the suitable internal representation. If the field is not a primitive type, then the user is presented with a button, which when clicked on, opens a new window that contains the definition of the concept. In Fig. 4, we can see the structure of a copyrightDescriptor, with a field "author" defined as a complex type (itself composed of firstName and lastName fields) and a field year defined as a primitive type.

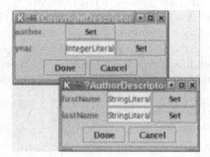

Fig. 4. Ontology setup

Search Query Creation. In order to create a search query, the user needs to create a set of descriptions (or description constraints) they want in the resource. They select each of the Descriptors that is necessary from a drop down list that is generated from the set of Descriptors known to the system. Descriptors can be added without recompiling the graphical interface. The selected Descriptor is then created and added to the descriptor set, in order to be used in the searches.

Actually, descriptors can be discovered using the search mechanism that we are describing: such a capability illustrates the reflexive nature of the system. However, a minimal set of descriptors is required (for instance, to discover descriptors), which can be found in a configuration file bundled with each peer.

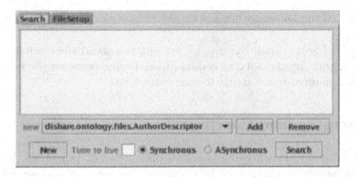

Fig. 5. Search

Once the set of Descriptors is complete, the user selects the type of search they want (synchronous or asynchronous), and sets how far they want the search to propagate via the time-to-live parameter (cf. Fig. 5). When the user clicks on the search button, the necessary search packet is constructed and passed to the ResultsAgent which fills in the rest of the necessary fields before sending the request out on the network.

Publishing Window. Publishing resources is made available through a user interface by which users can specify the resources to be made available for sharing. For each resource, the user is requested to attach a set of Descriptors describing the resource. The same interface is used here to edit these descriptors as when the user is creating a search request. The pairings between the files and their descriptor set are kept in a persistent database. Descriptors are allowed to be updated during program execution.

6   Related Work

Resource discovery is a central issue in distributed systems and numerous solutions exist, such as UDDI (www.uddi.org) for Web Services or Jini [13]. These solutions tend to adopt a client-server model; there are proposals to extend these so that resource information is replicated across multiple repositories.

Peer to peer systems have been widely publicised by systems such as Napster [4] and Gnutella [9]. JXTA (www.jxta.org) is a set of thin protocols for peer-to-peer computing supported by SUN Microsystems. A Google search on peer-to-peer computing also shows multiple commercial systems.

Gibbins and Hall [14] discuss the relationship between mediator-based systems for service discovery in multi-agent systems, and the technique of query routing used for resource discovery in distributed information systems. They provide a model of query routing which is used to examine the scalability of common architectures for resource discovery. The kind of search we implemented is illustrative of how we can engineer a peer-to-peer search system; our framework is suitable to implement other search algorithms as described by Gibbins and Hall.

Langley, Paolucci and Sycara [15] set out to extend the Gnutella architecture to support Agent-to-Agent communities. Dunne proposes the use of mobile agents in a manner not disimilar to our system [16].

7   Discussion and Conclusion

Asynchronous and synchronous searches offer different properties, in terms of result availability or anonymity. In particular, the asynchronous search requires the originator to be directly contactable by peers hosting resources matching queries. This may not always be a reasonable asumption in the presence of firewalls or disconnected networks. A combination of asynchronous and synchronous searches may therefore be a suitable solution to this problem.

Throughout the paper we have discussed how the system is designed to be open and how extra ontologies or agents can be added without re-compiling or re-deploying it. This can be taken further by looking at how new descriptors can be added to a system. They can be provided as an archive that contains a listing of them to be added to the list of available descriptors for the user interface and a jar file that contains their concrete implementations. These archives can then be added to the system at run-time and used as soon as the user has got access to them on their system. These resources can be discovered, either by using the FileSearchAgent already implemented or by creating a new set of descriptors especially for the task. The results of these searches can be transferred and installed on the originator's system when selected by the user.

In this paper, we have focused on the design and engineering of a resource discovery system using an agent framework. From an engineering viewpoint, this has allowed us to provide a system that is *extensible* because new descriptions and agents can be added dynamically, and *reflexive* because the search technique can be applied to aspects of the system itself. These properties allow such a system to be long lived, without requiring it to be re-compiled or re-deployed frequently.

We are planning to experiment with such a system in two different contexts. We intend to use it to discover resources and services in the context of a Grid application (www.mygrid.org.uk) and to make information accessible in the context of mobile users [17]; in particular, search results can be used as input of a recommender system.

References

1. Foster, I., Kesselman, C., eds.: The Grid: Blueprint for a New Computing Infrastructure. Morgan Kaufman Publishers (1998)
2. Cardelli, L.: Mobile computations. In: Mobile Object Systems: Towards the Programmable Internet. Springer-Verlag (1997) 3–6 Lecture Notes in Computer Science No. 1222.

3. Foster, I., Kesselman, C., Tuecke, S.: The Anatomy of the Grid. Enabling Scalable Virtual Organizations. International Journal of Supercomputer Applications (2001)

4. Napster. http://www.napster.com (1999)

5. Jennings, N.R., Sycara, K., Wooldridge, M.: A Roadmap of Agent Research and Development. Int. Journal of Autonomous Agents and Multi-Agent Systems **1** (1998) 7–38

6. Jennings, N.R., Wooldridge, M.: Agent-Oriented Software Engineering. In: Handbook of Agent Technology. AAAI/MIT Press (2001)

7. Wooldridge, M., Jennings, N.R.: Intelligent Agents: Theory and Practice. Knowledge Engineering Review **10** (1995)

8. Moreau, L., Gibbins, N., DeRoure, D., El-Beltagy, S., Hall, W., Hughes, G., Joyce, D., Kim, S., Michaelides, D., Millard, D., Reich, S., Tansley, R., Weal, M.: SoFAR with DIM Agents: An Agent Framework for Distributed Information Management. In: The Fifth International Conference and Exhibition on The Practical Application of Intelligent Agents and Multi-Agents, Manchester, UK (2000) 369–388

9. Gnutella. http://www.gnutella.com (2000)

10. Gruber, T.R.: Toward principles for the design of ontologies used for knowledge sharing. Technical Report KSL-93-04, Knowledge Systems Laboratory, Stanford University (1993)

11. Tel, G., Mattern, F.: The Derivation of Distributed Termination Detection Algorithms from Garbage Collection Schemes. ACM Transactions on Programming Languages and Systems **15** (1993) 1–35

12. Moreau, L.: Agents for the Grid: A Comparison for Web Services (Part 1: the transport layer). In Bal, H.E., Lohr, K.P., Reinefeld, A., eds.: Second IEEE/ACM International Symposium on Cluster Computing and the Grid (CCGRID 2002), Berlin, Germany, IEEE Computer Society (2002) 220–228

13. Oaks, S., Wong, H.: Jini In a Nutshell. O'Reilly (2000)

14. Gibbins, N., Hall, W.: Scalability issues for query routing service discovery. In: Proceedings of the Second Workshop on Infrastructure for Agents, MAS and Scalable MAS. (2001)

15. Langley, B., Paolucci, M., Sycara, K.: Discovery of infrastructure in multi-agent systems. In: Proceedings of the Second Workshop on Infrastructure for Agents, MAS and Scalable MAS. (2001)

16. Dunne, C.R.: Using Mobile Agents for Network Resource Discovery in Peer-to-Peer Networks. SIGecom Exchanges, Newsletter of the ACM Special Interest Group on E-Commerce, Vol. 2.3, pages 1–9 (2001)

17. Moreau, L., Roure, D.D., Hall, W., Jennings, N.: MAGNITUDE: Mobile AGents Negotiating for ITinerant Users in the Distributed Enterprise. http://www.ecs.soton.ac.uk/~lavm/magnitude/ (2001)

Peer-to-Peer Paradigm for a Semantic Search Engine

S. Bergamaschi[1,2] and F. Guerra[1]

[1] Dipartimento di Ingegneria dell'Informazione
Università di Modena e Reggio Emilia
Via Vignolese 905, 41100 Modena
[2] CSITE-CNR Bologna
V. le Risorgimento 2, 40136 Bologna
{bergamaschi.sonia,guerra.francesco}@unimo.it

Abstract. This paper provides, firstly, a general description of the research project SEWASIE and, secondly, a proposal of an architectural evolution of the SEWASIE system in the direction of peer-to-peer paradigm. The SEWASIE project has the aim to design and implement an advanced search engine enabling intelligent access to heterogeneous data sources on the web using community-specific multilingual ontologies. After a presentation of the main features of the system a preliminar proposal of architectural evolutions of the SEWASIE system in the direction of peer-to-peer paradigm is proposed.

1 Introduction

Peer-to-peer (hereafter P2P) consists of an open-ended network of distributed computational *peers*, where each peer can exchange data and services with a set of other peers called *acquaintances*. Peers should be autonomous in choosing their aquaintances. Moreover, it is usually assumed that there is no global control in the form of a global registry, global services, or global resources management nor a global schema or data repository. Gnutella and Napster [8] made the P2P paradigm popular as a version of distributed computing between traditional distributed systems and the web. Very recently a proposal in data management raised by this paradigm has been presented in [4]. In this context, each peer may have data to share with other peers and, in [4], it is assumed that each peer's database is relational and, since the data residing in different databases may have semantic inter-dependencies, peers are allowed to specify *coordination formulas*. Coordination formulas explain how data in one peer must relate to data in an acquuience and may also act as constraints or for propagating updates. Peer' s need an acquaintance initialization protocol where two peers exchange views of their databases and agree on levels of coordination and the level of coordination should be dynamic, i.e. peers should be able to establish and modify acquintances, with little human intervention. This is a crucial point and introduces a high degree of innovation into the traditional distributed databases and multi-database systems data management approach. The common assumption

G. Moro and M. Koubarakis (Eds.): AP2PC 2002, LNAI 2530, pp. 81–86, 2003.

in this area is, in fact, to have a global database schema, usually obtained by skilled databases designers [13,9]. In the new dynamic setting of P2P, we cannot assume the existence of a global schema for all databases in a P2P network or even those of the acquianted databases. Nevertheless, as proposed both in [4] and in this paper, the architecture of heterogeneous distributed databases or often called *multi-database systems* e.g. Multibase [11] , Momis [2,1,3], Garlic [5], TSIMMIS [6], and Information Manifold [7] is still valid. In most of these systems, a user issues queries to a global schema, and the system (called a *mediator* in [12]) maps the queries to subqueries on the underlying data sources. Each data source has a wrapper able to map subqueries into its native query language. A database designer is responsible for creating the global schema and the mappings with the data sources and for maintaining the schema and mappings with respect to evoution (i. e. data sources entering and leaving the system).

The SEWASIE system, presented in the paper, organizes and manages information in SINodes which follow the architecture of heterogeneous multi-database systems.

After a presentation of the main features of the system, Sect. 2, a preliminar proposal of architectural evolutions of the SEWASIE system in the direction of peer-to peer paradigm is proposed in Sect. 3.

2   The SEWASIE Project and Architecture

SEWASIE (Semantic Webs and AgentS in Integrated Economies) (IST-2001-34825) is a research project founded by EU on action line Semantic Web (May 2002/April 2005) (http://www.sewasie.org). The goal of the SEWASIE project is to design and implement an advanced search engine enabling intelligent access to heterogeneous data sources on the web via semantic enrichment to provide the basis of structured secure web-based communication. A SEWASIE user has at his disposal a search client with an easy-to-use query interface able to extract the required information from the Internet and to show it in an easily enjoyable format. From an architectural point of view, the SEWASIE prototype will provide a search engine client and indexing servers and ontologies.

The project will develop an agent-based secure, scalable and distributed system architecture for semantic search using community-specific multilingual ontologies; ontologies will be equipped with an inference layer grounded in WC3 standards. The developed system have to meet the needs of SMEs in a EU context.

The SEWASIE vision helps European enterprises to compete in a global market and to form strategic alliances at a European level by providing a sophisticated retrieval, brokering and communication service on basis of the semantic web technology. In particular, SEWASIE has to help European SMEs to find the right strategic information at the right time in a multinational environment; provide advanced and novel services for monitoring and linking information in the context of risk management and competitor analysis; provide ontology-based communication mechanisms for negotiation in multi-language environments; ease

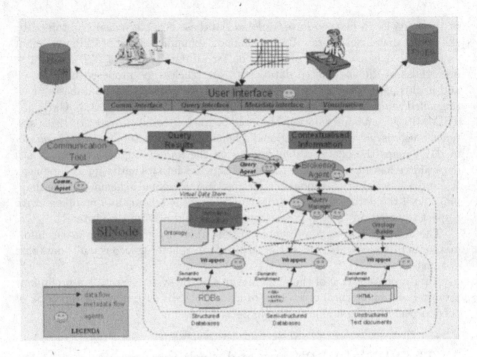

Fig. 1. The Sewasie architecture

the use of complex cross-language retrieval and data condensation tools by providing intuitive interfaces.

From an architectural point of view (see Fig. 1), the SEWASIE system will realise a virtual network, SEWASIE Virtual Network (SVN) whose nodes are SEWASIE Information Nodes (SINode):

- SINodes are mediator-based systems, each including a Virtual Data Store, an Ontology Builder, and a Query Manager;
- The managed Information Sources are heterogeneous collections of structured, semi-structured, or unstructured data, e.g. relational databases, XML or HTML documents;
- Ontologies are multilingual;
- In query solving phase, starting from a specified SINode, a Query Agent accesses other SINodes and thus collects partial answers;
- A Query Agent communicates with the Brokering Agent to acquire useful SINodes.
- The Brokering Agent maintains the knowledge related to the SEWASIE Virtual Network and the user profiles;
- The Brokering Agent classifies SINodes, it is responsible for handling the acquisition of a new SINode and for consequently updating of the SEWASIE Virtual Network.

3   SEWASIE in a P2P Architecture

In the general case, a P2P system has no centralized schema and no central administration. In the SEWASIE architecture we rely on two centralized aspects: the brokering agent (global control) that holds the knowledge of the overall network and the global schema or data repository of the network. Furthermore, SINodes are passive elements whose data and metadata are extracted by query agents and the brokering agent. How can we change the SEWASIE architecture in order to evolve towards a peer-to-peer paradigm?

We can define two alternative P2P networks (see Fig. 2):

- **Brokering Agents Network.** We can devise more brokering agents, one for each SINode, holding both SINode knowledge and coordination knowledge. Furthermore, within the Brokering Agents Network, each Brokering Agent communicates with other peers in order to have information about other information nodes.
- **INTER SINodes Network.** A SINode provides to other SINodes the knowledge about the involved information sources. It is possible to specify coordination formulas that explain how the data in one peer must relate data in an acquaintance.

The Brokering Agents P2P network generates a distributed knowledge about the involved information sources and may provide a support for generating coor-

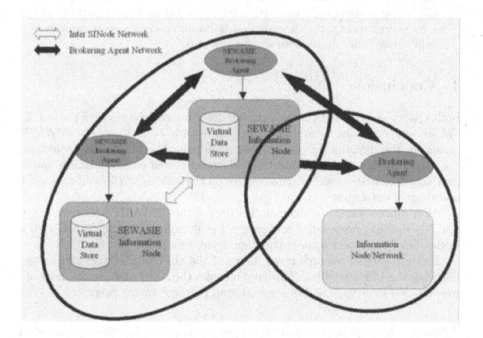

Fig. 2. The two alternative P2P networks

dination formulas (e.g. by using schema matching [10,2] , by deriving relations among the peers using inference techniques).

The Brokering Agents network supports the generation of the query plan in order to identify which SINodes have to be queried. In particular, the Network may:

- Generate interest groups with nodes that have similar content.
- Help the query optimization, by giving information to the query agent about the "data placement". A peer knows how data are distributed across the nodes and the query plan may take into account the existing resources and bandwidth constraints.

SINodes network is an alternative approach where the P2P pardigm is directly supported by SINodes. In this case, we may maintain a single brokering agent, holding the knowledge of the network topology and we need a P2P layer in each SINode holding the following functionalities:

- the P2P layer of a SINode needs a protocol for establishing an acquaintance dinamically;
- the P2P layer of a SINode could offer semi-automated support for generating coordination formulas, e.g. by using schema matching [10,2];
- the P2P layer of a SINode can use approaches for query processing of multi-database systems but also needs a policy to propagate subqueries through chains of P2P connections (i..e. the path for the query agents);
- the P2P layer of a SINode should be able to advertise its ontology presumably using a directory service (this service could be held/exported towards a brokering agent); this information is useful to create acquaintances and individuate other nodes with similar contents.

4   Conclusion

In this paper we provided, firstly, a general description of the research project SEWASIE and, secondly, a proposal of an architectural evolution of the SEWASIE system in the direction of peer-to-peer paradigm. The SEWASIE project has the aim to design and implement an advanced search engine enabling intelligent access to heterogeneous data sources on the web using community-specific multilingual ontologies.

After a presentation of the main features of the SEWASIE architecture system a preliminar proposal of architectural evolutions of the SEWASIE system in the direction of peer-to-peer paradigm have been proposed.

The next step of research is the design of the SEWASIE system architecture following the P2P paradigm. This step includes the study and development of a coordination laanguage and of a negotiation protocol among peers.

Acknowledgements. This work is supported in part by the 5th Framework IST programme of the European Community through project SEWASIE within the

Semantic Web Action Line. The SEWASIE consortium comprises in addition to the author' organization (Sonia Bergamaschi is the coordinator of the project), the Universities of Aachen RWTH (M. Jarke), Roma La Sapienza (M. Lenzerini, T. Catarci), Bolzano (E. Franconi), as well as IBM Italia, Thinking Networks AG and CNA as user organisation.

References

1. D. Beneventano, S. Bergamaschi, S. Castano, A. Corni, R. Guidetti, G. Malvezzi, M. Melchiori, and M. Vincini. Information integration: The momis project demonstration. In *VLDB 2000, Proceedings of 26th International Conference on Very Large Data Bases, September, 2000, Cairo, Egypt*, pages 611–614. Morgan Kaufmann, 2000.
2. S. Bergamaschi, S. Castano, D. Beneventano, and M. Vincini. Semantic integration of heterogenous information sources. *Journal of Data and Knowledge Engineering*, 36(3):215–249, 2001.
3. S. Bergamaschi, S. Castano, and M. Vincini. Semantic integration of semistructured and structured data sources. *SIGMOD Records*, 28(1), March 1999.
4. P.A. Bernstein, F. Giunchiglia, A. Kementsietsidis, J.M., L. Serafini, and I. Zaihrayeu. Data management for peer-to-peer computing: A vision. In *Proceedings of Fifth International Workshop on the Web and Databases(WebDB2002) Madison, Wisconsin*, Jun 2002.
5. M.J. Carey, L.M. Haas, P.M. Schwarz, M. Arya, W.F. Cody, R. Fagin, M. Flickner, A. Luniewski, W. Niblack, D. Petkovic, J. Thomas II, J.H. Williams, and E.L. Wimmers. Towards heterogeneous multimedia information systems: The garlic approach. In *RIDE-DOM*, pages 124–131, 1985.
6. S.S. Chawathe, H. Garcia-Molina, J. Hammer, K. Ireland, Y. Papakonstantinou, J.D. Ullman, and J. Widom. The tsimmis project: Integration of heterogeneous information sources. In *Proceedings of the 10th Meeting of the Information Processing Society of Japan, October 1994*, pages 7–18, 1994.
7. A.Y. Levy, A. Rajaraman, and J.J. Ordille. Querying heterogeneous information sources using source descriptions. In *Proc. of VLDB 1996*, pages 251–262, 1996.
8. A. Oram. *Peer-to-Peer: Harnessing the Power of Disruptive Technologies*. O'reilly, 2002.
9. M.T. Ozsu and P. Valduriez, editors. *Principles of Distributed Database Systems*. Prentice Hall, 1999.
10. E. Rahm and P.A. Bernstein. A survey of approaches to automatic schema matching. In *The VLDB Journal: Volume 10 Issue 4 (2001)*, pages 334–350, 2001.
11. J.M. Smith, P.A. Bernstein, U. Dayal, N. Goodman, T. Landers, K.W.T. Lin, and E. Wong. Multibase – integrating heterogeneous distributed database systems. In *Proceedings of 1981 National Computer Conference*, pages 487–499. AFIPS Press, 1981.
12. G. Wiederhold. Mediators in the architecture of future information systems. *IEEE Computer*, 25:38–49, 1992.
13. W. Litwin, L. Mark, and N. Roussopoulos. Interoperability of multiple autonomous databases. *ACM Computing Surveys*, 22(3):267–293, 1990.

Modeling and Evaluating Cooperation Strategies in P2P Agent Systems

L. Penserini[1], L. Liu[2], J. Mylopoulos[2], M. Panti[1], and L. Spalazzi[1]

[1] Istituto di Informatica, University of Ancona, Ancona, Italy
{pense,panti,spalazzi}@inform.unian.it
[2] Dept. of Computer Science, University of Toronto, Toronto, Canada
{liu,jm}@cs.toronto.edu

Abstract. Distributed computing is becoming a fundamental technology for information exchange and cooperation. However, for such a technology to gain wide use, it must cater to users who do not own sophisticated (hardware and software) platforms and permanent network connections. For such users, the recent Peer-to-Peer (P2P) computing model has many advantages over classical client-server and web-based distributed models. However, the P2P computing model in its current form has a number of other limitations in the data exchange and the protocols it supports. To overcome some of these, we proposed an agent based P2P system model whose nodes are agents (*Peer Agents*). In this paper, we adopt the i* graphical framework to help the modeling and evaluating of Peer Agent's cooperation strategies. Although, the highly dynamic nature of P2P networks complicates the evaluation procedure, we propose three possible evaluation criteria in order to characterize the best strategy related to a particular failure symptom.

1 Introduction

There have been many proposals for models and technologies in order to support information sharing and cooperation among distributed users in a dynamic environment where connections constantly change. The recent Peer-to-Peer (P2P) computing model [1,2,3] is a simple and natural approach to the problem, and offer many advantages over classical client-server and web-based distributed computing models. In particular, the P2P model doesn't assume sophisticated infrastructure, allows for constant evolution of acquaintance relationships among peers, and does away (in its more interesting, pure form) with central coordination, global schema, central services or registry. Each peer shares information and collaborates only for the time necessary to deal with a given task with least deterministic interactions. Each node is an equal (peer) to all others, and can operate as a router, client, or server according to circumstances. The P2P style of computing is suitable for collaborating enterprise groups, such as virtual enterprises, small operative units inside a health care system, virtual communities, etc. In such a network, partners are connected to each other through ever-changing acquaintance connections. Many tools have been built already in

G. Moro and M. Koubarakis (Eds.): AP2PC 2002, LNAI 2530, pp. 87–99, 2003.

order to support P2P computing. However, such tools have fundamental limitations [4]:

(a) *Expressiveness of exchanged messages.* Current tools use very simple languages for exchanged messages. In fact, these languages can only talk about objects/data that are well defined and uniquely identified by their names (i.e., MP3 files, image files, etc.) instead of information with complex semantics.

(b) *Data models.* The information that is exchanged is based on a very simple data model consisting of file directories.

(c) *Data transformation/integration.* Current P2P systems work on a uniform environment that doesn't allow for heterogeneity, inconsistency and all the other phenomena one expects when dealing with distributed data.

To overcome these limitations, we have proposed an agent-based P2P system model [5,6,7], in which the capabilities of each peer (*peer agent*) are distributed into several abstract roles, e.g., wrapper, mediator, facilitator, etc. However, because of dynamic connections and the lack of global visibility, other peers' behavior may be unpredictable, requiring different cooperation strategies on the part of a given peer. In this paper, we adopt the i* modeling framework to help with the modeling and evaluation of peer agent cooperation strategies. The i* framework is designed to model intentional relationships among agents [8,9]. In i*, actors have freedom of action, but operate within the constraints of a network of social relationships. Specifically, they depend on each other for goals to be achieved, tasks to be performed, and resources to be furnished. This paper models alternative cooperation strategies as tasks. In addition, the failures to be avoided are modeled as softgoals to be achieved. In i*, the softgoal concept is used to model quality attributes for which there are no a priori, clear-cut criteria for satisfaction, but are judged by actors as being sufficiently met ('satisficed') on a case-by-case basis [8,9]. Moreover, in order to allow a peer agent (the planner) to choose a better strategy related to a specific failure symptom, evaluation criteria are required. Although, the highly dynamic nature of P2P coalition complicates such an evaluation procedure, we propose three possible evaluation approaches in order to characterize the best strategy related to a particular failure symptom. Note that this paper does not address architectural issues for a peer agent. Instead, it focuses on the modeling and analysis of the system in terms of actors, their relationships, goals to achieve, and tasks to be performed. The rest of the paper is organized as follows. The next section presents an overview of the peer agent system used as reference model. Section 3 describes the planner actor, which is one of the components of a peer agent, through the i* Strategic Rational model. Section 4 discusses the symbolic, scenario-based, and quantitative evaluation respectively for cooperation strategies. Finally, Sect. 5 offers conclusions and directions for further research.

2   A Peer Agent Architecture

As stated above, the peer agent architecture we propose aims to enhance data management in loosely connected and constantly evolving environments. For example, in a world of hospitals, ambulances, family doctors, pharmacists and patients data have to be exchanged regarding a particular patient. The reference model, depicted in Fig. 1, is intended to support the principal capabilities required to deal with such settings. We assume that each peer node includes a peer (human or social entity) and a (software) peer agent which helps/assists the peer. The Strategic Dependency model of i* (SD), in Fig. 1 relates a peer agent's capability to those of its peer's goals. For instance, a peer depends on its peer agent to 'Deal with Problem Requested', and to give 'Solutions'. Also, the peer expects the peer agent to be 'Failure Tolerant', and to have good performance in terms of 'Good Bandwidth Optimization'. Moreover, each peer agent plays one or more of the following roles to support the needs of its peer:

Wrapper (Source Interfacing). This role is responsible for the interfacing with the peer's local environments. In fact, the figure shows that the peer agent benefits from its wrapper role for information needs and actions. Namely, the wrapper serves the peer agent's 'Information Needs' (resource dependency) by 'Perform (certain) Actions' (task dependency). The actions performed can be data management operations, coordination actions, and complex task sequences (workflows) among several sources.

Facilitator (Registration and Searching). In a decentralized P2P environment, each peer does not know a priori which partners to communicate with. The facilitator role provides a peer agent with searching and registry capabilities, which allow the peer agent to get to know other peer agents with useful skills (to establish new *acquaintances*). This kind of collaboration is driven by the locality principle [1], which means that each peer's global behavior emerges from local interactions.

Mediator (Reformulation and Integration). This role provides a peer agent with reformulation and integration capabilities [5]. Using these, a peer agent can reformulate the original problem (i.e., the initial request) in terms of a set of tasks/actions (i.e., the correct workflow), in agreement with some soft inter-database constraints (i.e., coordination rules [10]), each targeted at selected sources.

Planner (Strategy Generation). This role provides the peer agent with the skill of distributed problem reformulation. Thus, when a failure results from the peer agent inability to satisfy a request locally, the planner can help to build up a cooperation strategy in order to overcome the underling failure.

These four roles provide a peer agent with the skills to propagate over a P2P network four different kinds of knowledge: (a) data/information, (b) peers' addresses and service names, (c) tasks in terms of data management operations and coordination rules, and (d) the best cooperation strategies in order to overcome local failures.

We adopt the following data structure to represent the basic element (say case) of the knowledge base: $\langle P, R, I \rangle$ [5,6]. P is the problem to be solved, e.g., a workflow as a set of actions, queries towards DBMS or the Web, update DB operations, etc. In the example of Fig. 2, P is an 'insert' operation in the 'Patient' table of the dermatologist's database (DE_database). R is the internal PA's problem representation (say reformulation) in order to correctly fulfill each

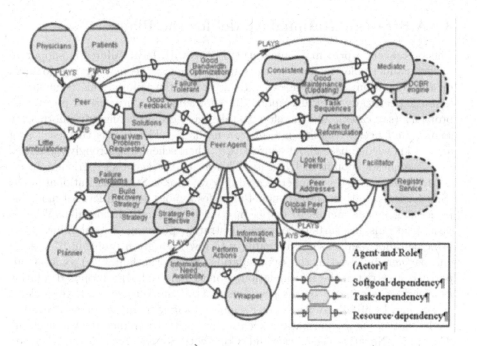

Fig. 1. P2P agent system architecture reference model

C P **INSERT INTO Patient IN (DE_database)**
        [attributes] VALUES [values]
R {a₁ = **INSERT INTO P_Visit IN (DE_database)**
        [attributes] VALUES [values],
    a₂ = **INSERT INTO P_Results IN (DI_database)**
        [attributes] VALUES [values],
    a₃ = **INSERT INTO Patient IN (FD_database)**
        [attributes] VALUES [values]]
I {<a₁,P₁ >,<a₂,P₂ >,<a₃,P₃ >}
    P₁ = {PA(DE)}, P₂ = {PA(DI₁),PA(DI₂)},
    P₃ = {PA(FD)}

Fig. 2. A case (C) in the knowledge base of the dermatologist's peer agent (PA(DE))

operation involved for the problem solution. In such a case, Fig. 2 shows three
updating coordinated actions (a_1, a_2, a_3) towards three physicians' databases,
i.e., respectively dermatologist (DE), dietician (DI), and family doctor (FD). I
is an interpretation of the problem (its reformulation), e.g., the execution of P
if the problem is a coordination action, the results of P if the problem is a query
towards a DB, etc. In particular, the current Peer Agent (Fig. 1) considers I as a
pair like this (Fig. 2): $\langle R, peer\ addresses \rangle$, where R is the problem reformulation
and *peer addresses* the peers able to give a solution to the problem reformulation.

3   A Strategic Rational Model for the Planner

The peer agent's principal capability to cope with local failures is supported by its planner role. In fact, when a failure occurs, the planner has to build up a cooperation strategy in order to overcome the failure. This behavior allows the peer to dynamically update its knowledge, i.e., in terms of peers' past problems (say cases), and therefore to take into account changes in information sources and peer's complex information needs [5]. This means that each peer agent's knowledge base about sources (e.g., their schema) is strongly influenced by the requests submitted by peers. This forms the agent's experience. In order to characterize the planner's capability we exploit Strategic Rational model (SR) features. Indeed, the SR model provides a more detailed level of modeling by looking 'inside' actors to model internal intentional relationships. When a peer agent fails, it resorts to cooperation strategy planning. A local failure arises principally for four reasons: a) inability to rewrite a given problem; b) at least one partner, involved in the reformulation, causes the failure; c) at least one partner, involved in the reformulation, is not connected; d) a proposed solution to a partner is rejected by the peer agent. As a consequence, we have modeled these main local failures as Planner's internal softgoals to be achieved, respectively, 'Satisfy New Information Need', 'Cope with Unpredictable Connection', 'Cope with Negative Feedback', and 'Cope with Source Dynamism'. Moreover, Fig. 3 indicates that a peer agent depends on its planner through the 'Provide Effective Strategy' task dependency. To deliver on this responsibility, the planner needs to understand the failure that occurred (i.e., 'Decide Failure Type' task dependency) and then it has to select a suitable strategy (i.e., 'Build Recovery Strategy' task dependency). As indicated above, a local failure is caused by deficiencies in a peer agent's capabilities. To 'Decide Failure Type', the planner relies on the peer agent to provide 'Failure Symptoms' information. In particular, the 'Decide Failure Type' resulting process consists in a failure type description (see Fig. 3). Therefore, this ability allows the planner to understand the principal reasons of a failure. Moreover, the alternative ways to fulfill the collaboration are represented as task nodes in i* model, which are:

Choose Partner. When a peer agent (say PA) fails, it can cooperate with other peer agents asking them to rewrite the problem according to their own knowledge base. If they succeed, PA can store the result as a new element (say case) in its knowledge base. The 'Choose Partner' task dependency represents one of the coordinates that planner can use in order to build up the suitable strategy. In particular, we have focused on the following principal groupings of collaborative partners:

- *All Peers*. They represent the set of all of PA's acquaintances ($\mathcal{AC}(PA)$).
- *New Peers*. In such a case, PA tries to interact with peers it was never acquainted with in the past. Namely, peers that do not belong to the PA's acquaintances ($\{new\} \notin \mathcal{AC}(PA)$). In particular, this task is strictly correlated with the facilitator's searching ability.
- *Peers Temporarily Disconnected*. This peer set is part of the PA's acquaintances set ($\{disconnected\} \in \mathcal{AC}(PA)$), but these peers are currently dis-

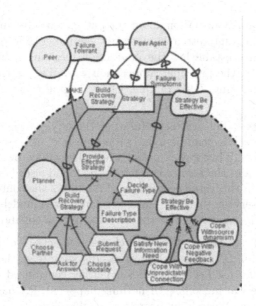

Fig. 3. Strategic rational model for the planner

connected from the network (not active). The PA can generally contact such peers after some time is passed.

- *Active Peers.* This peer set is the complement of the peer disconnected set. In particular, $\{active\} \cup \{disconnected\} = \mathcal{AC}(PA)$.
- *Peers That Succeed.* This peer set is a part of the PA's acquaintances ($\{succeed\} \in \mathcal{AC}(PA)$), and these peers are those that PA successfully collaborated with in the past.
- *Peers That Failed.* This peer set is the complement of the successful peer set. In particular, $\{succeed\} \cup \{failed\} = \mathcal{AC}(PA)$.

Submit Request. PA can send the original request (P) or its reformulation (if any). In particular, each time a local failure occurs, PA can exchange three request types towards another peer in order to fulfill collaboration:

- *Send the Original (P).* It is the initial request/problem that PA received and it was not able to solve locally.
- *Send a Reformulation (R).* In order to revise a component of its local knowledge ($\mathcal{KB}(PA)$) that failed (i.e., R).
- *Send the Failed Components.* Since, both P and R are sets of tasks (e.g., coordination activities, data management operations, etc.), PA can send only the problem or reformulation components that failed in evaluation.

Choose Modality. When PA has to collaborate with a partner temporarily disconnected a reaction modality in order to overcome such a failure is required. This modality principally depends on the involved collaboration type, e.g., a physician (a peer) has to interact with a specific partner (another peer), a physician has to ask some information about the patients' results under specific treatments, a physician is interested to increase the number of his collaborators, etc. Modality capability establishes the interaction mechanism between two peers in order to support the principal cooperation ways, i.e., centralized and decentralized P2P computing. For example, let us assume that PA is looking for a service:

- *Search for Peers*. This way is useful when the service owner is not connected, but the same service can be found elsewhere (e.g., new peers);
- *Wait for Peers*. This way is useful when the service owner is temporarily disconnected and the service can hardly be found elsewhere;
- *Send Email*. In this case the initiator (PA) knows that only this owner owns the required service, therefore PA uses a centralized model (email) to be sure that the service owner receive the message (e.g., a collaboration request).

In particular, for the *Search for Peers* choice, PA acts in a decentralized way, while in *Send Email* PA relies on a centralized system (e.g., the SMTP and POP services). The *Wait for Peers* modality is neither centralized nor decentralized, because after the waiting phase (if nothing happens), PA has to decide which modality to use, i.e., 'Search for Peers' or 'Send an Email'.

Ask for Answer. Finally, cooperation strategy can be classified according to the answer. PA can ask for rewriting the request in order to update its knowledge base with a reformulation obtained from its collaborators. PA can also ask for data that answer the request. Therefore, each time a peer agent collaborates with another one it does so in the following ways:

- *Ask for Data*, e.g., look for services, processing data management operations;
- *Ask for Reformulation* of a given problem, e.g., knowledge updating, knowledge consistence maintenance;
- *Ask for both Data and Reformulation* at the same interaction time.

Then, each time planner receives a failure symptom it has to be able to answer as automatically and better as possible to the question '*what is the best strategy to adopt in order to overcome the failure occurred?*'. Figure 3 indicates that one of the planner's main objectives is the achievement of the four softgoals that compose the 'Strategy Be Effective' softgoal. Indeed, as already indicated, each of the planner's internal softgoals is related to the principal failure symptoms. Nevertheless, the planner could use several task combinations in order to deal with such softgoals. As a consequence, we need to understand what is each softgoal's contribution from each task in order to classify the best strategy related to a specific failure. Indeed, each strategy is a four element structure (plan) $\langle partner, answer, modality, request \rangle$, where each element contains several alternatives.

4 Evaluation Mechanisms for Strategies

This section aims to describe three possible approaches in order to analyze and evaluate the contribution relationship between the planner's solutions (tasks)

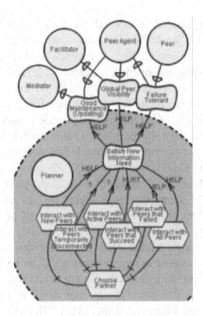

Fig. 4. Partner choices contribution relationships in order to achieve the 'satisfy new information need' softgoal

and expectations (softgoals). In particular, we are interested in identifying and characterizing the best strategies for coping with a peer agent's local failures. Namely, here we will describe 'why' and 'how much' each choice is better than another one in order to achieve each softgoal showed in Fig. 3. As shown in the Fig. 4, some external softgoals, e.g., 'Good Maintenance', 'Global Peer Visibility', and 'Failure Tolerant', are influenced by the planner's internal softgoals. This means that each peer agent is influenced by the roles (mediator, facilitator, wrapper, planner) they are playing. Each contribution link is characterized by a label that specifies the contribution type and strength. The positive contribution types for softgoals are HELP (positive but not by itself sufficient to meet the higher goal), MAKE (positive & sufficient), SOME+ (partial positive contribution), and '?' (unknown). The dual negative types are HURT, BREAK, and SOME-, respectively [8,9]. Moreover, for evaluation simplicity, let us assume that for each problem (initial request) always exists a solution that is distributed over the P2P coalition.

4.1 Symbolic Evaluation Approach

In such an analysis, the tasks' contribution estimation is established principally on general considerations about the system components in terms of knowledge base, peer acquaintances, and peer grouping relationships. Namely, contributions to softgoal are considered using a qualitative reasoning approach.

Evaluation Example 4-1. Let us analyze the contribution relationships furnished by some of the 'Chose Partner' sub-tasks to the 'Satisfy New Information Need' softgoal, as shown in Fig. 4. In such a case, a peer agent (PA) has to satisfy a new information need ($\mathcal{C}$). That is, it has to solve a new problem never considered in the past, for which it is not able to give a solution locally, i.e., $\mathcal{KB}(PA) \cap \mathcal{C} = \emptyset$. Alternatively, the PA can partially solve $\mathcal{C}$, i.e., $\mathcal{KB}(PA) \cap \mathcal{C} = \mathcal{C}'$ with $\mathcal{C}' \subset \mathcal{C}$. The peers, which successfully collaborated with PA in the past, have already shared part of their knowledge base with PA (e.g., $\mathcal{C}'$). In general, each peer updates its knowledge base on the basis of the information need (interests) that it has to satisfy. Therefore, peers with same interests (e.g., groupings of family doctors, cardiologists, physiologists, etc.) are also characterized by similar knowledge base. Thus, we can assume, without losing in generality, that PA often interacts with these succeed peers. As a consequence, we state the following: $\exists \mathcal{C}' \neq \emptyset$ s.t. $\mathcal{C}' = \mathcal{KB}(succeed) \cap \mathcal{KB}(PA)$ with $\mathcal{C}' \subset \mathcal{C}$ or $\mathcal{C}' \cap \mathcal{C} = \emptyset$, this formula means that if PA decides to collaborate with the peers that succeed in the past in order to satisfy $\mathcal{C}$, it probably will fail, i.e., we consider this as an HURT contribution. On the contrary, peers that failed in the past are characterized by different information needs in respect to the PA's one. Namely, we can state the following: $\mathcal{KB}(PA) \cap \mathcal{KB}(failed) \simeq \emptyset$. Therefore, it is a good choice to collaborate with peers that failed in order to overcome a failure due to a new information need, i.e., this is considered as an HELP contribution.

4.2   Scenario-Based Evaluation Approach

This scenario-based approach is used to describe the behavioral features and architectures of the Peer Agent system in a specific context in order to achieve some implicit purposes. Therefore, by the scenario-based evaluation some implicit system goals are made explicit. This analysis focuses more on Peer Agent interactions in terms of how many interactions are involved in a collaboration, what kind of information are exchanged, and how the information exchanged influences the PA's knowledge base.

Evaluation Example 4-2. Let us analyze the contribution relationships produced by 'Ask for Answer' sub-tasks in order to 'Cope with Unpredictable Connection' softgoal achievement. In particular, let us assume that a Peer Agent PA_1 interacts with another one PA_2 to solve a problem 'P', e.g., data (related to I), as shown in Fig. 5. The figure depicts three possible interaction scenarios. In particular, if PA_1 uses the (A) scenario it has to rely on PA_2 each time a request, similar to P, arrives. As a consequence, each time PA_2 is temporarily disconnected, PA_1 is not able to obtain the solution; we consider this as an HURT contribution. In contrast, in (B) and (C) scenarios, PA_1 after the first interaction is able to interact directly with the problem's solution/reformulation owners, i.e., this is considered as an HELP contribution. On the contrary, if PA_1 is interested to store the data too, the (C) cooperation model seems to be better than the other ones. In such a case, PA_1 also needs PA_3's and PA_4's addresses for data freshness checking (dotted lines).

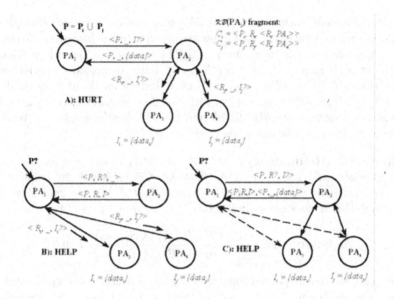

Fig. 5. Typical cooperation scenarios with different 'answer asked' choices in order to achieve the 'cope with unpredictable connection' softgoal

4.3 Quantitative Evaluation Approach

Often, in order to judge if a strategy is better than another one it is useful to preemptive know the effect of such a strategy over the principal system's components. Nevertheless, the high dynamism, the no global peers' visibility, and the unpredictable peers' connections of a P2P coalition make complex the application of any simple evaluation criteria. In particular, it is important to know 'how' and 'how much' the knowledge base varies during and after a long collaboration (collection of interactions). Moreover, in sharing information among several peer agents it is also interesting to consider and evaluate knowledge redundancy aspects. Another feature, worth of notice in a P2P environment, is the amount of bandwidth generated (and incurred) by each collaboration strategy. The latter, for space reasons, is not discussed in this paper. Therefore, we just introduce some parameters and their definition adjusted into the new peer agent system in order to support a quantitative evaluation approach.

Definition 1 (Recall and Precision). *Let $p_1, ..., p_m$ be m peers. Let $\mathcal{C}$ be a view (set of cases) of $p_1, ..., p_m$. Let PA be a peer agent such that PA interacts with $p_1, ..., p_m$ when PA fails. Let $\mathcal{KB}_n(PA)$ be the knowledge base of PA after n interactions with $p_1, ..., p_m$. Then:*

$$Recall: \quad \lim_{n \to \infty} \frac{card(\mathcal{KB}_n(PA) \cap \mathcal{C})}{card(\mathcal{C})} \in [0, 1] \tag{1}$$

$$Precision: \quad \lim_{n \to \infty} \frac{card(\mathcal{KB}_n(PA) \cap \mathcal{C})}{card(\mathcal{KB}_n(PA))} \in [0, 1] \tag{2}$$

In the previous definition, $\mathcal{C}$ denotes PA's information need, distributed among peers, in order to satisfy a particular request/problem. Moreover, *Recall* gives us an indication about 'how much' $\mathcal{KB}(\text{PA})$ is closer to the information need ($\mathcal{C}$). That is, it measures the $\mathcal{KB}(\text{PA})$'s capability to provide a correct answer for satisfying $\mathcal{C}$. While, *Precision* gives us an indication about 'how good' is the $\mathcal{KB}(\text{PA})$ (in term of its content) in order to do not provide wrong answers for $\mathcal{C}$. Nevertheless, how fast the *Recall* and the *Precision* are going to tend to '1' depends on the cooperation strategy chosen by PA.

Definition 2 (Redundancy). *Let PA_1 and PA_2 be two peer agents such that PA_1 interacts with PA_2 when PA_1 fails. Let $\mathcal{KB}_n(PA_1)$ be the knowledge base of PA_1 after n interactions with PA_2. Let $\mathcal{KB}_n(PA_2)$ be the knowledge base of PA_2 such that it does not change while PA_2 interacts with PA_1. Then:*

$$Recall: \quad \lim_{n \to \infty} \frac{card(\mathcal{KB}_n(PA_1) \cap \mathcal{KB}(PA_2))}{card(\mathcal{KB}(PA_2))} \in [0,1] \qquad (3)$$

When two (or more) peers cooperate with each other, some knowledge is exchanged among them. The strength of this exchange is captured (measured) by the *Redundancy* (3), e.g., *Redundancy*=0 means that two peers have no knowledge element (case) in common, *Redundancy*=1 means that two peers have the same knowledge base.

4.4 Evaluation Results

The evaluation criteria described above have been applied to all the contribution relationships among planner tasks and softgoals. Table 1 gathers all contributions and their numerical evaluation. This evaluation consists of a value, in the [-1,1] interval, corresponding to each i* contribution symbol, i.e., MAKE = +1, HELP = +0.5, ? = 0, HURT = -0.5, and BREAK = -1. Moreover, we have established for the unknown positive (negative) contribution a value between MAKE and HELP (BREAK and HURT), i.e., SOME+ = +0.75 (SOME- = -0.75). Using this table, the planner can decide (read from the table) the best strategy to adopt for a given failure symptom. Obviously, the contribution table is only intended to support the most complex decision making activities. Table 1 shows the contribution relationships among task dependencies and the principal softgoals related to the planner.

5 Conclusions

This work focuses on modeling and evaluating of cooperation strategies in a P2P agent system. In particular, we have adopted, as reference model, the system described in [5,6,7] and we have detailed its Planner actor capabilities. Inside the Peer Agent, the Planner's role is to build and manage cooperation strategies. Moreover, in both modeling and evaluation phases the i* framework is used to visualize the intentional relationships among actors and the rational within an

Table 1. Contribution relationships among task dependencies and the principal softgoals

Abbreviations used in the table:
  A: Satisfy New Information Need,
  B: Cope with Unpredictable Connection,
  C: Cope with Negative Feedback, and
  D: Cope with Source Dynamism.

	Partners (peers)						Request			Answer			Modality		
	New	Disconn.	Active	Succeed	Failed	All	Original	Reform	Failed C.	Data	Reform	Data&R.	Search	Wait	Email
A	.5	0	0	-.5	.5	.5	1	-1	.5	.5	.5	.5	1	-.5	-.5
B	.5	.5	.5	0	0	.75	.75	.75	.75	-.5	.5	.5	1	.5	.5
C	1	-.75	-.5	-.5	-.75	-.75	1	.5	.5	-.5	.5	.5	1	.5	.5
D	.5	.5	-.75	1	-.5	0	1	.5	1	.5	1	1	.5	.5	.5

actor. The softgoals and contribution concepts in i* fit very well for the modeling and evaluating of alternative strategies of peer agent's planner. Although, the highly dynamic nature of P2P coalitions makes the evaluation procedure even more complex, we propose three possible evaluation criteria in order to identify and characterize the best strategy related to a particular failure symptom. The three evaluation approaches, proposed in this paper, evince that the Planner's decision-making knowledge of multiple forms can be unified into symbolic or numerical forms for comparison. As a consequence, a contribution table has been produced from the analysis (Table 1). The methodology discussed in this paper can be adopted by any P2P agent system involved in similar decision-making activities.

References

1. Aberer, K.: P-Grid: A Self Organizing Access Structure for P2P Information Systems. In: Proc. of 9th International Conference on Cooperative Information Systems (CoopIS 2001). Volume 2172 of Lecture Notes in Computer Science., Berlin, Germany, Springer Verlag (2001) 179–194
2. Clarke, I., Sandberg, O., Wiley, B., Hong, T.: Freenet: A Distributed Anonymous Information Storage and Retrieval System. In Federrath, H., ed.: Designing Privacy Enhancing Technologies: International Workshop on Design Issues in Anonymity and Unobservability, Berlin, Springer (2001)
3. Graham, R.L.: Peer-to-Peer: Towards a Definition. Some lecture notes in 2001 International Conference on Peer-to-Peer Computing (P2P2001). Proceedings of the IEEE (2001) Linköpings unversitet, Sweden, 27-29 August 2001.
4. Gribble, S., Halevy, A., Ives, Z., Rodrig, M., Suciu, D.: What Can Peer-to-Peer Do for Databases, and Vice Versa? In: Proc. of the Fourth International Workshop on the Web and Databases (WebDB). (2001)
5. Panti, M., Spalazzi, L., Penserini, L.: A Distributed Case-Based Query Rewriting. In: Proc. of 17th International Joint Conference on Artificial Intelligence (IJCAI-01), San Mateo CA, Morgan Kaufmann Publisher (2001)

6. Panti, M., Penserini, L., Spalazzi, L.: A pure P2P approach to information integration. Technical Report 2002-02-19, Istituto di Informatica, University of Ancona, Ancona, Italy (2002)
7. Penserini, L., Panti, M., Spalazzi, L.: Agent-Based Transactions into Decentralised P2P. In: Proc. of The First International Joint Conference on Autonomous Agents & Multi-Agent Systems (AAMAS 2002), Bologna, Italy, ACM Press (2002)
8. Yu, E., Mylopoulos, J.: From E–R to 'A–R' – Modelling Strategic Relationships for Business Process Reengineering. Int. Journal of Intelligent and Cooperative Information Systems **4** (1995) 125–144
9. Yu, E., Liu, L.: Modelling Trust for System Design Using the i* Strategic Actors Framework. In R. Falcone, M. Singh, Y.T., ed.: Trust in Cyber–Societies – Integrating the Human and Artificial Perspectives. Volume 2246 of LNAI. Springer, Berlin (2001) 175–194
10. Bernstein, P., Giunchiglia, F., Kementsietsidis, A., Mylopoulos, J., Serafini, L., Zaihrayeu, I.: Data Management for Peer-to-Peer Computing: A Visions. In: Proc. of the Fifth International Workshop on the Web and Databases (WebDB). (2002)

A Distributed Implementation of the SWAN Peer-to-Peer Look-Up System Using Mobile Agents

Erwin Bonsma and Cefn Hoile

Intelligent Systems Lab, BTexact Technologies
Adastral Park, Ipswich, IP5 3RE, UK
{erwin.bonsma,cefn.hoile}@bt.com

Abstract. We present an agent-based implementation of the SWAN system. SWAN is a peer-to-peer look-up system that functions by letting the participating nodes self-organise in a virtual Small World Network. We have used DIET, a lightweight ecologically inspired multi-agent platform, to implement a test application of SWAN. We describe the implementation of the test application and present experiments in which the application runs on a cluster of computers. Our results show that the system is robust to failure and shows promising scalability.

1   Introduction

Recently there has been much interest in peer-to-peer applications, such as file sharing, file storage and collaborative working. Many of these applications require the ability to look-up items, ideally by a location-independent identity so that items can easily be moved and duplicated. How to implement a look-up system in peer-to-peer systems is an interesting question because ordinary, centralised solutions are typically not suitable. Various distributed look-up systems have been proposed, including Chord [1], Pastry [2], CAN [3] and SWAN [4].

Here we look at the SWAN look-up system. More specifically, we extend our initial work where we simulated the system [4] by using the DIET multi-agent platform [5,6] to build a test application that can run across multiple computers.

This paper is organised as follows. Section 2 and 3 provide the relevant background by respectively introducing the DIET platform and the SWAN system. Section 4 then describes the implementation of SWAN using DIET that is the subject of this paper. Some preliminary results about the performance of the system can be found in Sect. 5. Finally, Sects. 6 and 7 discuss the results and conclude the paper.

2   The DIET Platform

The DIET (Decentralised Information Ecosystem Technologies) platform is a multi-agent platform in Java that is being developed as part of the DIET project.

G. Moro and M. Koubarakis (Eds.): AP2PC 2002, LNAI 2530, pp. 100–111, 2003.

The DIET project is a 5th Framework project funded by the European Commission under the Future and Emerging Technologies area [7]. One of the main goals of the project has been to design a multi-agent platform that is open, robust, adaptive and scalable, using a substantially bottom-up and ecosystem-inspired approach. As a result, the DIET platform differs significantly from most other multi-agent platforms.

In DIET there is one *world* per Java Virtual Machine (JVM) which can contain one or more environments. An *environment* provides a location for agents to inhabit and can host one or more agents. DIET agents access the DIET kernel functionality by way of their environment. Each environment can have *neighbourhood links* to other environments, potentially to environments in a different world. These neighbourhood links allow agents without any a-priori knowledge of other environments to explore the DIET universe by migration. The neighbourhood links are specified on start up of the world, but can be changed dynamically while the world is running. There is no need for a central registration of worlds when you run DIET across multiple computers, so the architecture is effectively peer-to-peer.

Agents in DIET are very lightweight. Their minimal memory footprint is small and they can give up their thread when they do not need it. The DIET kernel will then attempt to give the agent a thread when it needs it, for instance to handle incoming messages. The lightweight nature has allowed us to run simulations with several hundred thousand agents in one JVM on a single, ordinary desktop computer.

For both communication and agent migration the kernel support is minimal. For instance, the platform has no specific communication protocol built into it, remote communication is not directly supported and migration is unreliable. This means that there is no unnecessary overhead and execution can be rapid. However, if need be, more sophisticated functionality can be built on top of the basic functions provided by the kernel, in a way best suited to the conditions in which it is used.

Robustness is explicitly addressed in the DIET kernel by directly exposing agents to potential failure. The kernel only fulfills a request when it can easily do so, and fails when it cannot. For instance, local message delivery fails when the receiving agent cannot be assigned a thread, or its message buffer has reached full capacity. In this way, no extra resources are spent when the system is apparently already overloaded. Additionally, by exposing the agents to failure they can adapt accordingly. For more details about the DIET platform refer to [5,6].

3   The SWAN System

The SWAN (Small World Adaptive Networks) system provides distributed look-up functionality for peer-to-peer infrastructures. In SWAN it is assumed that a collection of virtual *nodes* is connected by a communication infra-structure. A node can send a message to any other node given the *address* of the node. Each node also has a potentially arbitrary *identity* that is independent of its address.

The purpose of SWAN is to provide look-up of node addresses by identity, using a fully decentralised architecture.

Each node maintains information about a limited number of other nodes, mostly their addresses and identities. Storing a node's address represents a unidirectional *link*. Nodes maintain *short-range links* and *long-range links* which together form a virtual *SWN* (Small World Network) that is used to find nodes. Each node also has a few *bootstrap links* which are used to create the SWN. On start up, the only links a node needs are a few random bootstrap links to other nodes.

The nodes self-organise into a SWN that is based on their identities. Each node identity is mapped to a position in a multi-dimensional *identity space*. The SWN is created according to distances in this identity space.

The short-range links are formed by letting nodes periodically send Notify messages. These are randomly passed along the bootstrap links to reach an arbitrary position in identity space. Subsequently, the message is routed back to the originating node, along the current SWN links. When the originating node is not reached, some nodes will update their links accordingly. As a result, each node will eventually obtain short-range links to nodes that are nearby in identity space.

The second part of the self-organisation is the formation of long-range links. They are to nodes that are further away in identity space. Their distances are chosen such that the SWN meets the properties suggested by Kleinberg [8,9], which guarantees that the average effort required to find a node scales well with the total number of nodes. Each node gradually improves its long-range links by issuing Find queries for identities that are at a desired distance from its own identity.

Nodes use their short-range and long-range links to handle Find queries. When a node receives a Find message, it forwards the message along a link to a node that is closer to the target (in identity space). The properties of the SWN are such that the average number of messages that is required to find a node is polynomial in $\log N$, where N is the number of nodes. Experiments have shown that the self-organisation process that creates and maintains the SWN also has good scalability. More details about SWAN can be found in [4].

3.1   SWAN API

A prototype of the SWAN protocol has been implemented in Java. Most of the details of the protocol are hidden from applications that want to use SWAN. This is achieved by using the two interfaces shown below.

```
interface SwanEngine {

    /* Sets up and activates the SWAN protocol engine.
     */
    void activate(SwanIdentity id, SwanEngineContext context,
                  SwanAddress internal_address,
```

```
                         SwanAddress external_address);

  /* Provides the SWAN node with an additional bootstrap link.
   */
  void addBootstrapLink(SwanAddress address);

  /* Handles incoming SWAN messages.
   */
  void handleMessage(SwanMessage msg);

  /* Initiates a SWAN Find query.
   */
  void find(SwanIdentity target_id);
}

interface SwanEngineContext {

  /* Called by the SWAN engine to send outgoing SWAN messages.
   */
  void sendMessage(SwanMessage msg);

  /* Called by the SWAN engine to signal it wants a bootstrap
   * link.
   */
  void requestBootstrapLink();

  /* Called by the SWAN engine to return Find query results.
   */
  void findDone(SwanIdentity target_id, SwanIdentity subject_id,
                SwanAddress subject_address);
}
```

The *SwanEngine* interface is implemented by a generic SWAN protocol engine. The *SwanEngineContext* interface must be provided by the object that hosts the protocol engine, and provides the protocol engine with a context to interact with the application. For instance, the protocol engine does not send any messages, but uses the context to do so. In this way, the application can use a message delivery mechanism that is most suited to it. The protocol engine also uses the context to request bootstrap links. The application can use the SwanEngine interface to issue Find queries, and the results are returned to it by way of the SwanEngineContext interface.

There are two addresses associated with the SWAN node, both are set when the SWAN protocol engine is activated. The *internal address* is where all SWAN messages are received. These are low-level messages that are used to create and maintain the SWN, and to handle Find queries. The *external address* on the other hand, is reserved for application-level messages. This address is returned in response to external Find queries. It is therefore the address where any subsequent application-specific messages are received.

4   Implementation of SWAN Using DIET

To investigate how SWAN performs when it runs across multiple computers, we have implemented a test application in DIET. We have used DIET because its agent communication and migration capabilities provide a useful framework for developing distributed peer-to-peer applications. Furthermore, DIET's approach to robustness suits SWAN very well because SWAN does not require reliable message delivery. Moreover, it is desirable to quickly expose SWAN nodes to failure, so that the SWN can adapt as soon as possible. DIET's lightweight nature is also useful, because self-organisation in SWAN requires the sending of many, small messages.

At the heart of the application are the types of agent listed in Table 1. Multiple *ServiceProvider* agents are created. Each ServiceProvider makes itself accessible as a node in the SWAN system. On creation, each agent effectively generates a random node identity for itself. The agent also creates a SWAN protocol engine that is responsible for establishing the agent as a node in the SWAN network. The ServiceProvider agent uses the SWAN network to handle queries from other agents to find specific ServiceProvider agents. It does not offer any additional functionality here, but it would in a more realistic application. In a file-sharing application, for instance, each agent could be responsible for hosting a file and the identity of the SWAN nodes could be based on the filename. In this way, files can be retrieved by name, even after they are moved to a different location.

The *SwanEngineManager* is the most advanced agent of all. It manages one or more SWAN protocol engines. On start up, each ServiceProvider hands over its SWAN protocol engine to a local SwanEngineManager agent. From then on, the SwanEngineManager is responsible for receiving and sending all SWAN messages for these protocol engines. However, any messages related to the services provided by the ServiceProviders are sent to these agents directly. In this way, communication with ServiceProvider agents is not affected by the SwanEngineManager, and agents that use the ServiceProvider can be fully unaware of the SwanEngineManager. This is achieved by setting the internal and external SWAN addresses for each node as shown in Table 2. The `local ID` is an

Table 1. The different types of agents that are used

Type	Functionality
ServiceProvider	Makes itself accessible in the SWAN system
SwanEngineManager	Manages one or more SWAN protocol engines
Carrier	Performs basic remote communication
BootstrapScout	Finds suitable SWAN bootstrap links
Tester	Periodically samples the state of the SWAN network
TargetFinder	Used by the Tester to discover random Find targets

Table 2. The two different addresses per node in SWAN

Type	Address
internal	`<SwanEngineManager address><local ID>`
external	`<ServiceProvider address>`

identifier local to the SwanEngineManager, which is used to efficiently forward each incoming SWAN message to the appropriate SWAN protocol engine.

The SwanEngineManager makes use of two types of agent: Carriers and BootstrapScouts. *Carrier* agents are part of the standard DIET platform. They can perform remote communication, i.e. send a message to an agent in a different environment. A Carrier does so by migrating to the remote environment, connecting to the target agent and delivering the message to it. *BootstrapScout* agents are specific to SWAN. They discover SWAN nodes in other environments, which are then used by the SwanEngineManager to provide each SWAN node with suitable bootstrap links. BootstrapScouts find these other nodes by performing a random walk, along environment neighbourhood links.

The locally-centralised management of SWAN protocol engines has several advantages. Firstly, ServiceProvider agents do not receive any SWAN messages. They can therefore easily give up their thread. If a ServiceProvider temporarily needs a thread, for instance when it is contacted by another agent, the DIET kernel attempts to give it one so that it can respond. This makes sense from a resource point of view: Why permanently give a thread to agents that are inactive most of the time? It also helps to scale up the number of ServiceProviders that can be hosted in a single JVM.

Secondly, use of SwanEngineManagers makes it straightforward to improve the remote communication mechanism that is used. Currently, Carrier agents are used to carry messages to agents in different environments. This uses agent migration, which is implemented using TCP sockets. In SWAN many messages are sent to potentially many different destinations, but message delivery does not need to be reliable. Therefore connection-less UDP would be more efficient than reliable connection-based TCP. The SwanEngineManager can set up a UDP port to receive SWAN messages for all engines it is managing. It can forward each message to the appropriate engine, similar to how it currently forwards messages.

Note that the "centralisation" added by the SwanEngineManager does not negatively affect the robustness. The reason is that all agents reside in the same JVM, and thus share the same CPU, memory and network connection. If there is a hardware failure, or the system is temporarily overloaded, all agents in the same environment are affected anyway, even if each ServiceProvider would manage its own SWAN protocol engine.

The task of the *Tester* agent is to test the progress of the self-organisation, but it does not contribute to the self-organisation process. It samples the quality of the SWAN network by periodically issuing a Find request. It uses a *TargetFinder* agent to randomly find a target ServiceProvider agent. The TargetFinder does this by starting a random walk along neighbourhood links. In the environment where it ends, it randomly contacts one of the ServiceProviders and asks for its SWAN node identity. It then migrates back to its home environment where it reports back to the Tester with the identity. The Tester then contacts one of the local ServiceProviders and asks it to issue a Find query for the given identity to see if it can indeed be found.

Next to the agents, which make up most of the application, there are some monitoring and visualisation components. On start up, these attach themselves to environments, agents and SWAN protocol engines such that they are notified of relevant events. These components amongst others monitor the total number of messages that is sent, the links that are currently maintained by certain SWAN nodes and the state of the overall SWAN network.

5   Running SWAN Using DIET

We have run the application on a Beowulf cluster [10] consisting of eighteen computers, each with Dual Pentium 450 MHz CPUs. On each computer that we use, we run a single DIET world containing a single environment. On start up, each environment is filled with a single SwanEngineManager, a single Tester and multiple ServiceProviders. The other agents are created as and when they are needed. The Tester is configured such that it issues a Find query once every second. The swan protocol engines are configured so that the node activity leads to an overall CPU usage of approximately 50%.

Experiment 1 demonstrates how the system adapts to the arrival and departure of nodes. First we start up a single world, World 1, with one hundred ServiceProviders. After the SWN has sufficiently self-organised, we start up a second world, World 2, with another hundred ServiceProviders. Once the SWN has sufficiently self-organised again, we abruptly terminate World 2 and wait for the SWN to adapt, after which we terminate World 1. More precisely, we start up World 2 after ten subsequent find queries in World 1 have been successful. We then terminate World 2 after, in both worlds, ten subsequent find queries have been successful. We finally terminate World 1 once ten subsequent find queries have been successful again.

Table 3 gives an idea of the time and effort required for the SWN to adapt. It shows at various moments during run, the total number of agents that were created and that arrived in World 1, as well as the total number of messages sent by these agents. Figures 1 and 2 both show the SWN as seen from World 1, at different stages of the experiment. Both figures only show the short-range links, as the figures would be very cluttered otherwise. Finally, Fig. 3 shows a screenshot of a visualisation components. The component shows all the links maintained by a SWAN node in World 1. The address column shows that the node has several links to nodes in World 2, on a different computer.

The entire run took approximately five and a half minutes, which shows that the SWAN system can adapt fairly rapidly. In fact, the system was configured such that links would be removed after two subsequent message delivery failures.

Table 3. The total time and total agent and message activity in World 1 at various stages of Experiment 1

	Time [s]	Agents created	Agents arrived	Messages sent
Start of World 1	0	0	0	0
Start of World 2	60	467	0	1435
End of World 2	168	3278	3424	6162
End of World 1	327	4324	3424	7138

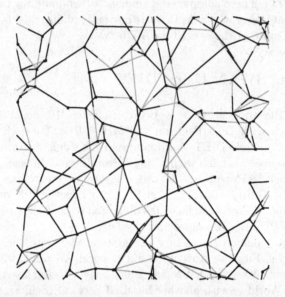

Fig. 1. The short-range links in World 1 just before World 2 started in Experiment 1. The nodes are shown in identity space, i.e. the node positions are derived from the node identities. The shading of the links indicates the directionality of each link. When a link originates from a node, the corresponding half of the link is dark

Lowering this threshold to one failed message per link would let the SWN adapt even more quickly after World 2 is terminated.

The aim of Experiment 2 is to see how the application performs when there are many nodes. We start a world on each of the eighteen computers in the cluster, and place six hundred ServiceProviders in each world to create 10800 SWAN nodes in total. We run the application for six hours.

Figure 4 shows the results of the Find queries generated by one of the Tester agents. The plots are generated by taking a sliding average over one hundred seconds. It can be seen that it takes thirty-five minutes before half of the Find queries succeeds. It is not surprising that the self-organisation takes longer than it did in Experiment 1. Not only did the total number of nodes increase from 200 to 10800, the available CPU time per node also decreased by a factor six.

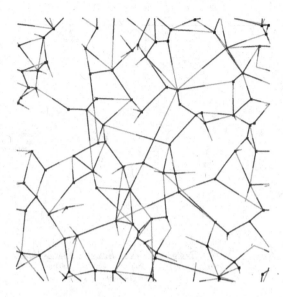

Fig. 2. The short-range links in World 1 just before World 2 ended in Experiment 1. The nodes in World 2 and the links that they maintain are not drawn, which explains why there is not a node at the end of every link

Identity	Type	Created	Sent	Rec	Address
	Boot	14:12:01	5	5	049bbf7ea-0fdf16d43@10.0.0.1:...
	Boot	14:12:02	8	8	049bbf7ea-0fdf16d43@10.0.0.1:...
	Boot	14:12:12	4	4	049bbf7ea-0fdf16d43@10.0.0.1:...
[623b][f729]	Long	14:12:16	2	2	049bbf7ea-0fdf16d43@10.0.0.1:...
	Boot	14:12:22	3	3	049bbf7ea-0fdf16d43@10.0.0.1:...
	Boot	14:12:32	5	5	049bbf7ea-0fdf16d43@10.0.0.1:...
	Boot	14:12:41	4	4	049bbf7ea-0fdf16d43@10.0.0.1:...
[7645][58ab]	Short-1	14:13:09	9	9	08f9dcf61-0fdf16d43@10.0.0.3:...
[7715][5811]	Short-2	14:13:13	13	12	08f9dcf61-0fdf16d43@10.0.0.3:...
[980a][42fb]	Short-1	14:13:27	9	9	049bbf7ea-0fdf16d43@10.0.0.1:...
[2e43][799f]	Long	14:13:37	1	1	08f9dcf61-0fdf16d43@10.0.0.3:...
[7750][660c]	Short-1	14:13:40	9	9	08f9dcf61-0fdf16d43@10.0.0.3:...
[9e79][5b0e]	Short-2	14:13:47	6	6	08f9dcf61-0fdf16d43@10.0.0.3:...
[6935][25f1]	Long	14:13:57	3	3	08f9dcf61-0fdf16d43@10.0.0.3:...
[6c76][9113]	Short-2	14:14:17	3	3	049bbf7ea-0fdf16d43@10.0.0.1:...
[8b89][952a]	Long	14:14:36	0	0	08f9dcf61-0fdf16d43@10.0.0.3:...

Fig. 3. Visualisation component that tracks the links for one or more SWAN nodes. The screenshot it taken just after World 2 ended in Experiment 1

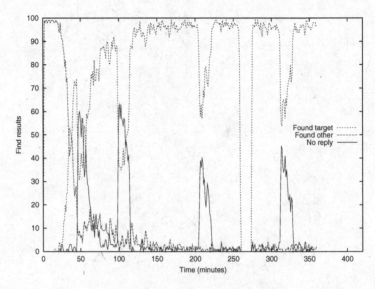

Fig. 4. The Find query results in Experiment 2 gathered by one of the Tester agents. It shows the number of Find queries for which a node with the requested identity was found (*found target*), for which a node with a different identity was found (*found other*), and for which no reply was received in time (*no reply*)

There are also five obvious dips in the performance. What exactly causes these unexpected dips is yet unknown. After debugging the application it appears that it happens because a thread that writes data into a socket blocks even though the world at the other end of the socket is ready to read incoming data. This results in a lack of threads in the world with the blocked writing thread, so that no agents can be created or migrate into this world. For the fourth dip, the world that has no spare threads is the world where the Tester resides. The Tester can therefore not create any TargetFinder agents, and as a result, does not issue any Find queries. The other dips are caused by failures in the other worlds. After approximately fifteen minutes the socket times out and is destroyed, so that the world resumes its normal functioning.

Although we have not yet been able to prevent this intermittent problem, it is very encouraging that the application keeps on functioning. Considering that six hundred SWAN nodes become unaccessible at once, the dip in the performance is relatively small, and after a while the application recovers entirely.

6   Discussion

We found that implementing the system in DIET was advantageous in several ways. Firstly, we think that an agent-based approach is in general a useful paradigm for developing peer-to-peer systems. The autonomous execution of agents and their ability to interact makes implementing peer-to-peer applications straightforward. The use of agents also make it natural to support multiple peers per computer.

Secondly, the lightweight nature of DIET was ideal for the application presented here. SWAN relies on the passing of many small messages, so it is important that this can be done efficiently. Additionally, the fact that agents do not permanently need to have a thread assigned to them helps to increase the number of nodes that can be supported.

Thirdly, the robustness of DIET has been important. When the application is ill-configured, or due to temporary glitches, parts of it can become overloaded. If the platform would try to ensure that all messages were handled anyway, this would inevitably cause the entire system to grind to a halt as more and more resources are needed to store and deliver pending messages. However, if messages and agents are discarded when overload occurs the system as a whole can keep on functioning. This only works properly if the application does not rely on perfect message delivery, but this is a sensible design approach for peer-to-peer systems anyway.

There is still plenty of scope for future work. Firstly, the experiments presented here have been limited. We are planning to perform additional experiments. It would be useful to generate more quantitative results, which for instance show how the number of nodes affects the speed of the self-organisation process. Additionally, it would be useful to test the adaptability and robustness of the system, by constantly introducing new nodes, removing arbitrary existing nodes, and changing the location of nodes.

Secondly, the system presented here can be enhanced in various ways. For instance, as mentioned in Sect. 4, the SwanEngineManager agent could be extended to use UDP for delivering messages. This would reduce the overhead associated with sending each message, and also reduces the number of sockets that is needed per JVM. The latter becomes important when you want to run the application on many more machines.

Thirdly, the software can be used to build actual applications. Amongst others, we are currently working on applications in the area of file sharing and file storage.

7 Conclusion

We have presented a distributed implementation of the SWAN look-up system using the DIET multi-agent platform. DIET's approach to robustness and its lightweight nature make it very suitable for running SWAN. An important feature of SWAN is that it is robust to failure, which has been demonstrated by the experiments. The experiments also show that the system is able to self-organise relatively quickly when it runs across multiple computers. The fact that ten thousand SWAN nodes could be hosted on only eighteen computers is also encouraging.

References

1. Stoica, I., Morris, R., Karger, D., Kaashoek, M.F., Balakrishnan, H.: Chord: a scalable peer-to-peer lookup service for internet applications. In: Proc. ACM SIG-COMM, San Diego CA (2001)
2. Rowstron, A., Druschel, P.: Pastry: Scalable, decentralized object location and routing for large-scale peer-to-peer systems. In: Proc. IFIP/ACM Int. Conf. on Distr. Sys. Platforms, Heidelberg, Germany (2001)
3. Ratnasamy, S., Francis, P., Handley, M., Karp, R., Shenker, S.: A scalable content-addressable network. In: Proc. ACM SIGCOMM, San Diego CA (2001)
4. Bonsma, E.: Fully decentralised, scalable look-up in a network of peers using small world networks. In: Proc. of the 6th World Multi Conf. on Systemics, Cybernetics and Informatics (SCI2002). Number 6, Orlando (2002) 147–152
5. Marrow, P., Koubarakis, M., van Lengen, R., Valverde-Albacete, F., Bonsma, E., Cid-Suerio, J., Figueiras-Vidal, A., Gallardo-Antolín, A., Hoile, C., Koutris, T., Molina-Bulla, H., Navia-Vázquez, A., Raftopoulou, P., Skarmeas, N., Tryfonopou-los, C., Wang, F., Xiruhaki, C.: Agents in decentralised information ecosystems: the DIET approach. In: Proc. of the AISB 01 Symposium on Information Agents for Electronic Commerce, York, UK (2001) 109–117
6. Hoile, C., Wang, F., Bonsma, E., Marrow, P.: Core specification and experiments in DIET: A decentralised ecosystem-inspired mobile agent system. In: Proc. 1st Int. Conf. on Autonomous Agents and Multi-Agent Systems (AAMAS2002). Number 2, Bologna, Italy (2002) 623–630
7. European Commission IST Future and Emerging Technologies: Universal information ecosystems proactive initiative. http://www.cordis.lu/ist/fethome.htm (1999)
8. Kleinberg, J.: The small-world phenomenon: An algorithmic perspective. Technical Report 99-1776, Department of Computer Science, Cornell University, Ithaca NY 14853 (1999)
9. Kleinberg, J.M.: Navigation in a small world. Nature **305** (2000) 845
10. Ridge, D., Becker, D., Merkey, P., Sterling, T.: Beowulf: Harnessing the power of parallelism in a pile-of-PCs. In: Proc. IEEE Aerospace. Volume 2. (1997) 79–91

HyperCuP – Hypercubes, Ontologies, and Efficient Search on Peer-to-Peer Networks

Mario Schlosser[1,*], Michael Sintek[2], Stefan Decker[3], and Wolfgang Nejdl[1]

[1] Stanford University, Stanford, USA
schloss,nejdl@db.stanford.edu
[2] German Research Institute for Artificial Intelligence, Kaiserslautern, Germany
sintek@dfki.uni-kl.de
[3] Information Sciences Institute/USC, Marina del Rey, USA
stefan@isi.edu
http://p2p.semanticweb.org

Abstract. Peer-to-peer networks are envisioned to be deployed for a wide range of applications. However, P2P networks evolving in an unorganized manner suffer from serious scalability problems, limiting the number of nodes in the network, creating network overload and pushing search times to unacceptable limits. We address these problems by imposing a deterministic shape on P2P networks: We propose a graph topology which allows for very efficient broadcast and search, and we describe a broadcast algorithm that exploits the topology to reach all nodes in the network with the minimum number of messages possible. We provide an efficient topology construction and maintenance algorithm which, crucial to symmetric peer-to-peer networks, does neither require a central server nor super nodes in the network. Nodes can join and leave the self-organizing network at any time, and the network is resilient against failure. Moreover, we show how our scheme can be made even more efficient by using a global ontology to determine the organization of peers in the graph topology, allowing for efficient concept-based search.

1 Introduction

Peer-to-peer networks are envisioned to find a broad range of applications, moving way beyond their current applications as infrastructure for file sharing and exchange such as in Gnutella or Morpheus [1]. For example, P2P networks for Semantic Web Services can be used to provide distributed access to these services without requiring a central service directory [2]. [3] uses a global service ontology which enables efficient service discovery and composition of web services. However, a fundamental building block of large-scale P2P networks is still missing: scalability. In almost all P2P networks requests for services use flooding algorithms which are based on inefficient broadcast mechanisms. We achieve efficiency by organizing peers in a P2P network into a graph structure based on hypercubes in our system HyperCuP (Hypercube P2P) which we describe

---

* Work done while authors were at Stanford University.

G. Moro and M. Koubarakis (Eds.): AP2PC 2002, LNAI 2530, pp. 112–124, 2003.
© Springer-Verlag Berlin Heidelberg 2003

in this paper. Section 2 describes the graph topology and its suitability for efficient broadcast and search. Section 3 presents a distributed algorithm which is capable of maintaining the graph structure efficiently, and elaborates the algorithm on a detailed example. In Sect. 4, we further extend this infrastructure by sketching the use of ontologies for partitioning the network. We briefly discuss related work in Sect. 5 and conclude in Sect. 6.

2   A Hypercube P2P Topology

Scaling a P2P network to a large number of peers while maintaining certain properties such as low network diameter requires controlling the evolution of the network topology upon peer joins and departures. We organize peers in a P2P network into a hypercube (or, more general, a Cayley graph) topology.

2.1   Organizing Peers into a Hypercube Graph

Figure 1a depicts a hypercube for a base $b = 2$, a topology that has been studied before in the area of multiprocessor machines [4], but under different assumptions. A complete hypercube graph consists of $N = b^{L_{max}+1}$ nodes and is defined by the fact that all nodes have $(b - 1) \cdot (L_{max} + 1)$ neighbors, $(b - 1)$ in each 'dimension' - where $L_{max} + 1$ is essentially the number of dimensions spanned by the cube (in Fig. 1, the cube has three dimensions, and L_{max} is 2). The network diameter, defined as the shortest path between most distant nodes in terms of node hops, is $\Delta = log_b N$. As visible, this structure is symmetric, i.e. no node incorporates a more prominent position than others. This is crucial for load balancing in the network: Every node can become the source of a broadcast (the root of a spanning tree of the network), yet the load will always be shared equally. The topology provides redundancy - its connectivity (the minimum number of nodes to be removed in order to partition the graph) is optimal, i.e. equal to $nodedegree - 1$. Power-law networks such as Gnutella can easily be partitioned by bringing down highly connected nodes in the network through denial of service attacks, the hypercube topology is far less vulnerable to such attacks. The hypercube base b can be chosen to adjust the network diameter and node degree. Note at this point that the construction algorithm that will be described in Sect. 3.1 works well with node numbers that are not equal to those in complete

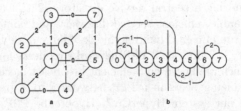

Fig. 1. a. Hypercube graph b. Serialized notation (links incomplete)

hypercubes, allowing for any number of peers in the network. To describe the topology of a graph $G = (V, E)$, we state some definitions. In the following, we will deal with hypercubes with a binary base for brevity. (Refer to [5] for an extension to bases $b > 2$.) Edges in the graph are labeled: Node Y is dubbed i-neighbor of node X or $Y = iN(X)$ iff node Y is X's neighbor in dimension i. For example, in Fig. 1, node 5 is the 2-neighbor of node 4. Node 5 is also dubbed 4's neighbor in dimension 2. Edges in the graph are undirected, i.e. node 4 is also 5's 2-neighbor. A node can have extended neighbors $Y = N(X) = \{x_0, x_1, \ldots\}(X)$, where N is termed neighbor link set, and it denotes the sequence of i-neighbors one would have to follow in the complete hypercube graph to reach node Y from node X and vice versa. In our example, the neighbor link set $\{0, 1\}$ leads from node 1 to node 7 and back, i.e. $1 = \{0, 1\}(7)$ and $7 = \{0, 1\}(1)$. Edge labels start at $i = 0$. The maximum dimension of a node is termed L_{max}. A node associates each of its neighbors with a link set and a transport network address.

2.2   Broadcast and Search Algorithm

Based on this terminology, we can define a broadcast scheme which guarantees that the set of nodes traversed strictly increases during a forwarding process, i.e. nodes receive a message exactly once. It is guaranteed that exactly $N - 1$ messages are required to reach all nodes in a topology. Furthermore, the last nodes are reached after $\log_b N$ forwarding steps. Any node can be the origin of a broadcast in the network, satisfying a crucial requirement. The algorithm works as follows: A node invoking a broadcast sends the broadcast message to all its neighbors, tagging it with the edge label on which the message was sent. Nodes receiving the message restrict the forwarding of the message to those links tagged with higher edge labels. As an example, refer to the serialized notation of the network graph in Fig. 1b (for clarity, only the links used in the example are depicted - however, one can just copy all links in 1a into this notation to arrive at the full picture): Node 0 sends a broadcast - at first to all its own neighbors, viz. nodes 4, 2 and 1. Node 4 receives the message on a link tagged as a dimension 0 link, i.e. it forwards the message only to its 1- and 2-neighbors, namely 6 and 5. At the same time, node 2 which has received the message on a dimension 1 link forwards it to its 2-neighbor, node 3. In the third forwarding step, node 6 relays the message to node 7, again its 3-neighbor. The characteristic path length [5] in this scheme can be calculated as $L = \frac{1}{L-1} \cdot \sum_{i=1}^{\log_b N} \frac{(b-1)^{\log_b N - i + 1}}{(\log_b N - i)!} \cdot \prod_{j=0}^{\log_b N - i}(i + j)$ which is about $0.5 \cdot \log_b N$. A search in a hypercube is essentially a broadcast with a time-to-live, i.e. a broadcast with a limited scope. It also has a monotonically increasing neighbor set which means that the maximum number of nodes is reached with a given number of messages.

3   Building and Maintaining Hypercube Graphs

In the following, we outline a distributed algorithm which allows nodes to build a hypercube topology. Here, the major challenges in P2P networks are as follows: To maintain network symmetry, crucial for P2P networks, any node in the network should be allowed to accept and integrate new nodes into the network. Furthermore, joining and leaving the network are to consume a reasonable amount of message transmission to limit the traffic imposed on the transport network. Clearly, a joining node should not have to register with all nodes in the network, i.e. we would like the protocol to beat a message number of $O(n)$ for node joins and removals.

3.1   Topology Construction and Maintenance Algorithm

In the following, we will describe our construction and maintenance of a hypercube P2P topology. The formal description of the algorithm and a proof of its completeness can be found in [5]. The algorithm can be used to build a general class of graphs, the so-called Cayley graphs [6]. Hypercubes are Cayley graphs, as well as a graph called star graph [6] which features even better (sub-logarithmic) properties than a hypercube. Yet, the algorithm can be more easily explained with hypercubes, hence we focus on them through the course of this paper. We will walk through an example by having 9 peers joining a network, and one peer leaving during the process, to elaborate the basic idea of the construction and maintenance algorithm. The construction and maintenance algorithm is based on the notion that nodes in an evolving hypercube graph take over responsibility for more than one position in the hypercube. The idea is to have the hypercube topology of the next biggest complete hypercube graph already implicitly present in the current topology state, i.e. in the link sets of all participating nodes. Upon arrival of new nodes, the complete hypercube topology unfolds as needed. Upon removal of nodes, other nodes jump in to cover the positions previously covered by the node that left the topology, prepared to give these positions up again as new nodes join. Since the complete hypercube topology is implicitly preserved, the broadcast and search algorithms do not have to change either - still, every peer receives a broadcast message exactly once.

Start. At the beginning, only peer 0 is active.

Step a. Peer 0 is contacted by node 1 which wants to join the P2P network. Peer 0 integrates peer 1 as 0-neighbor since it does not currently have any other neighbor: The peers establish a link between each other which is tagged with the neighbor set {0}, as depicted in Fig. 2. Generally, a peer integrates a joining peer in its first vacant dimension, the dimensions are ordered such that lower dimensions always come first.

Step b. Peer 2 contacts one of the two peers (here, we assume that it contacts peer 1) to join the network. The first vacant dimension of peer 1 is 1 since

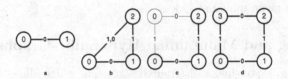

Fig. 2. Network Topology Construction

it already maintains a 0-neighbor, peer 0. Essentially, peer 1 opens up a new dimension for the hypercube, as depicted in Fig. 2b. Peer 1 becomes the so-called integration control node for the complete integration of peer 2 into the network: It is responsible for providing peer 2 with all necessary links - at the end of the integration process, peer 2 has to have neighbor links connecting it all currently existing dimensions, in order to be able to carry out complete broadcasts. Since peer 1 currently has two neighbors, a 0- and a 1-neighbor, it knows that it has to provide peer 2 with a 0- and a 1-neighbor, too. Peer 1 itself has become peer 2's 1-neighbor. Since there is currently no alternative, peer 1 selects peer 0 as the new 0-neighbor for peer 2. However, peer 0 can only become a temporary 0-neighbor for peer 2 because it already has another 0-neighbor, namely peer 1 - and we said before that a peer can only have one neighbor per dimension. Essentially, peer 0 now covers a vacant position in the hypercube, i.e., it acts as if it occupies two positions in the hypercube, as depicted by the thin copy of peer 0 in Fig. 2c. To mark the link between peers 2 and 0 as temporary relationship, it is tagged with the link set $\{0,1\}$ (instead of $\{0\}$): This link set denotes the path from peer 2 via the position at which the link set is originally aiming to peer 0, the peer which currently covers this position. (This path is also well visible in Fig. 2c.) Temporary link sets are always constructed by this rule.

Step c. Peer 3 wants to join the network. We compare three cases, viz. peer 3 contacting peer 0, 1 or 2 to join the network. In case peer 3 contacts peer 0 to join, peer 0 follows the general rule to integrate the peer in its first vacant dimension - which is 1, since peer 0 has a 0-neighbor, but no 1-neighbor. As its new 1-neighbor, peer 3 will now cover the temporary position that peer 0 used to maintain in the hypercube: Hence peer 0 can pass on links that are associated with this position to peer 3. Due to the construction rule of edge labels for temporary link sets, peer 0 is able to determine that link $\{0,1\}$ to peer 2 is a link that is to be passed on to peer 3. Peer 3 then establishes a link tagged by link set $\{0\}$ to peer 3, as depicted in Fig. 2d. In case peer 3 contacts peer 2 to join, peer 2 decides to integrate peer 3 as its new (and non-temporary) 0-neighbor. However, it does not carry out the integration itself: Since peer 0 currently covers the position that will soon be occupied by peer 3, the integration control responsibility has to be forwarded to peer 0. Peer 2 can do so via peer 0. Note that it is always possible for peers in the network to reach the node to which they have to forward the control integration, if necessary, in one hop. We prove this in [5]. Peer 0 carries out the integration just as described above, arriving at Fig. 2d. In case peer 3 contacts peer 1, peer 1 will integrate peer 3 in dimension 2, i.e., it opens up a new dimension for the hypercube. This leads to a momentary imbalance in the hypercube with some peers maintaining more links than others. To preserve network balance, joining nodes carry out a random walk (at maximum of length $\log_b N$) with increasing probability of choosing the currently visited node as integration champion. Simulations show that e.g. power-law join behavior observed in Gnutella-style networks leads to a fairly balanced network using this technique.

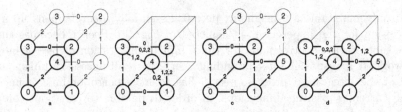

Fig. 3. Network topology construction continued

Step d. Peer 4 arrives and contacts peer 0. Now, the network crosses a threshold - a hypercube with 2 dimensions cannot accommodate 5 peers, hence a third dimension is opened up. Peer 0 integrates peer 4 in its first vacant dimension as its new 2-neighbor. Peer 4 needs 3 neighbors, one in each dimension - but neither peer 0's 1-neighbor, peer 3, nor peer 0's 0-neighbor, peer 1, are linked to their own 2-neighbor which they could provide as a new neighbor to peer 4. Thus, peer 3 acts as temporary 1-neighbor for peer 4, whereas peer 1 acts as temporary 0-neighbor for peer 4, indicated once again by the link sets {0, 2} and {1, 2} among these peers (see Fig. 3b). Figure 3a shows the existing peers in the network in bold style and the positions that are additionally covered by them in thin style. Once again, note that the positions that are additionally covered by peers determine the temporary connections the peers have to maintain, plus their edge labels. Figure 3a also demonstrates another basic rule: Peers that are 'closest' to a vacant position in the hypercube structure are always chosen to cover it. Here, 'closest' means that the peer in the highest dimension to a vacant position covers it. (In the more complicated case when a peer has to cover several positions, a peer covers the power set of its vacant dimensions.) Among the other peers in the network, adding another dimension to the graph means the multiplication of existing links, too: For example, peers 1 and 2 could now both integrate 2-neighbors, which would then be linked in dimension 1. Thus, they tag their already existing {1} link additionally as {1, 2, 2} link. So do peers 2 and 3 with their already existing {0} link.

Step e. Peer 1 is contacted to integrate the newly arriving peer 5. Peer 1 is still lacking a 2-neighbor, thus peer 5 will be integrated on this position (Fig. 3d). Now, peer 1 can get rid of its {1, 2, 2} link to peer 2: It is moved to peer 5. However, since 2 is not peer 5's final 1-neighbor either, the link stays temporary: Peers 2 and 5 now maintain a {1, 2} link among them. Peer 5 takes over peer 1's temporary {0, 2} link to peer 4, which still lacks its final 0-neighbor. It has found one now, namely peer 5.

Step f. Let us assume that peer 0 suddenly leaves the network. In the maintenance protocol, it is obliged to carry out a peer removal process: Basically, it decides which existing peers that it knows will be chosen to take over responsibility for the positions it gives up. In our example, peer 0 leaves only one position vacant, its original position in the graph - however, a node which covers multiple positions will have to find successors for each of its positions in the graph. Peer

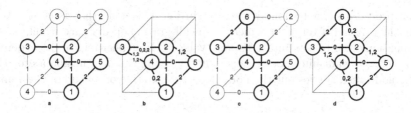

Fig. 4. Network topology construction continued

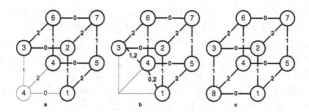

Fig. 5. Network topology construction continued

4 takes over peer 0's position, establishing temporary links to the former neighbors of peer 0, peers 1 and 3. Figure 4a shows the new distribution of covering responsibilities, Fig. 4b depicts the link structure that arises from this network state.

Step g. Peer 4 is contacted by peer 6 and decides to integrate it as its new 1-neighbor. This position is currently covered by peer 3, hence peer 4 forwards the integration control to peer 3, just as described in step c. In the example, all temporary links that are currently owned by peer 3, but originally belong to the new position of peer 6, are restored and passed on to peer 6. Additionally, peer 3 integrates peer 6 as its new 2-neighbor, arriving at Fig. 4d.

Step h. Peer 6 is contacted by peer 7, leading to peer 7's integration as peer 6's new 0-neighbor. Figure 5a and Fig. 5b depict the state of the network: Almost all positions of a complete hypercube graph with 3 dimensions are held by active peers, only peer 4 still covers two positions in the hypercube. What if several peers want to join the network simultaneously? We are currently working on turning our protocol into a real-time protocol, dealing with simultaneous node joins and departures. For example, parallel joins can be executed easily when join actions are time-stamped. We have also implemented the protocol on a JXTA-based P2P infrastructure [7] [8] and we are extending the implementation into a JXTA-based test platform for P2P overlay protocols.

Step i. On integrating peer 8, peer 4 pushes its links {1,2} and {0,2} to its new 2-neighbor, arriving at a complete hypercube topology again.

Link Failures. A link failure in the network leads to a node's immediate departure from the P2P topology, not being able to send any departing messages. If that happens, the topology must be able to recover and head back to a normal state. In the hypercube graph, we can always recover from a sudden node loss.

The procedure can be found in detail in [5]: The node that is closest to the vanished node (in terms of a metric we call graph hop distance which uses the dimension order to compute a distance value between positions in the hypercube) contacts the vanishing node's neighbors by asking its own neighbors for them. The node then carries out the node departure routine on behalf of the vanished node.

3.2 Complexity

Assuming a relatively balanced graph structure, the algorithm as described above yields an $O(\log_b N)$ complexity in terms of messages that have to be sent in order to join or leave the network. More precisely, this holds when there are only nodes in the graph that have $\lfloor \log_b N - 1 \rfloor$ or $\lfloor \log_b N \rfloor$ non-missing dimensions. Note that this allows for any number of nodes in the graph. To arrive at this complexity order, the algorithm uses optimizations not explained in detail in the walk-through in Sect. 3.1. For example, if a new hypercube dimension is opened up by integrating an additional peer (as has happened above in step d), this information is not broadcasted to all peers in the network - instead, it is propagated only when necessary, i.e. once again when nodes communicate on the issue of removing or integrating a peer. Networks that reach a large number of nodes can scale down again to a small number of nodes (as long as this takes place relatively balanced, see Sect. 3): Higher dimensions that are added during the construction process are removed again if no peer in the network has any neighbor in a dimension any more. Once again, this information is not broadcasted in the network but locally inferred by every peer by observing its set of neighbor link sets it maintains.

4   Ontology-Based Routing

A HyperCuP empowered P2P network features good scalability and search times. However, in the case of Semantic Web applications such as Semantic Web Services, additional knowledge is available that can be used to further improve the P2P network performance: Oftentimes, information or services that peers are able to provide can be categorized as belonging to general concepts. Concepts can in turn be organized in a (global) ontology which defines the relationships between existing concepts. In the following, we describe which role ontologies play in the domain of Semantic Web Services and how they can be used to improve the search properties of a P2P service network.

4.1   Ontologies and Semantic Web Services

An ontology [9] is a shared formalization of a conceptualization of a domain, to state a popular definition. In the Semantic Web, ontologies are used to assign commonly agreed upon semantics or interpretation to particular concepts. Semantic Web Services can be described by using various ontologies in parallel,

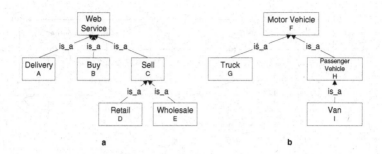

Fig. 6. Service ontology and domain ontology

augmenting a service ontology (see an example in Fig. 6a) by domain ontologies (e.g. as in Fig. 6b). A car retailer Web Service would describe itself by combining concepts from the service ontology with concepts from the car domain ontology, for example $C \wedge G \wedge I$. Semantic Web research has spawned many results on the design of and distributed negotiation on such ontologies which can well be reused to create service and domain ontologies, also in the domain of Semantic Web Services [10].

4.2   Ontology-Based Network Organization

Ideally, the P2P service network should allow for issuing a query to be sent to exactly those peers that can potentially answer the query. For example, a query $B \wedge I \wedge \neg G$ is to be broadcasted among those peers that buy vans, but are not interested in trucks. To allow for such broadcast containment, we introduce concept clusters into the hypercube network topology as described in Sect. 2: Peers with identical or similar interests or services are grouped in concept clusters which are in turn assigned to a specific logical combination of ontology concepts that describes best the peers belonging to the cluster. These concept clusters are organized into a hypercube topology to enable routing to specific concept clusters in the topology. Concept clusters themselves, too, are hypercubes or star graphs (the construction algorithm is capable of 'mixing' different Cayley graph topologies).

Concept Coordinates. These coordinates address a concept cluster on the 'outer' hypercube. A set of structuring concepts is chosen to build this hypercube (see Sect. 4.4). A structuring concept is contained in one of the ontologies that are available to describe Web services participating in the network, i.e. in the service or domain ontologies. Each selected structuring concept is represented by a single ontology coordinate whose binary value in a concept cluster address reflects the support of peers in the addressed concept cluster for the respective structuring concept.

Storage Coordinates. A concept cluster will contain more than one peer. Hence an additional address space is needed to accommodate multiple peers within a concept clusters. Storage coordinates denote the location of a peer

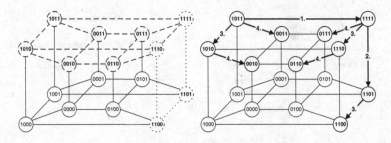

Fig. 7. a. Concept hypercube topology b. Routing example

within a specific concept cluster on the selected storage topology. Concept clusters form sub-graphs of the 'outer' ontology-based hypercube - however, their internal topology can be based on hypercubes, star graphs or any other Cayley graph topology.

4.3   Routing and Broadcast

Querying the network works in two routing steps: First, the query is propagated to those concept clusters that contain peers which the query is aiming at. Second, a broadcast is carried out within each of these concept clusters, optimally forwarding the query to all peers within the clusters. This involves shortest-path routing in the concept coordinate system as well as restricted broadcast in the concept and storage coordinate systems.

Query Minimization. A query that is issued by a peer undergoes logic minimization (e.g. Karnaugh minimization) to identify its logical minterms (conjunctions of structuring concepts). Minterms denote a group of concept clusters. All concept clusters pointed to by a single minterm are direct neighbors of each other in the network topology. Figure 7a depicts the 'outer' concept hypercube of a network that is organized by structuring concepts A, D, E and F from the ontologies in Fig. 6. The query $E \vee A \wedge D$ consists of minterms E as well as $A \wedge D$ and asks for some peer that is a wholesale service or a combined retail and delivery service.

Minterm Analysis. Distinct minterms resemble distinct groups of concept clusters in the network. To each of these groups, one copy of the query message has to be delivered to enable them to carry out broadcasts within the group. These groups may overlap or are adjacent. Figure 7a depicts the 4-dimensional concept hypercube that is created by using concepts A, D, E and F as structuring concepts. Each node in the network represents a concept cluster (for example, node 0101 represents the concept cluster containing peers which are motor vehicle retailers). However, note that not all clusters will actually be built: The outer hypercube will only be complete in the case of a flat ontology, i.e. a keyword list. In all other cases, is-a relations prohibit the conjunction of certain concepts. The corresponding clusters will never be built, the clusters will be interconnected in the usual HyperCuP way as described in Sect. 3.1. The two minterms in our query are associated with two (overlapping) groups of concept clusters, highlighted in Fig. 7a.

Routing to Concept Clusters. A copy of the broadcast message is delivered to each concept cluster addressed in the query. If queries span groups of concept clusters, this can be accomplished by carrying out restricted broadcasts in the concept coordinate system. Figure 7b depicts the broadcast steps that are executed in order to inform all concept clusters addressed by the query $E \vee A \wedge D$. The broadcast algorithm modifies the algorithm described in Sect. 2.2: A concept cluster group associated with a minterm is described by the set of dimensions in which it exists (directly associated with the concepts it supports). Broadcast is carried out only in those dimensions and branches out into additional dimensions at peers which belong to more than one minterm or are adjacent to peers belonging to another minterm. In order to start the broadcast, the broadcast message has to reach any peer within the concept cluster group - this is achieved by shortest-path routing from the querying peer to the closest peer in the group (by correcting one address bit in each routing step).

Broadcast in Concept Clusters. All informed concept clusters broadcast the query message among all their member peers. Broadcasting is carried out in the storage coordinate system, restricting it to the peers that belong to the broadcasting concept cluster.

Peer Feedback. Once the query message has arrived at a peer, the peer is able to react to the message - for example, by contacting the issuer of the query in order to establish a business relationship.

4.4 Topology Construction

Peers can join the ontology-based topology by contacting any peer already in the network. The peer reveals its capabilities in terms of concepts contained in any of the available global ontologies, and it is to be integrated in the concept cluster matching its description. If the peer describes itself with concepts that are not used as structuring concepts in the network, it is integrated in the most specific existing concept cluster. A join message is then routed to any peer in this cluster, using shortest-path routing. The contacted peer then integrates the new peer into the concept cluster using precisely the algorithm described in Sect. 3.1. Although it is possible to select all concepts contained in available service and domain ontologies as structuring concepts, it is reasonable to choose a subset as structuring concepts upfront which are empirically expected to be frequently used in peer descriptions. We are currently experimenting with an algorithm which chooses structuring concepts on the fly during network operations.

5 Related Work

Making P2P networks scalable has recently received much attention. Distributed hash table approaches [11] such as CAN [12] and Chord [13] aim at enforcing a deterministic content distribution instead which can be used for routing point queries. While similar in terms of message complexity for joining and departing nodes, our approach specifically performs well at optimizing the network load in broadcast and multipoint search, without requiring hash functions, and allows for more detailed queries, viz. logical combinations of ontology concepts. [14] constructs an efficient P2P topology, yet does not provide means of clustering peers with similar capabilities. Building a Semantic Service Web on a P2P infrastructure is opposed to centralized approaches such as UDDI [2]. Automated composition and verification of Semantic Web Services is addressed in [10], building on the service description framework DAML-S [3]. Our approach facilitates service discovery as a major building block of automated service composition.

6   Conclusion

We have presented a topology to efficiently cluster peers in a P2P network which features efficient broadcast and search algorithms without any message overhead during broadcast, logarithmic network diameter, and resiliency towards node failure. Super peers or central servers are not required. A set of globally known ontologies is used to categorize peers as providers of particular services to efficiently route and broadcast queries. Organizing peers in this manner allows for enhancing Semantic Web Services technology with the flexibility and dynamics of P2P networks while ensuring scalability to a large number of nodes.

References

1. Gnutella website: www.gnutella.com. (2002)
2. White paper: UDDI. (2002) available at www.uddi.org.
3. Martin, D., et al.: DAML-S: Semantic Markup for Web Services. (2001) White paper, available at www.daml.org/services/daml-s.
4. Johnsson, S.L., Ho, C.T.: Optimum Broadcasting and Personalized Communication in Hypercubes. IEEE Transactions on Computers **38** (September 1989) 1249–1268
5. Schlosser, M., Sintek, M., Decker, S., Nejdl, W.: HyperCuP. (April 2002) Technical Report, Stanford University.
6. Akers, S.B., Krishnamurty, B.: A group-theoretic model for symmetric interconnection networks. IEEE Transactions on Computers **38** (April 1989) 555–566
7. Nejdl, W., et al.: EDUTELLA: A P2P Networking Infrastructure based on RDF. In: Proceedings of the 11th World Wide Web Conference. (May 2002)
8. White paper: Project JXTA: An open, innovative collaboration. (2002) available at www.jxta.org.
9. Uschold, M., Gruninger, M.: Ontologies: Principles, Methods and Applications. Knowledge Engineering Review **11** (1996)
10. McIlraith, S., Son, T., Zeng: Semantic Web Services. IEEE Intelligent Systems. Special Issue on the Semantic Web **16** (March/April 2001) 46–53
11. S. Ratnasamy, S.S., Stoica, I.: Routing Algorithms for DHTs: Some Open Questions. In: Proceedings of 1st International Workshop on P2P Systems. (March 2002)

12. Ratnasamy, S., Francis, P., Handley, M., Karp, R., Shenker, S.: A scalable content-addressable network. In: Proceedings of ACM SIGCOMM. (August 2001)
13. Stoica, I., et al.: Chord: A scalable P2P lookup service for internet applications. In: Proceedings of ACM SIGCOMM. (August 2001)
14. Pandurangan, G., Raghavan, P., Upfal, E.: Building low diameter P2P networks. In: Proceedings of the 42nd Annual IEEE Symposium on the Foundations of Computer Science. (2001)

Messor: Load-Balancing through a Swarm of Autonomous Agents

Alberto Montresor[1], Hein Meling[2], and Özalp Babaoğlu[1]

[1] Department of Computer Science, University of Bologna
Mura Anteo Zamboni 7, 40127 Bologna, Italy
{babaoglu,montresor}@CS.UniBO.IT
[2] Department of Telematics, Norwegian University of Science and Technology
O.S. Bragstadsplass 2A, N-7491 Trondheim, Norway
meling@item.ntnu.no

Abstract. Peer-to-peer (P2P) systems are characterized by decentralized control, large-scale and extreme dynamism of their environment. Developing applications that can cope with these characteristics requires a paradigm shift that puts adaptation, resilience and self-organization as primary concerns. *Complex adaptive systems* (CAS), commonly used to explain the behavior of many biological and social systems, could be an appropriate response to these requirements. In order to pursue these ideas, this paper presents Messor, a decentralized load-balancing algorithm based on techniques such as multi-agent systems drawn from CAS. A novel P2P grid computing system has been designed using the Messor algorithm, allowing arbitrary users to initiate computational tasks.

1 Introduction

Informally, *peer-to-peer* (P2P) systems are distributed systems based on the concept of resource sharing by direct exchange between *peer* nodes (i.e., nodes having same role and responsibility). Exchanged resources include content, as in popular P2P file sharing applications [24,12,14], and storage capacity or CPU cycles, as in computational and storage grid systems [1,22,13]. Distributed computing was intended to be synonymous with P2P computing long before the term was invented, but this initial desire was subverted by the advent of client-server computing. The modern use of the term P2P and distributed computing as intended by its pioneers, however, differ in several important aspects. First, P2P applications reach out to harness the outer edges of the Internet and consequently involve scales that were previously unimaginable. Second, P2P by definition, excludes any form of centralized structure, requiring control to be completely decentralized. Finally, and most importantly, the environments in which P2P applications are deployed exhibit extreme dynamism in structure and load.

In order to deal with the scale and dynamism that characterize P2P systems, a paradigm shift is required that includes self-organization, adaptation and resilience as fundamental properties. We believe that *complex adaptive systems* (CAS), commonly used to explain the behavior of certain biological and social

G. Moro and M. Koubarakis (Eds.): AP2PC 2002, LNAI 2530, pp. 125–137, 2003.
© Springer-Verlag Berlin Heidelberg 2003

systems, can be the basis of a new programming paradigm for P2P applications. In the CAS framework, a system consists of a large number of relatively simple autonomous computing units, or *agents*. CAS typically exhibit what is called *emergent behavior*: agents, taken individually, may be easily understood, while the behavior of the system as a whole defies simple explanation. In other words, the interactions among agents, in spite of their simplicity, can give rise to richer and more complex patterns than those generated by single agents in isolation.

As an instance of CAS drawn from nature, consider an ant colony. Several species of ants, in particular those belonging to the *Messor Sancta* species, are known to group objects in their environment (e.g., dead corpses) into piles so as to clean up their nests. Observing this behavior, one could be mislead into thinking that the cleanup operation is being coordinated by some "leader" ants. Resnick [21] describes an artificial ant colony exhibiting this very same behavior in a simulated environment. Resnick's artificial ant follows three simple rules: (i) wanders around randomly, until it encounters an object; (ii) if it was carrying an object, it drops the object and continues to wander randomly; (iii) if it was not carrying an object, it picks the object up and continues to wander. Despite their simplicity, a colony of these "unintelligent" ants is able to group objects into large clusters, independent of their initial distribution.

What renders CAS particularly attractive from a P2P perspective is the fact that global properties like adaptation, self-organization and resilience are achieved without explicitly embedding them into the individual agents. In the above example, there are no rules specific to initial conditions, unforeseen scenarios, variations in the environment or presence of failures. Yet, given large enough colonies, the global behavior is surprisingly adaptive and resilient.

In order to pursue these ideas, we have developed *Anthill* [3], a novel framework for P2P application development based on ideas such as multi-agent systems and evolutionary programming borrowed from CAS [25,18]. The goals of Anthill are to provide an environment that simplifies the design and deployment of P2P systems based on these paradigms, and to provide a "testbed" for studying and experimenting with CAS-based P2P systems in order to understand their properties and evaluate their performance. An Anthill system is composed of a collection of interconnected *nests*. Each nest is a peer entity that makes its storage and computational resources available to swarms of *ants* – autonomous agents that travel across the network trying to satisfy user requests. During their life, ants interact with services provided by visited nests, such as storage management and ant scheduling.

Details of the design and implementation of Anthill can be found in a companion paper [3]. After having developed a prototype of Anthill, we are now in the process of testing the viability of our ideas regarding P2P as CAS by developing common P2P applications like file sharing [19] and grid computing over Anthill. In this paper, we present one of such application, called Messor. Messor is a grid computing system aimed at supporting the concurrent execution of highly-parallel, time-intensive computations, in which the workload may be decomposed into a large number of independent jobs. The computational power offered by a network of Anthill nests is exploited by Messor by assigning a set of jobs comprising a computation to a dispersed set of nests. To determine how to balance the load among the computing nodes, Messor use an algorithm inspired by the behavior of the artificial ant described above: Messor ants drop objects they are carrying only after having wandered about randomly "for a while" without encountering object concentrations. Colonies of such Messor ants try to disperse objects (more specifically, jobs) uniformly over their environment, rather than clustering them into piles.

Several computations can be profitably supported by Messor [1,7,2]. For example, in the Seti@Home project [1], the enormous amount of radio signals registered by radio telescopes are subdivided into a large number of data sets, that can be independently analyzed in the search for evidence of extra-terrestrial intelligence; Distributed.net [7] is an umbrella for several distributed computing projects, including cryptography challenges in which brute-force attacks are performed by subdividing key spaces into independent portions; the Anthrax Project [2] is an effort designed to help scientists to find a treatment for the Anthrax toxin, by performing screening analysis of large sets of molecules.

All these projects are based on a master-slave architecture, in which only the master node is enabled to generate and assign new jobs. Slave machines are relegated to a role of mere executors, thus in some sense betraying the peer-to-peer philosophy. Messor is completely decentralized, allowing every node in the system to generate new jobs and submit them to the network. An application designed in this way may be interesting for groups of entities that want to share their resources in order to exploit the resulting computing power cost effectively.

2   Anthill

An Anthill system is composed of a self-organizing overlay network of interconnected *nests*, as illustrated in Fig. 1. Each nest is a middleware layer capable of hosting resources and performing computations. The network is characterized by the absence of any fixed structure, as nests come and go and discover each other on top of a communication substrate. Nests interact with local instances of one or more *applications* and provide them with a set of *services*. Applications are the interface between the user and the P2P network, while services have a distributed nature and are based on the collaboration among nests. An example application may be a file-sharing system, while a service could be a distributed indexing service used by the file-sharing application to locate files.

An application performs *requests* and listens for *replies* through its local nest. Requests and replies constitute the interface between applications and services. When a nest receives a request from the local application, an appropriate service for handling the request is selected from the set of available services. This set is dynamic, as new services may be installed by the user. Services are implemented by means of *ants*, autonomous agents able to travel across the nest network. In response to a request, one or more ants are generated and assigned to a particular task. Ants may explore the network and interact with the nests that they visit in order to accomplish their goal. Anthill does not specify which services a nest

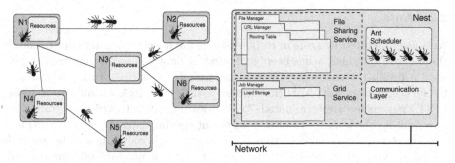

Fig. 1. Overview of a nest network   **Fig. 2.** The architecture of a nest

should provide, nor impose any particular format on requests. The provision of services and the interpretation of requests are delegated to ants.

2.1   Nests

Figure 2 illustrates the architecture of a nest that is composed of three logical modules: ant scheduler, communication layer and resource managers. The *ant scheduler* module multiplexes the nest computation resource among visiting ants. It is also responsible for enforcing nest security by providing a "sandbox" for ants in order to limit the resources available to ants and prohibit ants from performing potentially dangerous actions (e.g., local file access).

The *communication layer* is responsible for network topology (neighbor) management and for ant movement between nests. The set of remote nests known to a node are called *neighbors* of that node. Note that the concept of neighborhood does not involve any distance metrics, since such metrics are application dependent and is more appropriately chosen by developers. The collection of neighbor sets defines the nest network that might be highly dynamic. For example, the communication layer may discover a new neighbor, or it may forget about a known neighbor if it is considered unreachable. Both the discovery and the removal processes may be either mediated by ants, or performed directly by the communication layer.

Nests offer their resources to visiting ants through one or more *resource managers*. Example resources could be files in a file-sharing system or CPU cycles in a computational grid, while the respective resource managers could be a disk-based storage manager or a job scheduler. Resource managers typically enforce a set of policies for managing the (inherently limited) resource. Each service installed by a nest is associated with a set of resource managers. For example, the nest in Fig. 2 provides two distinct services: a file-sharing service based on a distributed index for file retrieval, in which a routing table is used by ants in making routing decisions, a file manager is used for maintaining shared files and a URL manager contains the distributed index; and a computational grid service, in which a job manager executes jobs assigned to it.

2.2 Ants

Ants are generated by nests in response to user requests; each ant tries to satisfy the request for which it has been generated. An ant will move from nest to nest until it fulfills its task, after which (if the task requires this) it may return back to the originating nest. Ants that cannot satisfy their task within a *time-to-live* (TTL) parameter are terminated. When moving, the ant carries its state, that may contain the request, results or other ant specific data. The ant algorithm is contained in a *run*() method, that is invoked at each visited nest. The ant code may be transmitted together with the ant state, if needed; appropriate code caching mechanisms are used to avoid to download the same algorithm more than once, and to update it when new versions are available.

Ants do not communicate directly with each other; instead, they communicate indirectly by leaving information related to the service they are implementing in the appropriate resource manager found in the visited nests. For example, an ant implementing a distributed lookup service may leave routing information that helps subsequent ants to direct themselves toward the region of the network that more likely contains the searched key. This form of indirect communication, used also by real ants, is known as *stigmergy* [10]. The behavior of an ant is determined by its current state, its interaction with resource managers and its algorithm, that may be non-deterministic. For example, an ant may probabilistically decide not to follow what is believed to be the best route for accomplishing a task, and choose to explore alternative regions of the network.

2.3 The Anthill Framework

A Java prototype of the Anthill runtime environment [23] has been developed, based on JXTA [11], an open-source P2P project promoted by Sun Microsystems. JXTA is aimed at establishing a programming platform for P2P systems by identifying a small set of basic facilities necessary to support P2P applications and providing them as building blocks for higher-level services. The benefits of basing our implementation on JXTA are several. For example, JXTA allows the use of different transport layers for communication and deals with issues related to firewalls and NAT.

In addition to the runtime environment, Anthill includes a simulation environment to help developers analyze and evaluate the behavior of their P2P systems. Simulating different P2P applications require developing appropriate ant algorithms and a corresponding request generator characterizing user interactions with the application. Each simulation study is specified using XML by defining a collection of component classes and a set of parameters for component initialization. For example, component classes to be specified include the simulated nest network, the request generator to be used, and the ant algorithm to be simulated. Initialization parameters include the duration of the simulation, the network size, the failure probability, etc. This flexible configuration mechanism enable developers to build simulations by assembling pre-defined and customized component classes, thus simplifying the process of evaluating ant algorithms.

Unlike other toolkits for multi-agent simulation [17], Anthill uses a single ant implementation in both the simulation and actual run-time environments, thus avoiding the cost of re-implementing ant algorithms before deploying them. This important feature has been achieved by a careful design of the Anthill API and by providing two distinct implementations of it for simulation and deployment.

3   Load Balancing in Messor

In this section, we present the Messor application and the services on which it relies. Messor is aimed at supporting the concurrent execution of highly-parallel, time-intensive computations, in which the workload can be decomposed into a large number of independent jobs.

3.1   System Model and Messor Specification

A Messor system is composed of a collection of interconnected Anthill nests configured to run the Messor software. Every such nest can submit *jobs* to the nest network, where each job is composed of some input data and the algorithm to be computed over these data. Jobs are scheduled and executed by the nest on which the job resides, by invoking the job algorithm. We say that a job is *completed* when its associated algorithm has been executed to completion. A completed job outputs a *result*, i.e. some data obtained from the job computation.

At each nest, Messor offers a very simple API to its users, enabling them to submit new jobs to be computed and collecting results once the jobs have been computed. The *originator* nest of a job is the nest where the job has been submitted. Once submitted, jobs may remain in the originator, or may be transferred to other nests in order to exploit their unused computational power. When a job is completed, the result is sent back to the originator. Once there, the user is either notified of the job result, or the result is stored locally; in the latter case, the user may periodically poll the nest to obtain the collected results. Messor guarantees that all jobs submitted to a *correct* originator will eventually be completed and their results delivered to the originator itself. Although this property may be satisfied by simply letting the correct originator compute all jobs, Messor attempts to disperse the load uniformly among cooperating nodes.

3.2   Messor Architecture

The architecture of a node supporting the Messor application is shown in Fig. 3. Messor nodes are composed of two main layers:

- the Messor Application Layer is responsible for interacting with the local user by accepting requests and collecting computed results on her behalf; furthermore, it is also responsible for keeping track of job assignments, in order to re-insert in the system, jobs assigned to nodes that may have crashed.
- the Messor Service Layer is responsible for job execution and load balancing.

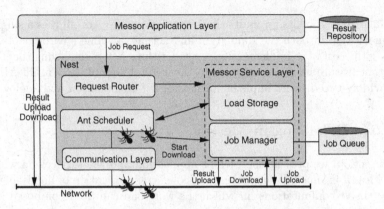

Fig. 3. The architecture of a node supporting Messor

The Application Layer receives jobs from the user, and delivers them as job requests to the Request Router contained in the nest. This module analyze the request and routes it to the appropriate service among those installed in the nest. In the case of Messor, job requests are delivered to the Messor Service Layer.

In order to achieve its goals, the Application Layer maintains a database of jobs originated by the local user and their status with respect to the computation. The status may corresponds to the computed results, if available, or to the identifier of the nest to which the job has been assigned. Results computed by remote nests are downloaded by the Application Layer out-of-band, i.e. outside the ant communication mechanism offered by nests, for efficiency reasons. A lease mechanism is used to keep track of operational nodes, in order to identify crashed nodes and opportunely re-insert jobs assigned to them.

The Service Layer exploits the ant communication and scheduling facilities provided by nests. Two main resource managers are employed: the Load Storage contains information about the estimated load of remote nests, while the Job Manager is responsible for executing the jobs assigned to the local nest. The Load Storage implementation is memory-based; it is the main data structure maintained by visiting ants, and its utilization is explained in the next section. The Job Manager maintains a database of jobs to be computed by the local nest, implemented as a queue, and acts as a scheduler that selects the next job from the queue and executes it. Once computed, the Job Manager is responsible for uploading the result to the Application Layer of the job originator. Jobs are inserted in the job queue either after the Messor Service Layer have received a local request through the Request Router, or by downloading them from other nests. The download process is triggered by Messor ants, that are responsible for load balancing, while the actual download is performed out-of-band, without the mediation of ants.

3.3 The Messor Ant Algorithm

The most interesting component of Messor is its ant algorithm. In order to understand the basic idea behind Messor, consider the following variation of the artificial ant algorithm described in the introduction: (i) when an ant is not carrying any object, it wanders about randomly until it encounters an object and picks it up; (ii) when an ant is carrying an object, the ant drops it only after having wandered about randomly "for a while" without encountering other objects. Colonies of such ants try to disperse objects uniformly over their environment rather than clustering them into piles.

The algorithm of Messor ants is inspired by the rules described above. The environment in which Messor ants live is given by the network of nests. The objects to pick-up and drop-off correspond to the actual jobs, existing within the nest network. During its life-time, a Messor ant may assume two different states: SearchMax and SearchMin. While in SearchMax state, the ant wanders about in the network until it finds an "overloaded" nest; at that point, the ant records the identifier of this nest and switch to the SearchMin state. While in SearchMin state, the ant wanders about looking for an "underloaded" nest. When such a nest is found, the ant requests the local Job Manager to transfer jobs from the overloaded nest to the underloaded one, and then switches back to the SearchMax state again; and the process repeats. The transfer process is performed by direct downloading between the two nests; this to avoid carrying potentially large amounts of data representing jobs from one node to another while wandering about, searching for underloaded nodes.

The *load* of a nest is defined as the number of jobs currently in the job queue of that nest; alternatively, if information about the potential computing power needed to perform jobs is available, the load of a nest may be defined based on this information. The concepts of overloaded and underloaded nests are relative to the average load of the nests recently visited by an ant. This definition enable ants to make decisions about job transfers between nests with unbalanced loads on the basis of local information only, i.e. without global knowledge.

The SearchMax and SearchMin walks are not performed completely at random. When wandering, ants collect information about the load of the last visited nests. This information is then stored in the Load Storage component in each nest, and is used by subsequent ants to drive their SearchMax and SearchMin phases: at each step, the ant randomly selects the next node to visit among those that are believed to be more overloaded (in SearchMax) or underloaded (in SearchMin). In this way, ants move faster towards those regions of the network in which they are more interested. To avoid that the system become biased toward a subset of nests (those believed to be more over- or underloaded), ants may occasionally, based on an *exploration probability*, select the next nest using a uniform distribution, enabling the exploration of the entire network.

The Messor algorithm is shown in Fig. 4. The state of each ant is represented by the set of variables listed in the preamble. The current state (SearchMax vs SearchMin) of the ant is stored in variable state. A circular queue, visits contains nest identifiers and load information of the last N visited nests; this information is

```
integer state = MAX;
Queue visits = new Queue(N);
integer maxLoad, minLoad;
NestId maxNest, minNest;

method doSearchMax() {
  if ((minLoad/maxLoad) ≤ TargetRatio[MAX]
    and not tossCoin(KeepSearchProb[MAX])) {
    state = MIN;
    doSearchMin();
  } else
    goNextNest();
}


method doSearchMin() {
  if ((minLoad/maxLoad) ≤ TargetRatio[MIN]
    and not tossCoin(KeepSearchProb[MIN])) {
    state = MAX;
    mng.forceTransfer(maxNest);
    clearMaxMin();
    doSearchMax();
  } else
    goNextNest();
}
```

```
method run(AntView view) {
  JobManager mng =
    view.getManager(JOBMANAGER);
  LoadStorage strg =
    view.getManager(LOADSTORAGE);
  initMaxMin(mng.getLoad(), view.getId());
  if (state == MAX)
    doSearchMax();
  elseif (state == MIN)
    doSearchMin();
}

method goNextNest() {
  if (tossCoin(ExplorationProb[state])) {
    list = strg.getNeighborList(view);
    nextNest= uniformRandom(list);
  } else {
    list = strg.getOrderedList(state, view);
    nextNest= normalRandom(list, Dev[state]);
  }
  strg.addLoads(visits);
  visits.add(mng.getLoad(), view.getId());
  view.move(nextNest);
}
```

Fig. 4. Pseudo-code description of the algorithm

used to update the load information stored in Load Storages. Variables maxLoad
and maxNest (minLoad, minNest) contain the load and the identifier of the nest
with maximum (minimum) load among those recently visited.

Whenever an ant reaches a nest, its $run()$ method is executed. The $AntView$
parameter passed to $run()$ is a proxy object used by ants to communicate with
the nest. The first action of $run()$ is to obtain references to the local Job Manager
and Load Storage; then, variables maxLoad, minLoad, maxNest and minNest are
initialized by the $initMaxMin()$ method (not shown in the figure), simply by sub-
stituting, the load value and the identifier of the nest with maximum or minimum
load. Finally, method run invokes methods $doSearchMax()$ or $doSearchMin()$,
depending on its current state.

The first step of method $doSearchMax()$ is to decide whether to keep travel-
ing through the network, searching for nodes with higher loads, or to switch to
the SearchMin state. An ant will explore the network until the ratio between the
maximum and the minimum load values stored in the ant state reaches a target value (represented by TargetRatio). Furthermore, each ant has a probability
KeepSearchProb to keep searching even when the target ratio has been reached,
providing a way for ants to continue their search for overloaded nests.

If the ant decides to keep searching, method $goNextNest()$ is invoked. This
method selects the next nest and moves there by invoking method $move()$ on
the $AntView$. The selection of the next nest depends on whether the ant decides
to explore the network completely at random, or to direct itself towards a region
of the network that is expected to be more overloaded. This decision is made by
tossing a coin with probability ExplorationProb. If the decision is not to explore,
the next nest is selected according to a normal distribution among the nests

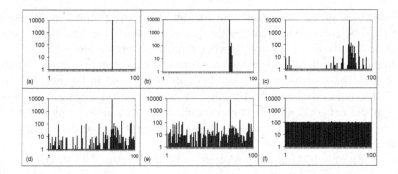

Fig. 5. Load distribution after 0, 5, 10, 15, 20, 50 iterations.

contained in the local Load Storage that are believed to be more overloaded. Before moving to the next nest, the ant updates the local Load Storage with its current content of visits, and then updates the visits variable with the load value and the identifier of its current nest.

Method *doSearchMin* is similar to *doSearchMax*; the only difference is when the ant decides to switch again to the SearchMax state, in which case the balancing operation (mediated by the involved Job Manager) is started and the variables are re-initialized.

4 Performance Evaluation

In this section, we present preliminary results for Messor, obtained through the Anthill simulator. Further details can be found in a companion paper [20]. Figure 5 illustrate how the load balancing process performed by Messor evolves over time. The results were obtained in a network of 100 idle nests, initially connected to form a ring (for visualization reasons). Initially, 10,000 jobs are generated in a single node. The different histograms depict the load observed in all the nests (x-axis) after 0, 5, 10, 15, 20, and 50 iterations of the algorithm. At each iteration, a set of 20 ants perform a single step, i.e. executes its run method and moves to the next nest. In each iteration, a node is limited to at most 200 job transfers to other nodes. As the figure illustrate, only 15-20 iterations are required to transfer jobs to all other nodes in the network, and after 50 iterations, the load is perfectly balanced. The first iterations are spent exploring the neighborhood in the ring network. After a few iterations, new connections are created and used to transfer jobs to remote parts of the network.

5 Discussion and Conclusions

We have argued that techniques borrowed from CAS could form the basis for a new paradigm for building P2P systems that are adaptive, resilient and self-organizing. To prove the viability of this idea, we have used Anthill to develope a P2P load-balancing algorithm that exhibit the above properties. Messor ants adapt their behavior to the load conditions, wandering about randomly when the load is uniformly balanced and moving rapidly towards regions of the network with highly unbalanced loads when these exist. The system is resilient to failures, as jobs assigned to crashed nodes are simply re-inserted in the network by the nest that generated them. And finally, Messor is self-organizing, as new nests may join the network, and their computing power is rapidly exploited to carry on the computation, as soon as ants discover the nest and start to assign it jobs transferred from other nests.

Our work may be compared with existing architectures for distributed computing. Several distributed computing projects [1,7] are based on the master-slave paradigm, in which a well-known centralized master is responsible for supplying slave machines with jobs. In Messor, every node of the network is capable of producing new jobs and introduce them in the network for computation.

Messor may be compared with so-called grid computing projects [9], such as Globus [8] and Legion [6]. The goals of Messor are more simplistic than those of these projects, that present complex architectures, capable to organize computations based on the memory, storage and computing requirements of jobs, as well as on the relationships between jobs. Nevertheless, Messor is interesting because, unlike these projects, presents a completely decentralized architecture.

Many systems already exist for achieving dynamic load distribution, in particular process migration systems [16] like MOSIX, Sprite, Mach and LSF. However, none of these apply a CAS based approach to this problem, and many of them employ a centralized load-balancing algorithm, making them unsuitable for deployment in grid computing applications. The MOSIX [4] system use a decentralized and probabilistic load balancing algorithm similar to the one adopted by Messor. However, MOSIX requires a prior knowledge of the distributed sytstems, while Messor is a self-configuring P2P system. Moreover, MOSIX is a kernel level process migration system, and thus unsuitable in heterogenous environments.

Anthill share its goals with project DIET (Decentralised Information Ecosystem Technologies) [15,5], aimed at the development of a robust, adaptable and scalable software platform for multi-agent systems applied to information processing.

We conclude by highlighting the fact that Messor is still a prototype. Many important features needed by distributed computing systems have not been implemented yet. For example, we have not considered issues related to security, apart from enclosing visiting ants in "sandboxes" that limit the set of actions performed by them. Mechanisms to authenticate users and to keep account over the number of jobs submitted and computed by nests are needed; these mechanisms may also prove useful as a defense against denial-of-service attacks. Further studies are needed to improve our understanding of the behavior of Messor ants. In particular, we are interested in obtaining an evaluation of the number of ants needed to manage a network. We plan to implement a mechanism to bound the number of ants present in the system simultaneously, by adding a module at each nest that kills ants when they are in excess, and creates new ants when the nest has not been visited recently. This module will also have an adaptive behavior, increasing the number of ants when the load is highly unbalanced.

References

1. D. Anderson. SETI@home. In A. Oram, editor, *Peer-to-Peer: Harnessing the Benefits of a Disruptive Technology*, chapter 5. O'Reilly, Mar. 2001.
2. The Anthrax Project. http://www.chem.ox.uk/anthrax.
3. Ö. Babaoğlu, H. Meling, and A. Montresor. Anthill: A Framework for the Development of Agent-Based Peer-to-Peer Systems. In *Proc. of the 22th Int. Conf. on Distributed Computing Systems*, Vienna, Austria, July 2002.
4. A. Barak and A. Shiloh. A Distributed Load Balancing Policy for a Multicomputer. *Software Practice and Experience*, 15(9):901–913, Sept. 1985.
5. E. Bonsma and C. Hoile. A Distributed Implementation of the SWAN Peer-to-Peer Lookup System Using Mobile Agents. In *Proc. of the 1st Workshop on Agent and Peer-to-Peer Systems*, Bologna, Italy, July 2002.
6. S. Chapin, J. Karpovich, and A. Grimshaw. The Legion Resource Management System. In *Proc. of the 5th Workshop on Job Scheduling Strategies for Parallel Processing*, Apr. 1999.
7. Distributed.net Home Page. http://www.distributed.net.
8. I. Foster and C. Kesselman. Globus: A Metacomputing Infrastructure Toolkit. *International Journal of Supercomputer Applications*, 11(2):115–128, 1997.
9. I. Foster and C. Kesselman, editors. *The Grid: Blueprint for a Future Computing Infrastructure,*. Morgan Kaufmann, 1999.
10. P. Grasse. La reconstruction du nid et les coordinations interindividuelles chez bellicositermes natalensis et cubitermes sp. *Insectes Sociaux*, 6:41–81, 1959.
11. Project JXTA. http://www.jxta.org.
12. G. Kan. Gnutella. In A. Oram, editor, *Peer-to-Peer: Harnessing the Benefits of a Disruptive Technology*, chapter 8. O'Reilly, Mar. 2001.
13. J. Kubiatowicz et al. OceanStore: An Architecture for Global-Scale Persistent Storage. In *Proc. of the 9th International Conference on Architectural support for Programming Languages and Operating Systems*, Cambridge, MA, Nov. 2000.
14. A. Langley. Freenet. In A. Oram, editor, *Peer-to-Peer: Harnessing the Benefits of a Disruptive Technology*, chapter 8. O'Reilly, Mar. 2001.
15. P. Marrow, M. Koubarakis, et al. Agents in Decentralised Information Ecosystems: The DIET Approach. In M. Schroeder and K. Stathis, editors, *Proc. of the Symposium on Information Agentsfor Electronic Commerce (AISB'01)*, pages 109–117, University of York, United Kingdom, March 2001.
16. D.S. Milojičić, F. Douglis, Y. Paindaveine, R. Wheeler, and S. Zhou. Process Migration. *ACM Computing Surveys*, 32(3):241–299, Sept. 2000.
17. N. Minar, R. Burkhart, C. Langton, and M. Askenazi. The Swarm Simulation System, A Toolkit for Building Multi-Agent Simulations. Technical report, Swarm Development Group, June 1996. http://www.swarm.org.
18. M. Mitchell. *An Introduction to Genetic Algorithms*. MIT Press, Apr. 1998.
19. A. Montresor, Ö. Babaoğlu, and H. Meling. Gnutant: Free-Text Searching in Peer-to-Peer Systems. Technical Report UBLCS-02-07, Dept. of Computer Science, University of Bologna, May 2002.
20. A. Montresor, H. Meling, and Ö. Babaoğlu. Messor: Load-Balancing through a Swarm of Autonomous Agents. Technical Report UBLCS-02-08, Dept. of Computer Science, University of Bologna, May 2002. In preparation.

21. M. Resnick. *Turtles, Termites, and Traffic Jams: Explorations in Massively Parallel Microworlds.* MIT Press, 1994.
22. A. Rowstron and P. Druschel. Storage Management and Caching in PAST, a Large-Scale, Persistent Peer-to-Peer Storage Utility. In *Proc. of the 18th ACM Symp. on Operating Systems Principles*, Canada, Nov. 2001.
23. F. Russo. Design and Implementation of a Framework for Agent-based Peer-to-Peer Systems. Master's thesis, University of Bologna, July 2002.
24. C. Shirky. Listening to Napster. In A. Oram, editor, *Peer-to-Peer: Harnessing the Benefits of a Disruptive Technology*, chapter 2. O'Reilly, Mar. 2001.
25. G. Weiss. *Multiagent Systems: A Modern Approach to Distributed Artificial Intelligence.* MIT Press, 1999.

Market Models for P2P Content Distribution*

P. Antoniadis and C. Courcoubetis

Department of Informatics
Athens University of Economics and Business
76 Patision Str., Athens, GR 10434, Greece
{antoniad,courcou}@aueb.gr

Abstract. The new p2p networking paradigms offer new possibilities for content distribution over the Internet. We propose a model that treats peers as independent economic agents buying and selling content and investigate the basic economic properties of such a market managed p2p content distribution network. Initially, we assume that no peer has the content, and there is a substantial initial cost to bring it within the peer group. The bargaining position and hence the price that can be posted by an agent having the content depends on the cost to transport the content to the requesting peer, its value, and the number of other agents providing the same content. We discuss the influence of parameters such as the maximum number of the competitive offers allowed by the system, content popularity, its value to the agents, and the transport costs, taking into account the risk of the first agent incurring the initial content cost.

1 Introduction

In contrast with existing content distribution paradigms such as multicasting, caching and content distribution networks (CDNs), in the p2p model the content is delivered in a fully distributed fashion. Each peer after receiving the content can act as a content provider making the content distribution much more efficient due to the lack of central management. As initially conceived, p2p networks assumed insignificant costs in terms of obtaining and transporting content and deployed minimum control mechanisms.

In such a simple model, an agent that needs the content will always obtain it, and will make it freely available to others. But content may be costly to obtain, since the bandwidth of the network may be restricted at places causing delay costs over particular distribution routes. Furthermore, making content accessible to others reduces a peer's access bandwidth and hence degrades his network access performance. If such costs become significant, the altruistic community spirit may not be enough to sustain the successful operation of the system. Deploying a market mechanism within the peer community may solve these problems and reduce unnecessary waste of resources resulting from peers requesting content for which their value is less than the cost imposed to others. This approach is

---

* This work is partly supported by EU's Fifth Framework project 'Market Management of Peer-to-Peer Services' – MMAPPS (RTD No. IST-2001-34201)

G. Moro and M. Koubarakis (Eds.): AP2PC 2002, LNAI 2530, pp. 138–143, 2003.

consistent with recent studies of the behavior of popular p2p file sharing applications such as Napster and Gnutella [1] [2] which conclude that free riders consist the majority of the participating peers of these systems. This behavior is allowed where no central management or market mechanisms exist to ensure the fair and economically justified allocation of resources. Recent game theoretic analysis [3] indicates that without some market mechanism in place there exist no suitable incentives for peers to contribute to the p2p community.

Market mechanisms lie somewhere between existing centralized solutions and the current unmanaged p2p systems. Peers are modeled as economic agents having incentives for obtaining revenue from distributing content. We may assume that there is a common cost W to bring the content to a p2p group, resembling to the case of a copyright cost or to the case where there is a substantial cost for transporting the content to any peer from its external source. We also assume that there is some intra-group cost for transporting the content, different in general for each pair of communicating peers and for each service direction. This can model delays or link performance degradation when bandwidth is a scarce resource, as in the case of network access.

Each time an agent requests a specific content we assume there exists a lookup service that provides cost and price information and can control the number of competitive offers allowed for each request. We compare two types of content distribution paradigms:

1. A *restricted competition* model, where at most t agents are randomly selected from the set S of all candidate content providers. This is an oligopoly model, where prices will depend on the number t of competing peers.
2. A *privileged provider* model, where the first agent to acquire the content[1] and hence to incur the initial cost W is granted the privilege to be the unique seller of this content within the group. The above agent has the power of a monopolist that can do personalized pricing.

In this paper we discuss the influence of restricting content availability information to the spreading of the content in the peer community. Granting different market power to agents selling the content affects their expected profits, and hence influences their decisions about buying the content and further reselling it. Allowing a highly competitive market has the positive effect of bringing prices low and resulting in higher social welfare since more agents will finally buy the content. On the other hand, it is not obvious that excessive competition will always benefit the system as a whole. Obtaining information about the quality of the content has always a positive effect by stimulating demand since low prices make it difficult for the agent that quires the content to recover his cost, and hence reduce his motivation to do so. It is hence reasonable to assume that the end result may depend on the size of the system and on the costs of initially acquiring the content and further distributing it within the group compared to the value of the content to the agents.

---

[1] Since this agent has different characteristics from the rest of the group we will assign him index 0.

We propose a simple economic model that takes into account all the above parameters and results in tractable analytic solutions of the underlying games. It can be used to analyze the sensitivity of various performance metrics such as the social welfare and the expected net benefit of the agents with respect to parameters such as the initial cost, the value and popularity of the content, the available information, the transport costs, etc. These parameters affect the prices and the expected net benefit of the agents which in turn influence their decisions and the resulting content distribution.

2   A Simple P2P Content Distribution Market Model

Lets assume a group of N peer agents which may request some content, each agent i obtaining value u_i by using the content, where u_i is uniformly distributed in $[0, V]$. We assume that initially the content belongs to some external provider who charges a substantial fee W, high enough relative to V. So, once some agent purchased the content, it makes more sense for this agent to resale the content at lower prices within the group in order to recover his cost and even make some profit, instead of more agents paying this high fee to the content provider. This potential profit allows for agents with $u_i - W < 0$ to take the risk and purchase the content. The larger the size of the group, the greater $\max_i\{u_i - W_i\}$ will be, hence increasing the probability for such a decision. Clearly, the desicion whether to pay this fee W depends on the estimate of the average revenue that can be obtained by reseling it, and on the degree of agents' risk aversion.

On this level there is an interesting game to be played. Each agent waits for another agent to do this first move and pay the fee W. This 'free rider' problem may in some cases result in low probability of purchasing the content. We discuss next the part of the model that describes the internal market of the p2p group, which is used to compute the average revenue obtained by content resale.

An important aspect of our model is the cost associated with moving content around. We denote by c_{ij} the cost for moving content from agent i to agent j. This may be direct communication cost such as delay, information loss or payments to transport service providers, or indirect cost corresponding to performance deterioration of the access service of the agent giving away the content. Such a cost will be charged to the agent purchasing the content in addition to the payment for the content itself. Depending on the situation, c_{ij} may be known a priori only to j, or only to i, or to both. For instance, agent j may get back from the network the identity of agent i and the average throughput of a connection to this agent, while the agent i may only know that there is a potential customer. This uncertainty and asymmetry about the costs is crucial for deriving positive revenues. For instance, if agent j requests the content and there are two competing providers i and k which already have the content, where $c_{ij} = c_{kj} = 0$, then the equilibrium price is zero [4]! On the other hand, if costs are known to all parties involved and $c_{ij} > c_{kj}$, then k will win posting the price $c_{ij} - c_{kj}$. If the distribution of these costs is random with a known distribution, then one may calculate the average revenue from such a transaction. Our model allows various types of information asymmetry: costs may be random and known only by the customers, or each seller knows only his cost.

There are other important parameters such as content popularity, which can be modeled by the probability of an agent to request the content or by the number of agents that will eventually request the content (the equivalent size of the group with respect to the above content). Reputation may be modelled by associating different values for the same content obtained from different sellers. For instance, the value of agent i may be u_{ij} where j is the seller of the content.

2.1   Calculation of Social Welfare and Expected Revenue

We discuss next the market models and the resulting prices and revenues corresponding to different levels of competition. As we show, the degree of competition influences the agents' decisions and the social welfare of the system. Our goal is to convince the reader that our model leads in many interesting cases to analytically tractable solutions, which we hope that can provide better insight to the sensitivity of the performance with respect to the key parameters introduced.

The Case of a Privileged Provider

This is the extreme case of a monopoly, where agent 0 is granted the exclusivity right to resale the content after purchasing it for the initial price W. This agent, given the available information, must choose the optimal price w to charge for the content in order to maximize his expected revenue $\bar{R}_m$ obtained by selling the content to the peer group. Then he must compare this expected revenue to $W - u_0$ and decide if it is worth to him to undertake this effort.

We briefly describe how one may compute the expected revenue from resale. Let c_i be the cost to transport the content to agent i from agent 0. We assume for simplicity that the c_{ij}s are iid with uniform distribution in $[0, C]$. We also assume that the value of c_i is made known only to agent i that requests the content[2] whereas its distribution is known to agent 0. Similarly, the value u_i of the content to agent i is iid and uniform in $[0, V]$. Let w the price that agent 0 uses to respond to the request of agent i. If $u_i < w + c_i$, then agent i will refuse to buy the content resulting in zero revenue for agent 0. The optimization problem faced by agent 0 becomes

$$\max_w R(w) = wP[u > c + w],\tag{1}$$

where for simplicity we have omitted the subscript i. By solving (1) we obtain

$$0 \leq C \leq 2V/3 : w^* = V/2 - C/4, R^* = \frac{[V - C/2]^2}{4V},\tag{2}$$

$$2V/3 \leq C \leq V : w^* = V/3, R^* = 2V^2/27C.\tag{3}$$

The total average revenue $\bar{R}_m(N)$ is now obtained by multiplying R^* by N.

---

[2] One may make different assumptions about the disclosure of such information.

To compute the social welfare we must compute the average value of a peer that accepts such an offer, and then multiply it by the average number of such peers. In order to do this, one must compute the conditional distribution of the value of a peer given the fact that he accepted price w^*. The average number of peers that will eventually accept the offer is $NP[u > c + w^*]$. This allows us to compute the social welfare, given that the content is purchased, $SW_m = NP[u > c + w^*]\frac{7C^2 + 12CV - 36V^2}{24(C-2V)}$. Multiplying with the probability that at least one agent will finally decide to initially buy the content, $P_b = [1 - (1 - P[u > W + \bar{R}_m(N)])^N]$, we can compute the expected social welfare $\bar{SW}_m = P_b SW_m$.

The Case of Restricted Competition

In this case we allow t peers to compete for every content request. These are chosen randomly among the peers that have already purchased the content. We consider the illustrative case where $t = 2$. To simplify notation consider the case where peers 1 and 2 compete for a given request by some third peer. Let c_i and w_i, $i = 1, 2$, be the costs and prices corresponding to each of these peers.

Similarly to the priviledged provider case we can calculate the optimal price $w_1^* = \frac{C}{2}$ and the expected revenue $R_1(w_1^*) = \frac{C}{4}P[w_1^* + c < u] = \frac{C(V-C)}{4V}$ of each transaction. [3]

Lets evaluate now the revenue of agent 0. The first time he will resell the content he will use (1) since he is the unique agent that can sell the content. After that he will always use price w_1^*. How much revenue will he make in total? Assuming that agents are randomly chosen among the set S of candidate providers, the probability that agent 0 is chosen in the competing pair is $2/|S|$.

Conditioned on the event that M agents will eventually buy the content, the expected revenue of agent 0 in this duopoly case is

$$\bar{R}_d(M) = \frac{[V - C/2]^2}{4V} + \frac{C}{2}\frac{1}{2}\sum_{k=2}^{M}\frac{2}{k} \approx \frac{[V - C/2]^2}{4V} + \frac{C}{2}[\gamma + \ln M - 1], \quad (4)$$

where γ the Euler-Mascheroni constant and $M = NP[w_1^* + c < u]$.

Similarly to the case of the privileged provider we can compute the total value generated in this system. For instance, in the case where $C \leq 2V/3$, $SW_d = N\frac{13C^2 - 12V^2}{24V}$ and $\bar{SW}_d = [1 - (1 - \frac{V - W + \bar{R}_d(M)}{V})^N]SW_d$.

3   Evaluation of Results

Below we present some initial results we have obtained comparing the above two cases. The expected revenue of the restricted competition case is significantly reduced in comparison with the priviledged provider case, as it increases logarithmically with N. Thus, the probability that an agent will decide to initially

---

[3] For simplicity we have assumed that $V >> C$ and hence computed an approximation of (higher than) the optimal price.

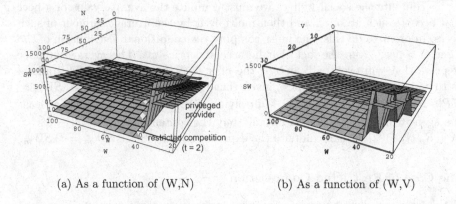

(a) As a function of (W,N)   (b) As a function of (W,V)

Fig. 1. Comparison of the expected social welfare between the two cases

take the risk and purchase the content is also reduced. However, if this probability is high enough, when W is close to V, the expected social welfare of the
system is significantly higher (see Fig. 1) since prices in this case are lower and
more agents will finally buy the content.

4   Conclusions and Future Work

In this paper we have presented some ongoing work regarding performance evaluation of market managed mechanisms for p2p systems. We have motivated a
cost model where simple good will incentives may not be enough to allow content
to propagate efficiently within the p2p group. Our model allows for the analysis
of the intricacies introduced by a market model, and in many cases produces
analytic results. Our next step is to interprete in more depth our results and
validate some of the conjectures made in this paper. We believe that complete
lack of control may be detrimental in certain cases where substantial costs are
involved. The goal of our model is to substantiate this and provide for some
quantitative results. We believe that although many of the assumptions regarding cost are of a rather theoretical nature, they capture some essential aspects
of the system and will help us understand the role of the key parameters.

References

1. Adar, E., Huberman, B.: Free riding on gnutella. First Monday **5** (2000)
2. Saroiu, S., Gummadi, P., Gribble, S.: A Measurement Study of Peer-to-Peer File
   Sharing Systems. In: Proceedings of Multimedia Conferencing and Networking, San
   Jose. (2002)
3. Golle, P., Leyton-Brown, K., Mironov, I., Lillibridge, M.: Incentives for Sharing in
   Peer-to-Peer Networks. In: Proceedings of WELCOM'01. (2001)
4. Varian, H.: Microeconomic Analysis. Norton (1992)

The Resource Management Framework: A System for Managing Metadata in Decentralized Networks Using Peer-to-Peer Technology

Steffen Rusitschka and Alan Southall

Siemens AG, Corporate Technology, Intelligent Autonomous Systems
Otto-Hahn-Ring 6, 81730 Munich, Germany
{Steffen.Rusitschka,Alan.Southall}@mchp.siemens.de

Abstract. Given the current explosion in peer-to-peer based protocol implementations, application developers require a means of abstracting the individual characteristics of specific peer-to-peer implementations away from their application logic. The *Resource Management Framework* provides a unified model of peer-to-peer computing which is independent of the underlying protocols. To this end, a data model and APIs for both application and peer-to-peer protocol developers are provided which hide many of the intricate details, such as database management and redundancy, inherent in all peer-to-peer systems. A first application of the Resource Management Framework has been demonstrated via the implementation of a FIPA compliant, distributed, ad-hoc Directory Facilitator for the Java Agent DEvelopment Framework (JADE).

1 Introduction

The peer-to-peer (P2P) paradigm is attracting an ever increasing amount of attention in both industrial and academic spheres. Over the past few years there has been an explosion in the number of P2P based routing protocols and platforms, e.g. Chord [4], Pastry [2], CAN [7], and JXTA [6]. Given such a large number of systems, one major concern for application developers is, however, which system to choose and whether applications written for one specific P2P solution will be usable with other P2P platforms. Similarly, P2P protocol developers often tend to reimplement the same features realized several times before in previous P2P protocols, e.g. database support, leasing and data redundancy.

The primary objective of the Resource Management Framework (RMF) [9] is to provide an active and collaborative information space for heterogeneous data which can be browsed or modified in order to share information between groups of all sizes based on a unified model of peer-to-peer computing which is independent of the underlying protocols. To this end, an extensible data model based on XML has been created which defines a base class called resource. Resources may be inter-linked to form trees and lists, and inherited to form new user defined types. Semantic Web [10] style applications are supported by the embedding of, for example, RDF [11] metadata in a resource.

The RMF architecture defines two APIs: one for application developers and one for P2P protocol developers. These APIs provide access to RMF functionality such as resource registration, lookup, data redundancy, etc.

G. Moro and M. Koubarakis (Eds.): AP2PC 2002, LNAI 2530, pp. 144–149, 2003.
© Springer-Verlag Berlin Heidelberg 2003

A powerful feature of the RMF is a content-based publish-subscribe [1] mechanism which is based on XML query language event subscriptions. Event subscriptions allow an application developer to monitor add, remove and modify states within an RMF database and provide a way of performing inter-process communication between applications.

2   System Architecture

The RMF architecture aims to provide P2P application developers with a simple, interoperable, well defined model of P2P computing, i.e. an application should be written to take advantage of the P2P paradigm and not a specific P2P protocol implementation. Similarly, the architecture supports the P2P protocol developer by providing many of the features required by P2P systems, e.g. a database and a redundancy mechanism. This not only simplifies the development of new P2P protocols, i.e. the protocol developer can concentrate on the network and routing features of the protocol, but also prevents the development of monolithic P2P systems all supporting the same features with varying, non-interoperable, implementations.

The RMF architecture has therefore been designed so that a level of abstraction between RMF applications and the underlying P2P protocol(s) is provided which supports the following features:

- A simple to use API which shields the user from any details of the P2P protocol(s) being used.
- An extensible data model for defining resources, i.e. a base class for resource definitions and a set of semantics for the base class which can be extended by the user in order to create user defined data types.
- A way of linking resources into list or tree structures which can be efficiently navigated by the user.
- A means of registering resources in a network of RMF peers.
- A means of querying a network of RMF peers, in order to find specific registered resources, using a text based query language which is independent of the structure and content of new user defined data types.
- An eventing model which can be used to monitor the state of registered resources.
- A redundancy mechanism to reliably store registered resources in the event of RMF peer failures.

The diagram given in Fig. 1 shows the layers of the RMF architecture. The application layer represents all applications which are developed to make use of the RMF. The RMF layer, which implements the resource registration, database, redundancy, leasing, lookup and event subscription mechanisms is sandwiched between the *RMF API* and the *Communicator API*. The RMF API, provides the registration, lookup and event subscription features of the RMF layer to the application developer. The Communicator API builds a layer of abstraction between the details of specific P2P protocol implementations and the RMF layer by providing an interface which must be implemented by a specific P2P protocol before it can be used by the RMF layer. In addition to the Communicator API itself, a set of semantics relating to the use of the Communicator

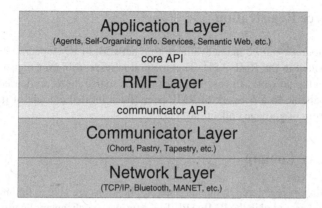

Fig. 1. The RMF architecture consists of four layers where each layer represents a functional unit required in the construction of non-monolithic P2P systems.

API have been defined to which the P2P protocol developer must adhere. The Communicator layer represents all P2P protocols which correctly implement the Communicator interface whilst the network layer represents all network protocols which are used by the communicator layer. It is the responsibility of the communicator layer to distribute resources, queries and event subscriptions to peers in an RMF network based on keys assigned to resources by the RMF layer. In our prototype, keys are integer values generated by a hashing algorithm and the communicator layer is an internally developed Chord [4] protocol implementation.

3   RMF Resources

The RMF provides a mechanism for describing *entities*, e.g. things which exist in the real or electronic world, in terms of metadata. To this end, a universal, extensible data model for entity descriptions is given using XML. The base type of this model is defined by the *base resource definition*. By using inheritance, the user may extend the base resource definition by creating *user resource definitions*[1]. Resource definitions consist of typed properties which represent the metadata information of an entity. Resource definitions may, for example, be described using RDF or XML schemas [13]. In the RMF, a *resource* is an instance of a resource definition. Therefore, a resource can represent, in terms of metadata, entities such as: files, web pages (e.g. by using web site descriptions in RDF [11]), services (e.g. by using WSDL [12] descriptions), people, books, cars, abstract data and associations.

---

[1] User resource definitions may also extend other user resource definitions.

4   Resource Registration

All RMF resources can be made available to a network of RMF peers via the register method provided in the RMF API[2]. This method is responsible for registering a given resource into the network. In case of peer failures, registrations are leased as to make resources available to a network of RMF peers for a limited amount of time and thus provides a form of garbage collection.

5   Resource Lookup

Once a resource is registered in the network, applications are able to find it by using the search method provided in the RMF API. To perform a search, an application must know at least one peer where a resource has been registered. An application may already know such a peer because, for example, it is aware of at least one of the resource's keywords and thus the search request can be directed to the peer responsible for this keyword.

6   An Alternative FIPA Directory Facilitator Based on the RMF

One application scenario for the RMF is a distributed directory service. In terms of FIPA [3] the directory facilitator (DF) has the functionality to register and discover software agents, i.e. their service descriptions, and federated DFs can form a distributed directory service that has similarities to a Gnutella network.

We have implemented an alternative DF, called the RMF-DF, for the JADE [5] platform which uses the RMF to register und discover agent service descriptions. By using the RMF, the DF benefits from peer-to-peer protocols such as Chord, to form a very efficient, potentially global, decentralized agent service description directory.

When an agent "XYZ" registers it's service description(s) at the RMF-DF, the description will be piggybacked into an RMF resource. This resource will be registered to the RMF information space. When another agent, running on a different machine but connected to the same RMF information space, searches for agent "XYZ" it queries its local RMF-DF which will look up that agent in the RMF information space and return its service description(s). The registration as well as the lookup of agent service descriptions with the RMF-DF is fully FIPA compliant from an agent's perspective.

7   Related Work

Pastry [2] provides a mechanism for building a self-organizing network of peers in which messages are routed using keys. It allows the user to publish and find objects in the network. Objects are identified by an object identifier which is supplied by an application when registering an object to the network. Objects can only be searched with their object identifiers. It is not possible to search objects based on their content.

---

[2] In addition to the register method, the RMF API supports the ability to remove resources from or modify resources in an RMF database.

JXTA [6] is a Java framework for building P2P applications. It provides mechanisms for announcing and finding peers, peer groups and services and for communication between peers. It does not provide any of the concepts of the RMF, e.g. resources, content-based publish-subscribe, searching and redundancy. However it is possible to implement an RMF communicator layer based on JXTA using, for example, a JXTA Chord implementation to simplify the bootstrap process of peers.

Jini [8] supports the registration, lookup and subscription of Java services based on metadata attributes. The matching algorithm however is very simple and does not, for example, allow sub-string searches. Additionally it does not efficiently scale to large networks, e.g. the Internet.

8 Conclusions

We have given a brief introduction to the RMF. The RMF attempts to offer a unified model of P2P computing which is independent of underlying protocols and offers support for both the P2P protocol and application developers. Unlike other P2P frameworks, the RMF offers a highly generic, extensible data model which allows complex, inter-linked data structures to be distributed and efficiently discovered across a network of peers. The layering structure of the RMF is such that all of these features are encapsulated into one reusable unit. To summarize, the RMF, in combination with an appropriate communicator layer, provides a fully distributed, self-organizing, object-oriented, active XML database.

As a network of RMF peers is active, it seems logical that a user cannot, and indeed has no desire to, personally handle all events generated by the network. Autonomous applications, i.e. agents, which can collect, analyze and react to events will, we believe, play a vital role in RMF applications. By using the RMF to build an efficient, distributed, ad-hoc DF we intend to further explore the possibilities of using agent technology in massively distributed systems.

The RMF prototype developed by Siemens Corporate Technology is currently under evaluation in an internal project. During the course of this project we intend to address security, reliability and scalability issues in large, inter-corporate, networks.

References

1. A. Carzaniga, D. S. Rosenblum, and A. L. Wolf: Design of a Scalable Event Notification Service: Interface and Architecture. Technical Report CU-CS-863-98, Department of Computer Science, University of Colorado, August 1998
2. A. Rowstron and P. Druschel: Pastry: Scalable, distributed object location and routing for large-scale peer-to-peer systems. IFIP/ACM International Conference on Distributed Systems Platforms (Middleware), Heidelberg, Germany, pages 329-350, November, 2001
3. FIPA: The Foundation for Intelligent Physical Agents. http://www.fipa.org
4. I. Stoica, R. Morris, D. Karger, M. F. Kaashoek, and H. Balakrishnan: Chord: A Scalable Peer-to-peer Lookup Service for Internet Applications, ACM SIGCOMM 2001, San Deigo, CA, August 2001, pp. 149-160
5. Java Agent DEvelopment Framework: http://jade.cselt.it/
6. Project JXTA. http://www.jxta.org

7. S. Ratnasamy, P. Francis, M. Handley, R. Karp and S. Shenker: A scalable content-addressable network. In Proc. ACM SIGCOMM, San Diego, 2001
8. Sun Microsystems: Jini Network Technology Specifications
    http://www.sun.com/software/jini/specs/
9. T. Friese: Selbstorganisierende Peer-to-Peer Netzwerke. Disploma Thesis, Department of Computer Science, Philipps-University Marburg, March 2002
10. T. Berners-Lee, J. Hendler and O. Lassila: The Semantic Web. Scientific American, May 2001
11. W3C: Resource Description Framework (RDF). http://www.w3.org/RDF
12. W3C: Web Services Description Language (WSDL) http://www.w3.org/TR/wsdl
13. W3C: XML Schema. http://www.w3.org/XML/Schema

Using an O-Telos Peer to Provide Reasoning Capabilities in an RDF-Based P2P-Environment

Martin Wolpers[1], Ingo Brunkhorst[1], and Wolfgang Nejdl[2,*]

[1] Institute for Information Systems, University of Hannover
Appelstr. 4, 30167 Hannover, Germany
wolpers,brunkhorst@kbs.uni-hannover.de
[2] Computer Science Department, Stanford University
nejdl@db.stanford.edu

Abstract. The open source project Edutella is an RDF-based Peer-to-Peer infrastructure for digital resources, focusing on learning materials. Building upon the established meta-data standard RDF(S) appropriate for the description of distributed resources in the World Wide Web WWW, it provides a general RDF-based meta-data infrastructure for P2P applications. In this paper, after a short introduction to the Edutella infrastructure, we describe how an Edutella peer based on the conceptual modeling language O-Telos, using the ConceptBase meta-database, can provide storage and reasoning capabilities on RDF meta-data in the P2P network. To provide this feature, we exploit the similarity of the O-Telos data model to the RDF(S) data model, and show how RDF(S) meta-data can easily be stored in the ConceptBase database. Finally, we describe how the Datalog-based Edutella query exchange language RDF-QEL can be naturally expressed by O-Telos query classes.

1 Introduction

The Edutella project [1] aims at providing access to distributed collections of digital resources through a P2P network. In contrast to already existing P2P networks, resources are not described using ad hoc meta-data fields (like Napster & Co), but use RDFS schemata [2] and RDF [3] meta-data[1] for their description. Our current main application area for Edutella is the exchange of learning resources, though the Edutella infrastructure is general enough to cater for any RDF-described digital resources on the Web.

In contrast to client/server architectures, clients do not need to address specific servers, but can use the services provided by Edutella provider peers in a P2P manner. In the case of query services, client peers connect to the Edutella network and send their queries which transparently reach the appropriate provider peers.

Within any P2P network, and consequently also in Edutella, the query service is the most basic service. Peers providing it must realize storage and query functionalities for RDF meta-data, based on the Datalog-based RDF-QEL query exchange language [4]. Queries within the Edutella P2P network basically address and retrieve meta-data about

---

* On leave from University of Hannover
[1] We will use the expression RDF(S) throughout this paper to refer to RDF schemas and RDF data.

G. Moro and M. Koubarakis (Eds.): AP2PC 2002, LNAI 2530, pp. 150–157, 2003.
© Springer-Verlag Berlin Heidelberg 2003

resources managed by the Edutella peers, resources are then retrieved directly from the appropriate peer.

The Edutella P2P architecture is based on the recently announced JXTA framework [5]. Initial services will be a Query Services providing standardized query and retrieval functionality of RDF meta-data, Replication Services providing data persistence, availability and workload balancing while maintaining data integrity and consistency, Mapping and Mediation Services for translating between different meta-data vocabularies and schemata to enable interoperability between different peers and Annotation Services to annotate materials stored anywhere within the network.

In this paper we describe storage, query and reasoning services provided by an O-Telos provider peer. This peer uses the ConceptBase database (see [6] and [7]) as a repository for storing, reasoning and managing meta-data about resources, which has been used in a variety of modeling contexts (see [8] for an overview) during the last 10 years. The ConceptBase system is a deductive object-oriented database manager that implements the language O-Telos [9], based on the TELOS modeling language [10,11]. O-Telos has been designed as an object-oriented meta-modeling language that provides facilities for unrestricted meta modeling levels, and has been axiomatized based on property quadruples (similar to RDF triples, but including an explicit ID for each tuple). Furthermore, the ConceptBase database implements a query and reasoning mechanism based on (negated) Datalog, first order formulas can be used in rules and constraints based on the Lloyd-Topor transformation [12]. This reasoning functionality is an important service needed in the Edutella network e.g. for enabling automatic data consistency based on the data content, for fast and highly flexible data retrieval, and for general reasoning purposes.

The O-Telos Peer implements two basic services in order to provide reasoning services to the network. The storage service is designed to import and store RDF(S) data in the ConceptBase repository. The storage service translate RDF(S) data into O-Telos which is used internally by the repository. The translation bases on the O-Telos-RDF axioms as described in [13].

The query service enables queries formulated in the Datalog-based RDF exchange language RDF-QEL [4] which the peer are translates into O-Telos queries, executes them in ConceptBase, and translates the results back into RDF statements.

In the next Sect. 2 we continue with a brief section describing Edutella in more detail. Section 3 then illustrates basically how RDF(s) data are stored in ConceptBase. Section 4 deals with the querying facility provided by this peer, specifically how we can use the advanced querying facilities of ConceptBase for querying RDF(S) data. Finally, Sect. 5 describes the technical issues concerned.

2   Edutella Architecture

The Edutella project uses the recently announced JXTA [14], [15] framework, an open source project managed and supported by Sun Microsystems, to provide a set of XML based protocols in a layered architecture for creating P2P applications. The layered approach supports Edutellas' structure: the JXTA service layer is complemented by the Edutella services, the Edutella peers reside on the JXTA application layer using its services in addition to the Edutella services.

RDF and RDFS are used as the common lingua franca which the various peers of Edutella use to communicate. Each peer makes the meta-data that describe its stored resources available to the network using RDF(S). Even the functionality of the Edutella network, Edutella services, are mediated within the network using RDF(S).

Among the Edutella services, the storage and query service is the most basic service. Peers register queries they may be asked through the query service i.e. by specifying the meta-data schemas they support. The queries are then sent through the Edutella network to various peers which have registered to be interested in this kind of queries. The resulting answers stated in RDF statements are sent back to the requesting peer.

3   Storing RDF Meta-data in ConceptBase

All resources exchanged in the Edutella network are described by appropriate RDF(S) data, which is also used as import and export format by the O-Telos peer. The example used throughout this paper is a small database containing the RDF description of some books. This database is taken from the Edutella [1] examples library.

In order to store the RDF meta-data in the ConceptBase database the peer has to translate RDF(S) to O-Telos. O-Telos itself is an object-oriented logic modeling language defined using 32 axioms [9]. Our translation is based on the discussion of O-Telos-RDF [13], which analyzed similarities and differences between RDF(S) and O-Telos.

The translation ensures that RDF(S) data is translated without any loss of information. At first we are changing the representation from XML serialization to its representation as triple statements. Each triple is extended with an unique id (as O-Telos extends the RDF triples by a fourth argument, the triple id). Additional quadruples not originally present in RDF(S) are included as well, as O-Telos-RDF employs explicit instantiation of properties, not only resources/objects [13]. This set of quadruples then forms the O-Telos database where each quadruple represents an O-Telos statement.

As a result of the translation we are able to easily express RDF(S) data in the O-Telos language and also to import it into the ConceptBase database. See [13] for a thorough discussion of the underlying fundamentals.

4   The Query and Reasoning Service

This section provides some insight into the way the RDF(S) data imported into the O-Telos Peer are queried, and how the reasoning facilities of ConceptBase are used for answering the RDF-QEL queries [4] sent over the Edutella network. Based on Data-log [16] RDF-QEL abstracts the various RDF storage layer query languages (e.g. SQL) and user level query languages thus providing the syntax and semantics for an overall standard query interface across heterogeneous peer repositories for any kind of RDF meta-data.

RDF-QEL does not distinguish between data and schema levels and allows querying of different modeling levels. In doing so, RDF-QEL conforms to the RDF(S) schema definitions and the more recent RDF model theory [17]. In order to describe and handle different query capabilities [4] defines several RDF-QEL-i exchange language levels with increasing expressiveness: RDF-QEL-1 queries (conjunctive queries) are expressed as unreified RDF graphs while the higher levels use reified RDF statements for increased expressiveness (e.g. RDF-QEL-3 covers relational algebra, RDF-QEL-4 incorporates Datalog). In this paper we will use examples in RDF-QEL-1 only for simplicity reasons. More advanced working examples with advanced features like negation can be found at `http://cip1-s.cip1.uni-hannover.de:3120/rdf2cb`.

```
eduquery(X) :- title(X,''Just Java'')
?- eduquery(X)
```

Example 4.1. The datalog representation of the example query

```xml
<?xml version='1.0' encoding='ISO-8859-1'?>
<!DOCTYPE rdf:RDF
 [ <!ENTITY a 'http://purl.org/dc/elements/1.1/'>
   <!ENTITY b 'http://www.edutella.org/edutella#'>
   <!ENTITY c 'http://www.w3.org/2000/01/rdf-schema#'>
   <!ENTITY rdf 'http://www.w3.org/1999/02/22-rdf-syntax-ns#'> ]>
<rdf:RDF xmlns:a="&a;" xmlns:rdf="&rdf;" xmlns:b="&b;"
         xmlns:c="&c;" >
  <b:QEL1Query rdf:about="#genQuery">
    <b:hasVariable rdf:resource="#X"/>
    <b:hasVariable rdf:resource="#Y"/>
    <b:hasResultType rdf:resource="&b;GraphResult"/>
  </b:QEL1Query>
  <b:Variable rdf:about="X" a:title="Just Java" c:label="X">
    <a:title rdf:resource="#Y"/>
  </b:Variable>
  <b:Variable rdf:about="Y" c:label="Y"/>
</rdf:RDF>
```

Example 4.2. The RDF-QEL XML representation of the example query

The RDF-QEL queries are translated into O-Telos queries which are then answered by the ConceptBase database. This translation uses the Edutella common data model (ECDM) which defines the interface between the Edutella network and the local data model for all Edutella peers. The ECDM is based on Datalog and represents the queries and their results (see [4]). O-Telos results are therefore translated to either a RDF graph result in XML serialization or the RDF triple format.

As an example we want to know from the book database which books have the title "Just Java". The respective query expressed in datalog is stated in 4.1 while being expressed in RDF-QEL-1 and XML in example 4.2.

The query asks for at least one resource in the database which has a property called dc:title with a value "Just Java". The resulting resource(s) are returned as an RDF graph in XML notation. The peer constructs from the RDF query representation the respective O-Telos representation using the ECDM, so the query is reformulated in O-Telos that it states that there is at least one resource in the database which has a property called dc:title with a value "Just Java". The set of all resources for which this holds is the solution set and is returned as result.

```
QueryClass EduQuery isA Individual with
     retrieved_attribute
          title : String;
          namespace : String
     constraint
          varX : $ exists Y/Individual A(this,title,Y)
                         and A(this,title,"Just Java") $
end
```

Example 4.3. The O-Telos frame representation of the query example

For querying the knowledge base in a simple way ConceptBase offers the O-Telos construct QueryClass. Queries are formulated using instances of the QueryClass construct. The query solutions are the instances of that query class, see the query class EduQuery stated in example 4.3 with the resulting solution stated in example 4.4 for an example.

Query classes can be inherited by other query classes thus enabling a feature similar to set intersection in relational algebra. In example 4.3 the query class EduQuery is an instance of ConceptBase's built-in class QueryClass. EduQuery is also a subclass of the O-Telos class Individual and thus has as answers other instances of the class Individual.

The QueryClass feature "retrieved_attribute" provides a feature similar to projection in relational algebra. This feature is used in example 4.3 for retrieving all attributes with label title and label namespace, both of type String. All solutions to the query must instantiate the retrieved_attribute thus all solutions to EduQuery have an attribute named title and named namespace holding some values of type String.

```
<?xml version='1.0' encoding='ISO-8859-1'?>
<!DOCTYPE rdf:RDF
  [ ENTITY rdf 'http://www.w3.org/1999/02/22-rdf-syntax-ns#'
    ENTITY a 'http://purl.org/dc/elements/1.1/' ]>
<rdf:RDF xmlns:rdf="&rdf;" xmlns:a="&a;">
  <rdf:Description rdf:about="http://www.xyz.com/jv.html"
    a:title="Just Java"/>
</rdf:RDF>
```

Example 4.4. The XML serialization of the query answer expressed in RDF

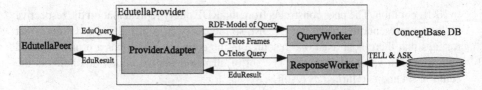

Fig. 1. Schematic representation of the architecture

ConceptBase offers a further feature called "query constraint" to query the knowledge base. A query class can define a constraint based on (negated) Datalog which is evaluated at execution time. The constraint can contain retrieved_attributes. In example 4.3 the constraint varX declares that all instances of the answer set must have an attribute named title and that this attribute holds the value "Just Java".

The answer to the example query in 4.2 consists of the RDF statements in example 4.4 declaring that there is a resource with URL http://www.xyz.com/jv.html. This resource is the domain of a property named title which has the range "Just Java". The title property is defined in the Dublin Core namespace.

5 The Edutella Wrapper

Due to place restrictions let us now only real briefly introduce the basic implementation of the Edutella wrapper for the O-Telos Peer, which is implemented in Java as is the whole Edutella project. The implementation consists of three parts: the servlet provides a simple user interface, the EdutellaPeer implementation realizes the Edutella peer service and the EdutellaProvider provides the actual query service[2].

As shown in Fig. 1 the ProviderAdapter receives EduQuery objects generated from a parser based on the Jena RDF parser API [18]. In a first step these are translated to O-Telos query objects by the QueryWorker. In a second step the ResponseWorker establishes a connection to the ConceptBase database, sends the query, receives the answer and returns the EduResult objects constructed from ConceptBases' answer. The ProviderAdapter itself returns the EduResult objects to either the servlet or the Edutella peer which in turn process them according to their respective needs.

6 Summary

The Edutella Peer-to-Peer network combines provider and client peers of various kinds, with the unifying characteristics that each peer describes its resources using the RDF(S) meta-data format, and that messages exchanged between peers also use this format. After a short introduction into the architecture of the Edutella infrastructure, we described the implementation of an Edutella peer with enhanced reasoning capabilities on RDF data. This provider peer uses the ConceptBase database to store RDF data based on its implementation of the meta modeling language O-Telos. Based on ConceptBase

---

[2] See http://www.cip1.uni-hannover.de:3120/rdf2cb/ for a demo.

and its reasoning capabilities the Edutella services storage and querying are realized: a repository for importing and storing RDF data and a query facility for the imported data.

As RDF(S) semantics is quite similar to the O-Telos semantics, mapping RDF(S) statements to O-Telos statements is not too difficult. The main differences compared to RDF(S) are statement IDs, explicit instantiation of properties and object-oriented property definitions in O-Telos, and each RDF(S) model can be translated into an O-Telos model without loss of information. Our storage service therefore uses an appropriate translation from RDF(S) to O-Telos and vice versa, which is also sketched in this paper. Based on this translation the query service translates RDF-QEL queries to O-Telos queries and the answers back to RDF(S), which is also quite straightforward, as ConceptBase query classes directly map to Datalog-based RDF-QEL queries.

The resulting O-Telos Peer is able to provide advanced storage and reasoning capabilities within the Edutella network, and thus indirectly extends basic RDF(S) with (negated) Datalog reasoning functionalities.

References

1. Nejdl, W., Decker, S., Wolf, B.: Edutella Project Homepage (2001) http://edutella.jxta.org.
2. Brickley, D., Guha, R.V.: Resource Description Framework (RDF) Schema Specification 1.0 (2002) http://www.w3.org/TR/rdf-schema.
3. Lassila, O., Swick, R.: W3C Resource Description framework (RDF) Model and Syntax Specification (2001) http://www.w3.org/TR/REC-rdf-syntax/.
4. Nejdl, W., Wolf, B., Qu, C., Decker, S., Sintek, M., Naeve, A., Nilsson, M., Palm r, M., Risch, T.: EDUTELLA: a P2P Networking Infrastructure based on RDF. In: WWW 11 Conference Proceedings, Hawaii, USA (2002) http://edutella.jxta.org/reports/edutella-whitepaper.pdf.
5. SUN Microsystems: JXTA v1.0 Protocols Specification. (2001) http://spec.jxta.org/v1.0/docbook/JXTAProtocols.html.
6. Jarke, M., Gallersdörfer, R., Jeusfeld, M., Staudt, M., Eherer, S.: ConceptBase - a deductive object base for meta data management. Journal on Intelligent Information Systems 4 (1995) 167 – 192
7. Jeusfeld, M.A., Jarke, M., Nissen, H.W., Staudt, M.: ConceptBase - Managing Conceptual Models about Information Systems. In Bernus, P., Mertins, K., Schmidt, G., eds.: Handbook on Architectures of Informations Systems. Springer Verlag (1998)
8. Jeusfeld, M., Team, C.: Application papers. Technical report, Chair of Computer Science V - Information Systems, RWTH Aachen (2000) http://www-i5.informatik.rwth-aachen.de/CBdoc/cblit.html#cb-app.
9. Jeusfeld, M.: nderungskontrolle in deduktiven Objektbanken. Infix-Verlag, St. Augustin, Deutschland (1992)
10. Kramer, B.M., Chandhri, V.K., Koubarakis, M., Topaloglon, T., Wang, H., Mylopoulos, J.: Implementing Telos. SIGART Bulletin 2 (1991)
11. Mylopoulos, J., Borgida, A., Jarke, M., Koubarakis, M.: Telos: A language for representing knowledge about information systems. ACM Transactions on Information Systems 8 (1990)
12. Lloyd, J.W., Topor, R.W.: Making prolog more expressive. Journal of Logic Programming 3 (1984) 225–240
13. Nejdl, W., Dhraief, H., Wolpers, M.: O-Telos-RDF: a resource description format with enhanced metamodeling functionalities based on O-Telos. In: Workshop on Knowledge Markup and Semantic Annotation at the First International Concerence on Knowledge Capture (K-CAP'2001). (2001) http://www.kbs.uni-hannover.de/Arbeiten/Publikationen/2001/kcap01_final.pdf.

14. Gong, L.: Project JXTA: A technology overview. Technical report, SUN Microsystems (2001)
    http://www.jxta.org/project/www/docs/TechOverview.pdf.
15. Corp., S.: Project JXTA Homepage. http://www.jxta.org/ (2001)
16. Ullmann, J.D.: Principles of database and knowledgebase systems. Principles of computer
    science series. Computer Science Press, Inc., Maryland, USA (1988)
17. Hayes, P.: RDF model theory. W3C working draft (2002)
    http://www.w3.org/TR/rdf-mt/.
18. Company, H.P.: The Jena Semantic Web Toolkit (2001)
    http://www.hpl.hp.com/semweb/jena-tob.html.

A Mobile Multi-agent System for Distributed Computing

Stefan Kleijkers, Floris Wiesman, and Nico Roos

International Institute of Infonomics / Universiteit Maastricht, Department of
Computer Science
P.O. Box 616, 6200 MD Maastricht, The Netherlands

Abstract. The paper describes a peer-to-peer distributed-computing
platform, called YACA, based on mobile agents. Next to the client agents,
which seek computational resources in a cluster, YACA consists of four
agents, who manage the computers within a cluster. (1) The Directory
Agent keeps track of the computers belonging to the cluster. These computers are called nodes. (2) The Weather Agent monitors the resources
of a node and (3) the Account Agent keeps track of the resources used by
each client agent. (4) The Controller Agent controls the access to a node
and migrates client agents to other nodes in the cluster if the node becomes overloaded. Experiments showed that YACA brings little overhead.
However, its load balancing algorithm has room for improvements.

1 Introduction

Despite the exponential growth of CPU speed, modern computers cannot cope
with the growing demand for computational resources that occur in areas such
as bio-informatics. Computer models are becoming more refined and often show
an exponential time complexity. Moreover, the amount of data to be processed
is growing rapidly. At the same time, there is a huge amount of unused computer
power available on the desks of people, especially after office hours.

The SETI@home project has demonstrated convincingly the scalability and
feasibility of distributed computing with spare CPU cycles. At the same time
Gnutella, KaZaa, and Morpheus have generated ample interest in peer-to-peer
(P2P) networks and have shown their utility. Combining these two approaches
is an obvious step. Mobile agents seem the ideal tools for such a unification,
because (a) they can react flexibly on the availability of resources, and (b) they
allow for new computational tasks to be created without the need for installing
new software on multiple hosts. This study investigates the possibility of mobile
agents for P2P distributed computing.

The remainder of this paper is organized as follows: Sect. 2 outlines existing
approaches to distributed computing, Sect. 3 describes our platform based on
mobile agents, and Sect. 4 presents the results of the experiments. Finally, Sect. 5
presents our conclusions.

G. Moro and M. Koubarakis (Eds.): AP2PC 2002, LNAI 2530, pp. 158–163, 2003.

2   Distributed Computing

The best-known conventional tools for distributed computing are PVM [1] and
MOSIX [2]. They consists of a set of libraries for distributing tasks and communication between tasks located on different computers. POPCORN [3] is a P2P
system for trading processor resources on the Internet. Buyers have to write
their programs using the POPCORN library; a program can be sent to the market to find a seller. PaCMAn [4] is a system for distributed computing based
on the Aglets mobile-agent platform [5]. A broker keeps track of the system
configuration, resources, and network load by dispatching special agents that
gather the required information. Messor [6] is a distributed-computing system
with load-balancing based on ant-like agents.

3   The Yaca Platform

At the start of the project five design goals were set. None of the existing platforms met all of these objectives: (a) the platform has to be operating system
independent, (b) the platform will be based on mobile agents, (c) the load must
be well-balanced over the nodes, (d) the overhead has to be low, and (e) it should
be possible to extend the platform with markets for computational resources.

In this section we describe our platform, YACA. Section 3.1 provides an
overview of the platform and Sects. 3.2–3.6 describe the various YACA agents.

3.1   Overview

The YACA platform consists of four types of management agents running on the
Aglets platform. Besides the management agents, there are *client agents*. They
are the agents performing tasks for users, but strictly speaking they are not part
of the YACA platform. Before a client can run on a particular host, the Aglets
platform must be started on that node together with the management agents.

The *Directory Agent* keeps a list of all hosts that are part of the cluster.
Hosts that belong to a cluster are called *nodes*. The *Controller Agent* controls
the node, the *Weather Agent* monitors the load of the system, while the *Account
Agent* keeps track of the resources being used by the clients. Figure 1 shows
which agents communicate with each other in a two-node cluster.

3.2   The Directory Agent

The first agent of the YACA platform is the Directory Agent. Only one Directory
Agent is required per cluster. The main task of the Directory Agent is managing
a list of all computers that take part in the cluster. When a computer wants to
join or leave the cluster it has to report this to the Directory Agent.

The Controller Agent can ask the Directory Agent for a list of other nodes in
the cluster, so as to decide to which node it will migrate a client when the load
gets too high. The Directory Agent does not return the complete list of nodes

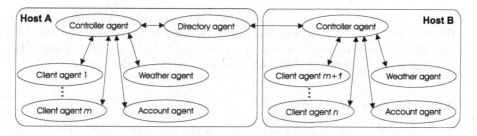

Fig. 1. Interaction between YACA agents on two hosts

but only a random selection.[1] If the Directory Agent would return the whole list, the node would have to query all the available nodes.

3.3   The Controller Agent

The second YACA agent is the Controller Agent. Each node in the cluster has one Controller Agent. This agent is the ruler of a node. It decides if and when agents will be migrated and where to. Furthermore it decides which agents are permitted on the node and what their restrictions are.

When a Controller Agent registers itself with the Directory Agent, the host of the Controller Agent is added to the list of nodes. After registering, the Controller Agent starts its job. First it will wait for a Weather Agent and an Account Agent to register themselves with the Controller Agent, then it will accept client agents. A client agent has to be registered with the Controller Agent otherwise the client will be removed. If the Weather Agent reports low resources, the controller will try to migrate clients to hosts with more resources.

3.4   The Weather Agent

The third YACA agent is the Weather Agent. Each node has one Weather Agent. This agent keeps track of the system resources. If the node runs out of resources it informs the Controller Agent. Currently the only resource monitored is the processor load, which is checked at regular intervals.

The level of processor load at which the Weather Agent informs the Controller Agent can be set at start up time or by the Controller Agent. In this way the Controller Agent can control the load of the node: it can decide to permit clients when the system is idle and refuse clients if the host is occupied by a user. To make the decision whether to inform the Controller Agent as easy as possible the Weather Agent only uses a single value for representing the load of the different system resources. If the Weather Agent would monitor more than one resource it would need a function to combine multiple values into a single one.

---

[1] This only happens when the total number of nodes is greater than a predefined threshold; otherwise the complete list is returned.

The Weather agent does not inform the Controller agent every time it checks the load of the system. It will first check the load several times and take the average of those samples. The average will be sent to the Controller Agent. This way the system can handle fast and short fluctuations in the load.

3.5   The Account Agent

The last of the four management agents is the Account Agent. The Account Agent is responsible for keeping track of the resources used by a client agent. This is necessary for the payment. If a client has paid for some resources YACA has to prevent the client from using more resources than was paid for.

When a client agent enters a node it registers itself with the Controller Agent, which then registers the client with the Account Agent. The Account Agent now monitors the client agent. If the client agent wants to migrate to another node it deregisters itself from the Controller Agent. The Controller Agent then deregisters the client from the Account Agent and asks the Account Agent for the resources being used by the client and writes this information to a log file.

The Controller Agent may migrate the client to another node in the cluster, because of low system resources at the current node. In this case the Controller Agent deregisters the client from itself and the Account Agent. After that it will register the client agent with the new node. The Controller Agent also asks the Account Agent for the resources being used by the client and informs the Account Agent at the new node about the resources being used by the client until that time.

3.6   The Client Agents

The agents that carry out the real work for the user are the client agents. All clients have to register themselves with the Controller Agent on the node they just entered. When a client migrates by itself it has to deregister itself from the Controller Agent and register itself with the Controller Agent on the new node. When the Controller Agent migrates a client, the Controller Agent will deregister the client from the current node and register it with the new node. Without registration the client will be removed by the Controller Agent of the new node.

A useful design pattern for YACA clients with homogeneous tasks is to build one main agent that holds all program code and data. After it is started, the main agent clones itself several times, thus creating child agents who carry out subtasks. After the child agents have finished, they return their results to the main agent.

4   Experiments

The experiments conducted on YACA concentrated on performance. On no parallel computing system the running time of a task will decrease linearly with

Table 1. Time used for all configurations and relative gain for the dual node cluster.

Number	Time used (s)			Dual node gain (%)
	Pure Java	Single node	Dual node	
20,000,000	152	154	155	-0.65
40,000,000	410	411	405	1.46
60,000,000	731	732	655	10.52
80,000,000	1103	1108	870	21.48
100,000,000	1518	1518	1215	19.96

the number of nodes of the cluster. There are three potential causes. First, the bookkeeping of the cluster and the migration of tasks require computational overhead. Second, it takes time to distribute tasks over nodes evenly. During this time some nodes become overloaded while others are still idle. Third, not every task can be split up in subtasks. In our research we do not focus on the latter problem, therefore our experiments use a task that can be split up easily.

So as to investigate to what extent the first two causes influenced the performance, a program was used that counts the number of prime numbers in a given interval. The program was implemented in two ways: as a pure Java program, running outside YACA, and as an agent, running inside YACA. The pure Java program uses no threads, hence it tests all numbers sequentially. The agent clones itself n times and assigns all children $\frac{1}{n}$ of the subtask, thus covering the entire interval to be searched. The agent program was tested in two different settings: on a single node cluster and on a dual node cluster. The agents on the single node cluster show the overhead of YACA, the agents on the dual node cluster show the overhead of the migration process and the balancing of the cluster. The pure Java program and the single node cluster experiment were both executed on a system with an AMD Athlon 900 MHz processor and 256 MB of RAM. The operating system used was Windows 2000 pro, running Aglets 1.1.0 with Java JDK 1.1.8. No other programs were running while conducting the experiments. The dual node cluster experiment was conducted on two of the above systems. The two systems were connected to each other in a 100 MBit Ethernet LAN. Thus the results were not influenced by network delay.

Table 1 shows the results of the experiments. All experiments started from 0 until the number in the first column. The columns 2–4 display the time in seconds the algorithm needed for finishing the task with the pure Java program, the single node cluster, and the dual node cluster, respectively.

As can be seen, there is no significant difference between the native Java program and the single node cluster. In the beginning there is also no real difference between the single node cluster and the dual node cluster. As the search interval grows and the time increases the balancing algorithm of YACA starts working and a difference can be seen between the single node cluster and the dual node cluster. The last column of Table 1 shows the relative gain in percentage of the time between the single and dual node cluster (the theoretical maximum is 50 percent). As can be seen, the gain increases with larger tasks where the overhead of migration is smaller than the gain in time.

Some conclusions can be drawn from the results presented in the previous section. First, the YACA platform itself has little overhead, as shown by the small differences in time between the pure Java program and the agent on the single node cluster. This indicates that YACA consumes little resources for itself. Second, to be effective YACA needs large tasks. With small tasks, which take little time to complete, no gain can be achieved by using multi-node clusters. As can be seen from the results the gain with large tasks does not come close to the 50 percent, thus the balancing algorithm is not efficient enough and needs more tuning; this holds especially for the Weather Agent and the Controller Agent.

5   Conclusions

We have described YACA, a platform for P2P distributed computing based on mobile agents. The experiments that were carried out with the implementation showed that YACA brings little overhead. However, YACA's load balancing algorithm turned out to be not satisfactory. Fortunately, the algorithm has ample room for improvements.

In future research on YACA we will extend the Weather Agent with monitoring of memory usage, disk usage, and other resources. Moreover, we plan to investigate how the introduction of a market mechanism can lead to more dynamical load balancing. The introduction of payment for computational tasks also will increase the flexibility for the client agents; a task with a high priority can be given more resources by offering a higher price. In [7] we provide more details on the possibilities of market mechanisms for distributed computing. Finally, for YACA to become a reliable system, its security needs further attention.

References

1. Geist, A., ed.: PVM: Parallel Virtual Machine. MIT Press, Cambridge (1994)
2. Barak, A., Guday, S., Wheeler, R.G.: The MOSIX Distributed Operating System. Lecture Notes in Computer Science, Vol. 672. Springer Verlag, New York (1993)
3. Nisan, N., London, S., Regev, O., Camiel, N.: Globally distributed computation over the Internet — the POPCORN project. In: Sixth International World Wide Web Conference, Santa Clara, California USA (1997)
4. Evripidou, P., Samaras, G., Panayiotou, C., Pitoura, E.: The PaCMAn metacomputer: Parallel computing with Java mobile agents. In: Proceedings of 25th Euromicro Conference, Milan, Italy (1999)
5. Lange, D.B., Oshima, M. In: Programming and Deploying Java Mobile Agents with Aglets. Addison Wesley, Reading, Massachusetts (1998)
6. Montresor, A., Meling, H., Babaoglŭ, O.: A mobile multi-agent system for distributed computing. In: Agents and Peer-to-Peer Computing 2002. Lecture Notes in Computer Science 2530, Springer-Verlag (2002)
7. Kleijkers, S.: Distributed computing with multiagent systems (2001) M.Sc. Thesis Universiteit Maastricht, Department of Computer Science, CS–01–04.

Implementation of a Micro Web Server for Peer-to-Peer Applications*

F. Callegati, R. Gori, P. Presepi, and M. Sacchetti

D.E.I.S., University of Bologna, Via Rasi Spinelli 176, 47023 Cesena, Italy
fcallegati@deis.unibo.it
{rgori,ppresepi,msacchetti}@ingce.unibo.it

Abstract. In this paper we present a very low cost web server based on off-the-shelf microcontrollers, to be used for monitoring and control purposes by means of peer-to-peer standard Internet connections. The paper describes the design principles followed, with particular emphasis on choices adopted for the TCP/IP protocol stack implementation to overcome the hardware limitations.

1 Introduction

Peer-to-peer systems are widespreading over the Internet for applications of file and resources sharing. The famous Napster and more recently applications such as Gnutella etc. are examples that are very visible to everyone.

This application of peer-to-peer computing is indeed interesting for the final user and may reach a huge level of diffusion because of the very large number of users potentially involved. Nevertheless all these applications requires that the user terminal is an Internet enabled personal computer with up to date hardware facilities.

In this paper we want to address a different application scenario of peer-to-peer computing, where the key characteristic is the limitation of hardware resources available in most of the peers involved. We imagine a network of web enabled machines, with very limited hardware resources and cost, that will be called *micro-hosts (μ-hosts)*. These μ-hosts can dialog in a peer-to-peer fashion in order to realize monitoring and control tasks over a variety of controlled devices. By adopting the standard TCP/IP protocol suite the μ-hosts could introduce a real revolution in several environments where monitoring and control are already widely used, but with different, and often proprietary, architectural approaches.

Some examples of Internet enabled very low cost devices have already been reported. For instance in [1], an application based on a micro-controller of the Microchip PIC (PIC and PICDEM.net are registrered tardemarks of Microchip Corporation) family is described, that is also available as a demo product. Starting from this example we have adopted a similar architecture, aiming at an im-

---

* This work is partially funded by the Italian Region Emilia-Romagna under the Spinner program. The authors wants to thank Ing. Alberto Tabanelli for his help regarding the hardware implementation.

G. Moro and M. Koubarakis (Eds.): AP2PC 2002, LNAI 2530, pp. 164–169, 2003.

plementation of the TCP-IP stack with added functionalities, among which the implementation of a fully functional client/server serial link controller.

The paper is structured as follows. In Sect. 2 an overview of the application scenarios is provided. In Sect. 3 is described the system design followed in Sect. 4 by a description of the the protocol stack implementation. Finally some conclusions are drawn in Sect. 5.

2   The Scenario

The last twenty years have seen a considerable development of distributed systems with monitoring and control purpose. From conventional computer aided manufacturing to environmental control and building automation, these systems are based on fairly similar hierarchical master-slave architectures. Usually a number of peripheral devices based on low cost PLCs are connected to a control centre that acts as master and is usually based on a personal computer. From the pure data transmission point of view, meaning up to the link layer of the ISO-OSI architecture, the connection between master and slaves is usually realized either by means of conventional serial communication ports with an ad-hoc link control or by means of field buses. That of field buses is an area where several standards, supported by different groups of manufacturers, coexist. Most of these standards are proprietary and do not offer to the developers an open system environment. Only recently the Ethernet, thanks to the huge success experienced in the LAN market, is spreading towards the field bus application arena and hubs and switches suitable for industrial application have been presented. Above the data link layer, these architectures usually work with proprietary protocols. The final user may, in general interact just with an application located in the master, that manages the data collected from the slaves.

This brief discussion makes clear what we believe to be the major weakness of such systems from the final user perspective: *the lack of open communication standards*. This impares, for instance, the possibility to design ad-hoc applications based on data collected with a direct peer-to-peer communication between the end-user and the controlling/monitoring devices.

The best candiates to substitute proprietary applications and protocol to realize an open communication environment are the protocols of the Internet. The TCP/IP protocol suite and the World Wide Web with the http protocol have become the most widespread set of protocols for data communications, with implementation on virtually any hardware platform of a certain size, from palmtops to workstations and servers. Therefore the goal of the project presented in this paper is to bring the Internet as close as possible to the field, that is in direct contact with sensors and controllers used to interact with the environment whether it is the air temperature or the rotation angle of a shaft. In principle this could be done simply placing a personal computer wherever necessary but with a major impact on the final cost.

Therefore we believe that such concepts will spread only if the Internet enabling process has a cost that is just a fraction of the final appliances; in many case just normal commodities such as a washing machine or a microwave oven. The device needed is what we called a μ-host, a low cost hardware that can be placed wherever monitoring or control are needed, and acts as an Internet host with web server capability. In this case no ad-hoc client to control this servers would be needed. The normal web browser and related interface will be used to interact in a peer-to-peer fashion with the μ-hosts and their controlled devices.

3   System Design

A very versatile solution to pursue our goal is represented by microcontrollers. Following the basic ideas presented in [1] we designed the μ-host as a quite simple integrated circuit, useful to evaluate the application of a peer client connecting to an embedded web server. The choice for the core unit device is a PIC16F877. This micro cpu is part of a midrange family with a fully featured set of useful peripherals and equipped with 8 Kbytes of FLASH Program Memory, 368 bytes of Data Memory (RAM), 256 bytes of EEPROM data memory.

Enabling networking capability for a such small microcontroller means a completely new engineering of the entire protocol suite. The starting point were the original IETF RFCs to evaluate the minimum requisites for an internet host described in [5,6].

Some special techniques were needed to solve the problems and limitation introduced by the micro environment, in particular the lack of RAM. A network packet is usually 1,5 Kbytes but we have to deal with a small 96 bytes buffer, plus a serial hardware with a queue of only 1 byte. Therefore storing a datagram in RAM is out of question. The only way to realize a reasonable working system is to transmit outgoing frames on the fly, adding the control information at the right point of the bit flow, and decode received packets in the same way, storing in RAM only the control information that has to be processed. This arises the proplem of processing control information, like checksums for TCP and IP, that appear in the datagram header, but are calculated on the whole packet data.

4   Protocol Stack Implementation

4.1   The Point-to-Point Protocol (PPP)

PPP provides a standard method for transporting multi-protocol datagrams over point-to-point links, composed of a method to encapsulate multi-protocol datagrams, a Link Control Protocol (LCP) for establishing, configuring and testing the Data-Link connection and a family of Network Control Protocols (NCPs) for establishing, and configuring different network layer protocols.

The protocol requires an automaton state machine to configure the whole link. A reduced state machine was used here, structured as follows:

PHASE_DEAD : a phase where nothing is happening on the network interface;

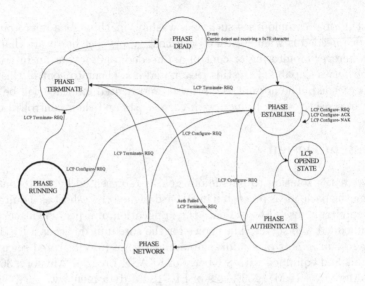

Fig. 1. The PPP automaton.

PHASE_ESTABLISH : a state where LCP packets are carried by the system
to configure the link;

PHASE_AUTHENTICATE : a successful LCP handshake have been completed and the peer try to authenticate itself;

PHASE_NETWORK : the authentication was a success and we are going to
configure the transport of data trough a network protocol;

PHASE_RUNNING : network protocol is running and the peers are exchanging data packets;

PHASE_TERMINATE : one side has asked to close the connection and the
system is going to unlink the channel.

In the implementation the first step is to accept and manage LCP packets
to configure the link. LCP support a couple of configure codes that makes the
system able to understand the available features at the peer. After a successful exchange of LCP packets the automaton starts the authentication phase. If
the authentication is successful, the Network phase follows, during which one
or more Network Protocol to carry data content can be configured. The present
implementation of PPP supports just the IP Configuration Protocol and every other requested protocol is rejected with a "Protocol-Reject" code. A state
diagram of the protocol implementation is presented in Fig. 1.

Client and server facilities were implemented, meaning that the system can
connect to the Internet itself upon an external event occurs or act a server
waiting for a end-user that wants to directly verify the device state. For instance
the client case could be used to implement a temperature control system that
reaching a critical threshold connects to the Internet and informs some end-user
by sending an e-mail.

4.2   IP and TCP

An important issue is the way to transmit a correct IP header with the small buffer we have reserved in RAM. The main problem is the *Total Lenght* IP header field that reports the length value of the whole datagram in bytes. In the packet handling solution implemented the user data of the datagram will be transmitted on the fly while reading them from the external EEPROM. Therefore the datagram length should be declare before the whole datagram is sent and its length known.

The solution to the problem is quite simple when the datagram should carry pre-defined user data, namely web pages already stored in the system EEP-ROM. Since RomFS [8] capability has been added to the software the external EEPROM organization is based upon this filesystem standard. Therefore the file length can be obtained from the file table of the RomFS.

The problem comes out when a web page that has to be sent to the peer contains dynamic data, that are acquired upon request. The general content of this page is stored in the external EEPROM too, but with some variable keycodes that are used to evaluate the device state on the fly and substitute the right value into HTML content, to forward to the peer a web the state of the controlled device. Obviously the size of the number of bytes corresponding to these variable information is not known a priori. To solve the issue the only choice was to impose some limitation to the system. We decided to assign $B = 100$ bytes to the maximum variable content in a web page, called *bonus* bytes. In this way we can read the file length from the RomFS, add to this value the B bonus bytes and operate the variable value substitution on the fly. Assuming the variable data sums up to v bytes, when the datagram has been completely sent, k padding bytes (blank characters) are added in order to reach the "Total length" declared value, where $k = B - v$. This method is not fully general and limits the variable part of web pages to the pre-defined value of B, but is flexible enough for this application. This also extends the solution presented in [1], where the size of variable data is fixed a priori.

A similar problem arises with the TCP "Checksum" field, that is calculated over the user data, the TCP header and the IP pseudo-header, that is a subset of the full IP header. Here we have the same problem as before but even more complex because the checksum depends not just on the amount of data to be send but on their actual value. Several solutions are suggested in [1]. One alternative is to parse the page twice, the former to compute the checksum and the latter to actually send it. This solution is suitable just for static pages and slows down the computation affecting the overall throughput achievable. Another possibility suggested in [1] is to transmit together with the variable, which length in pre-defined, an equal amount of information that make them negligible in the checksum calculation.

We have followed a similar approach, placing two bytes at the end of the web page, that are used to sum up with all the data and a pre-defined checksum in order to make them consistent.

4.3   Application Protocols

The Web server interface required the implementation of the HTTP protocol [7].
A basic HTTP sever has been added to the software with no relevant effort since
the techniques developed and applied to the lower layers granted to satisfy RFCs
requirements for communication with Internet hosts. Anyway, to fit TCP/IP
code in the small environment, we had to cut off some of its standard features
such as packet fragmenting or multiple sockets support.

The peer client can simply send the http request for the wanted resource,
the server will match it and will take the proper action. The RomFS filesystem
functions will manage the communication with the external EEPROM supporting the web site. If there is no file request specified the default answer will be
the default Web server page as any HTTP server does. The wanted file can be
a simple Web page, in this case the request will be served with no additional
operations, but if the resource has been associated to the microcontroller automation process, a dynamical parse of the web page content is performed and
the variable data is filled up with the state of the controlled device.

The device implements in less than 8Kbytes a standard PSTN Modem driver,
the PPP, LCP, PAP, IPCP link protocols, the TCP/IP stack with single socket
support, an HTTP Web Server, an SMTP client and a RomFS Filesystem for
web pages management.

5   Conclusions

In this paper we have described the hardware and software design principles to
realize a very low cost micro-host (μ-host) equipped with a TCP/IP protocol
stack and with a Internet web server. The μ-host can be used for monitoring and
control external analog and digital devices that interact with the field (air temperature, electro appliances, industrial machines etc.). The micro-host enables
the interaction with such devices in the fully functional peer-to-peer fashion that
characterize web-based applications.

References

1. J. Bentham, "TCP/IP Lean: Web Servers for Embedded Systems", CMP Books,
   USA 2001.
2. W. Simpson, Ed., "The Point-to-Point Protocol (PPP)", RFC 1661, July 1994.
3. J. Postel, "Internet Protocol", RFC 791, Sept. 1981.
4. J. Postel, "Transmission Control Protocol", RFC 793, Sept. 1981.
5. R.T. Branden, "Requirements for Internet Hosts – Communications Layers",
   RFC1122, October 1989.
6. R.T. Branden, "Requirements for Intenrent Hosts – Application and Support",
   RFC1123, October 1989.
7. T. Berners-Lee, R. Fielding, H. Frystyk, "Hypertext Transfer Protocol –
   HTTP/1.0", RFC1945, May 1996.
8. On line: http://romfs.sourceforge.net

Author Index